Play Therapy with Families

Play Therapy with Families

A Collaborative Approach to Healing

Edited by Nancy Riedel Bowers, PhD

JASON ARONSON
Lanham • Boulder • New York • Toronto • Plymouth, UK

Published by Jason Aronson
A wholly owned subsidiary of Rowman & Littlefield
4501 Forbes Boulevard, Suite 200, Lanham, Maryland 20706
www.rowman.com

10 Thornbury Road, Plymouth PL6 7PP, United Kingdom

British Library Cataloguing in Publication Information Available

Library of Congress Cataloging-in-Publication Data

Play therapy with families : a collaborative approach to healing / [edited by] Nancy Riedel Bowers.
p. cm.
Includes bibliographical references and index.
ISBN 978-0-7657-0808-3 (cloth) — ISBN 978-0-7657-0810-6 (electronic)
1. Play therapy. 2. Family psychotherapy. I. Riedel Bowers, Nancy, 1952- editor of compilation.
RJ505.P6P57 2014
618.92'891653—dc23
2013039252

∞™ The paper used in this publication meets the minimum requirements of American National Standard for Information Sciences Permanence of Paper for Printed Library Materials, ANSI/NISO Z39.48-1992.

Printed in the United States of America

Just as a plant needs sun and rain and good rich earth in order to attain its maximum growth, so the individual needs the permissiveness to be [one's self], the complete acceptance of one's self- by one's self as well as by others. . .

—V. Axline, *Play Therapy*, 1947

Contents

List of Figures

Acknowledgments

Mentorship in the field of play therapy has been both serendipitous and sought out. Walking in the footsteps, literally, of Virginia Axline around Columbia University in 2011, were special moments that have prompted this publication. Dr. Charles Schaefer provided the connection with Dr. Aronson for this book contract for which I am truly thankful; Dr. Garry Landreth facilitated my doctoral internship and research direction with gentleness; and, Dr. Eliana Gil, supervisor and teacher, is always informative, even at a distance. Dr. Frank Turner, my former dean and current colleague in many facets of social work, is always an inspiration. Colleagues who contributed to his book simply "get it," understanding that play and play therapy provide a special voice for children. Their work is very important and I learn from my colleagues every day. Winnie is most valued and we followed her requirements for formatting. Amy, our editor, was respectful and patient to the end.

It is my family that has provided a love for play. Sailboating on the Bay of Quinte, Ontario, Canada was always a privilege and is now a memory of much pride for which I thank my parents, Dr. and Mrs. Riedel and sisters, Janet and Susan. My children, with whom I have a very special relationship, provide unconditional love and encouragement. Anna, MA School Psych (UBC-2015) and Nick, MD (U of T-2014) share my ability to persevere. At the end of the day, it is my husband, Art, who provides laughter and patience in order to make each day a special one.

Chapter One

Play as a Voice for Our Children

Nancy Riedel Bowers and Anna Bowers

Around the world children are thriving and others are merely surviving. Some children have a community, family, and supports around them, others do not. But regardless of where families are, play provides a respite, a way of expressing, a "voice," and an opportunity for creativity. In different parts of the world children are encouraged to play, whether it be running in the streets of the Medina in Marrakech, playing with the latest technological tablets for self-expression, rolling a ball on a flat piece of land, or finding refuge in the hills.

Children and their support systems either heal together by being together and joining through family and community traditions, or they are left to heal from life's events alone. Play provides an opportunity for children to join with others to see their world for what it is and has been, to understand it a bit better, to express emotions about what has come their way, and to resolve a new way to survive. Play is "the natural medium of self-expression" for the child (Axline, 1947, p. 9) and, alone, provides a way of understanding and healing each and every day.

This book is intended to serve families, mental health workers, teachers, and children. It provides a better understanding of *play* and its relationship to family life with a special emphasis on healing alternatives through *play*. An understanding of the changing world of *family life* is presented with a focus on how play serves a pivotal role in the child's healing in today's world.

FAMILIES IN A CHANGING WORLD

Families are ever changing. Families are different in all corners of the world, within each country and within each community. The effects of time, history, and our changing world have placed demands on the family for the maintenance of separate identities and of some semblance of normal functioning. Additionally, all families experience stressful situations at some point in their life course and are thus faced with the challenge of finding ways to cope so as to bring the family back to equilibrium. While many families adapt successfully to difficult events they are faced with, for some this is not possible given that resources and opportunities vary for each unique family group.

The opportunity to heal from natural and man-made disasters, for many, is a privilege. Proximity to water, food, adequate shelter, and medical care along with the opportunity for emotional growth is not available to many, due to inadequate financial resources and political decisions. The opportunity to heal from an intra-familial crisis is dependent upon the pile-up of stressors, the tools and techniques used by the family to deal with those demands, and the meaning the family assigns to their situation, all in an attempt to restore balance in family functioning.

Some families rely on their own existing resources for everyday life and healing after trauma, loss, and emotionally laden events. Historically the community, faith-based settings, rituals, and beliefs provide a buffer as well as tools for family support. Other families expand their repertoire of resources by strengthening or developing new methods of dealing with a crisis. Nevertheless, there are many situations that arise when the "outsider" is invited in to assist in the healing process. Highlighting the natural healing resources may be part of this process as is reinforcing the strengths that the family can incorporate on their road to recovery.

Families, naturally, have playful tools for growth. We see music, dance, and games evident in countries where earthquakes, violence, and health concerns affect thousands of people at a single time. Laughter, even at a time of complex trauma and multiple losses, provides temporary relief and often comfort during the mourning and healing time. Play, whether through toys or another form, facilitates interactions among family members and provides a common language in times of uncertainty and hardship. Play also facilitates a safe and secure basis for families to explore and resolve issues together, drawing upon the unique perspectives while working through the needs of each family member.

Play has a special place in the lives of people throughout the world. Groups of children, whatever the form, interact and develop relationships that provide social connections and support that are cultivated through play. Families gather in usual and creative ways to join together, playing and healing simultaneously. They connect, share, understand their reason for being together, and many depart from one another. Playing provides an experience and purpose for joining. It facilitates the relationship and offers a link for connecting, healing, and attachment.

PURPOSE OF THIS BOOK

Through the compilation of experiences and theoretical review by experts in the field of healing for children, this book provides an overview of *play* as well as of *families*, their past, present, and changing definitions. An examination of how play acts as a tool for healing for biological, adoptive, and foster families inclusive of other types of "family" within the world today represents a substantial part of this book.

The variation of family life creates both an intriguing diversity in the world community and at the same time, a conundrum regarding how families survive. An overview of the "family" today provides a segue to interventions and healing alternatives within the world of counseling and therapy. Play, its therapeutic factors, and contribution to family healing provides a perspective that all families, anywhere in the world, can and will provide support and healing of their own. Professional interventions facilitate these opportunities. This book serves to highlight some of these models of healing.

PLAY AS A HEALING TOOL

Play is described as a phenomenon that provides socialization, relationships, and attachment opportunities. Models of play therapy, a researched and proven form of therapeutic intervention, highlight the power of play as a way of healing. Models of play therapy that incorporate family members within the ecosystem are featured and are integral to the application of the book's purpose: to provide tools for knowledge and practice.

Family therapy, its origin and evolution, as well as the incorporation of play within family therapy are explored. Using the Metaframeworks model (Breunlin, Schwartz, & MacKune-Karrer 2001) as a way to both include and transcend specific models of family therapy, case examples are used to explore the theory and practice of family and family play therapy.

Narrative Play Therapy and associated family involvement is described from its origin with the pioneering of Michael White and David Epstein and its application for family restructuring. Alternative activities and play-based healing provide direct application for professionals and families.

Theraplay and filial models, two play therapy models with a family focus, are described highlighting the therapeutic process for family growth. The phases of these researched models are described in detail leaving the reader with opportunities for direct application to work with families in the healing process. While the two models have a different focus, theraplay on building family attachments and filial on facilitating family play, they are most applicable to mental health interventions within diverse regions around the world.

Sandplay, a commonly used tool and method of healing, is described vis-à-vis the healing process for adoptive families. In an effort to begin and maintain a strong attachment, sandtray provides a medium for families who choose to adopt to share stories, feelings, and problem solve as the needs to do so arise. Direct application for those who study the sandplay approach is available within this chapter in the book.

A NEW MODEL FOR FAMILY HEALING: COLLABORATIVE PLAY THERAPY

The introduction of a new model of play therapy for children and families is presented at the outset of this publication. The *collaborative play therapy model* highlights the tools, genogram, ecomap, and timeline, for sharing of the family story, recognizing strengths and areas of challenge, planning opportunities for change, and sharing of the changing story through collaborative efforts. An opportunity for families, new, reconstituted, and restructured, will be presented so that healing through the medium of play is available to everyone. The three tools are useful for the development of an understanding for the child and family of life's events, family, and community relationships (i.e., The Genogram); for a view of significant events, both positive and challenging (i.e., Timeline), and a bird's eye view of the ecosystem and all aspects of available resources that exist for children and their family systems (i.e., Ecomap). While basic, these resources coupled with all that is creative (colors, collage work, music, materials and art work for expression, puppetry with or without technological inclusions) can "bring to life" those parts of the child's life.

The *collaborative* approach that involves the child with the family throughout the healing process, from assessment and intake to termination, is based on the understanding that children have a "voice" that can be heard through playful techniques and that this voice enhances self-expression, choices for healing options, and new attachments.

GENOGRAM:

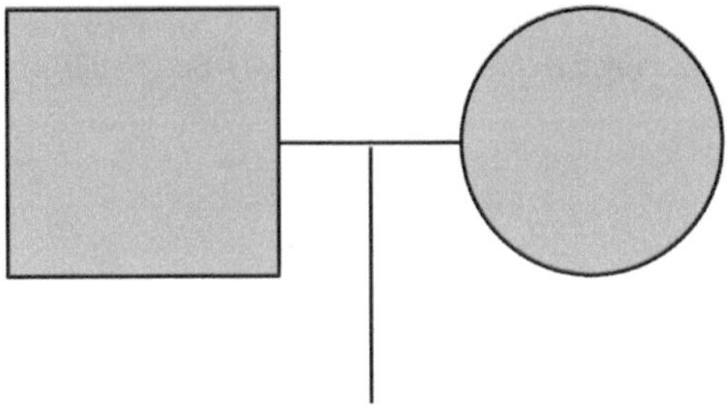

TIMELINE:

0 yrs **now**

ECOMAP:

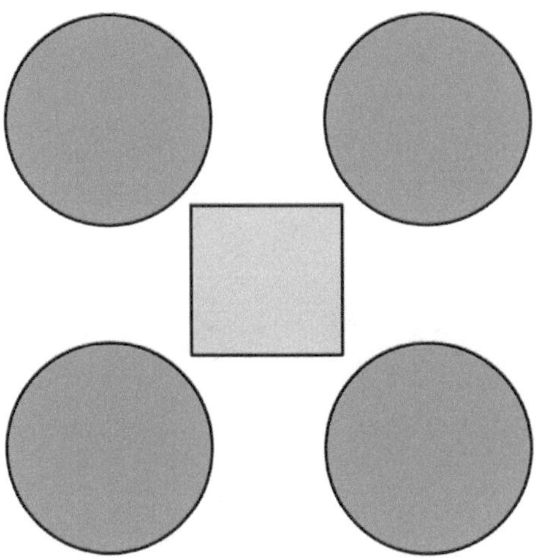

Figure 1.1. Tools for Collaborative Play Therapy

REFERENCES

Axline, V. (1947). Play Therapy. New York: Ballantine Books.
Breunlin, D., Schwartz, R., & Mac Kune-Karrer, B. (2001). Metaframeworks: Transcending the Models of Family Therapy. San Francisco, CA., Jossey-Bass Publishers.

Chapter Two

Setting the Context: Play and its Therapeutic Application

Nancy Riedel Bowers

WHAT IS PLAY IN A GLOBAL CONTEXT?

This chapter that presents "play" as a curative agent in the healing process has been conceptualized and started several times and in several places. It is by the Grand River in Waterloo Region of Ontario in Canada that this final draft is composed. It was on Nauset Light Beach on Cape Cod, USA that most of the work was put onto paper and it was in Morocco, Cannes and Hong Kong that children's play was observed as amazingly diverse and providing many different contexts for communication, family life, and collaborative healing. This chapter celebrates the notion that play provides "a voice" for the children of the world.

The family and its changing definitions offer the challenge of creating an idea, or many ideas, of how families heal through play. How is the family context understood around the world? What are "families"? How do families "play"? Do some families not "play'? Is play an activity, a natural part of the person's development? Is "play" evident from birth to death or is it just leisure activity, or both? Does play contribute to healing of loss, trauma, and daily events? The challenge of defining play is endless. Play and its function as well as curative factors are changing in our midst as we add new ways of playing. It is clear that "when children play, they are able to develop a wide range of adaptive skills and process emotions" (Christian, Russ, & Short, 2011, p. 179). We observe the "value of play for expression" (Brumfield & Christensen, 2011, p. 216) but how does play contribute to family relationships and healing through life's course? This book attempts to answer some of these questions and offers alternative forms of healing through play, thereby facilitating growth for children and their families. Actually, play is presented as pivotal to family cohesion and survival. Ultimately, we learn to play with life through children (Hart, 2003); families and community systems can learn from children about the healing power of play through their children. But what is play?

In one year I had the opportunity of observing children play without toys, just using their ability to run and be chased down the back streets of the Medina of Marrakesh, Morrocco followed by watching, at a distance, children playing on large boats off the coast of France. With this contrast in mind came a voyage to the new world of playing through technology as seen in Singapore, Japan, and Hong Kong where computer tablets of all sizes are held by all ages, shared with one another, and now provide new alternatives for play and creativity. At the end of this year of observation, I was left intrigued as to the changing conceptualization of play on the world stage.

I have been comforted by the notion that, ultimately, play is "a voice . . . self-actualization . . . empowerment" (Riedel Bowers, 2009, p. 176) evident in the normal growth and development most applicable to healing through play therapy. Bratton et al. (2013) reinforce the universality of play as a powerful tool of communication suggesting that "play therapy is a developmentally and culturally responsive intervention particularly suited to treat young children's social, emotional, and behavioural problems" (p. 30). At the risk of sounding too "academic" this chapter attempts to define play from a traditional point of view, then moves to presentation of play as a healing tool, and concludes with the application of play to the healing or therapy process, namely, to selected play therapy models that incorporate children, adults, communities, and families. Particularly, play and its connection to relationship development are highlighted as relevant to the formation and maintenance of family and community connections.

DEFINING PLAY

Play is a common activity for most, and yet a precise operational meaning of play has historically been difficult to achieve. With excitement abound within the last quarter of the twentieth century for further focus on play, Ellis (1973) indicates that "A new burst of theoretical activity is upon us, accompanying the increase in practical concern for play" (p. 4) with sporadic attention has been devoted to this phenomenon over the past fifty years. The concept of play continues to be defined in many ways and is discussed within a variety of contexts. Its profound importance to the child's growth and transition to adulthood has become increasingly understood. Play, as the foundation of life (Brown, 2010), suggests that play is integral to human growth.

Charles Schaefer (1983) notes that "it is somewhat difficult for anyone interested in play and play therapy to gain a clear understanding of what is meant by the term play because no single, comprehensive definition of the term has been developed" (p. 2). Moreover, one must be clear about the context within which play is being examined.

The etymology of the word, play, originates within the context of fighting and game playing. E. Mahon (1993) reviews the origin of the word play:

> Whereas the modern definition of play as "games, diversion" captures the lucid nature of the activity, the word derives from the Old English plega, which implied a less sportive intent—to strike a blow (asc-plega = playing with spears, that is, fighting with spears; or sword—plega = fighting with swords [Skeat, 1910]) . . . If we follow these etymological leads, play would seem to have begun with actions that were anything but "playful" in the modern usage of the word. (p. 173)

Modern dictionaries have offered a variety of definitions over the past many years that incorporate the game aspect of play implied in the original meaning of the word play along with other variations on this theme. Webster's Ninth New Collegiate Dictionary (1989) suggests that the meaning of play is "the spontaneous activity of children" (p. 902). The Oxford English Dictionary (1989) emphasizes play "as exercise, brisk or free movement or action" (p. 1011) and as "unimpeded movement" (p. 1012) and Merriam-Webster.com (2012) suggests that play is "a state of being active; operative and relevant; free and unimpeded motion." These definitions, along with other current ones, highlight "freedom" afforded by the process of play as well as "spontaneity" as recurring descriptive themes.

Prominent theorists have defined and described play. The following review of several classic and more contemporary theories of play will assist in a more thorough explanation. The contributions of play to the child's socialization and relationship development within the context of his or her world or surrounding environment are then summarized.

REVIEW OF SELECTED THEORIES OF PLAY RELATING TO RELATIONSHIP DEVELOPMENT

R. van der Kooij and Joop Hellendoorn (1986) comment on the fragmented compilation of theories of play that presently exist:

> the existence and importance of play has never really been in doubt . . . nevertheless, one cannot state that play is under scientific control, either from a theoretical or a methodological point of view. In the literature on play, a great number of different opinions can be found, and this divergence continues to exist today. In older theories on play, such as the work of Spencer, Hall,

> Lazarus and Groos (1901), only some aspects are elucidated. What would be our final judgment when we include in our analysis the modern theories on play of Piaget, Erikson, Chateau, Heckhausen, Buhler and Hetzer? We agree with Scheuerl (1975) who concludes: "The course of history of play theories has been a road of fragments which seldom fit together, are often opposites of each other, and also not connected to each other" (pp. 11-12)

The theories of some of these aforementioned theorists along with others assist in the organization of a better understanding of play. This understanding serves to identify the qualities necessary for the enhancement of the relationship between the individual and the environment in which he or she lives, inclusive of family, community, and general system.

A HISTORY OF PLAY THEORIES

An examination of the history of play reveals that play has been innate to many generations of civilization. R. Meares (1993) suggests that children's use of play serves to "project basic time-space patterns in their lives" (p. 119). He further comments,

> Artifacts from the earliest civilizations include miniature representations of people and animals, presumably used as toys. It is difficult not to conclude that the capacity of play is part of our genetic endowment, just as a potential for language creation is biologically given . . . this capacity depends upon the responsiveness of the environment. (p. 151)

The existence of play in the individual's growth process is timeless, often taken for granted and not thoroughly understood.

Rubin (1982) attempts an overview of classical and contemporary play theories, recognizing that the former are widely criticized but have an unrecognized impact on the study of play as it exists today. He summarizes early views of play which are reviewed in contemporary writings some of which have implications for relationship development:

1. Play allows the child to transform reality and thus to develop symbolic representations of the world (Schiller, 1954; Spencer, 1873; Groos, 1898, 1901; Piaget, 1962; Vygotsky, 1967; Singer, 1973).
2. There are qualitative differences in children's play which reflect different levels of ability. These play forms, originally described by Schiller (1954), Spencer (1873), and Groos (1898, 1901), range from sensori-motor activities to fantasy endeavors and games with rules.
3. One characteristic of play is its 'as-if' or non-literal nature (Bateson, 1956; Garvey, 1977; Matthews & Matthews, 1982).
4. Play aids in the development of creativity and aesthetic appreciation (Dansky, 1980; Lieberman, 1977; Singer, 1973).

5. Play in childhood permits the practice and mastery of activities which are later useful for more serious endeavors in adulthood (Groos, 1898; Bruner, 1972; Sylva, 1976). Moreover, the notion that play is related causally to mastery over one's environment is reaffirmed in the mid-twentieth-century Freudian theory.
6. Play serves a cathartic function in development (Hall, 1920; Axline, 1969). This view is found in contemporary psychoanalytic theory and practice and through the recognition of the benefits of play therapy (Axline, 1969).
7. Neural mechanisms are responsible for the existence of play (Berlyne, 1960).

(pp. 11-12)

Highlighted from Rubin's study of play are the contributions of Piaget and Groos pertaining to play and its symbolic value. As well, the concepts of creativity and mastery are stressed as being essential to the child's development of problem-solving skills. The cathartic function of play serves as a basic premise for modern play therapy methods.

The remainder of this section will attempt a more specific review of the tenets of play theories. Selected play theories, listed in chronological order, are presented as they relate specifically to the importance of games in play, symbolic play, play as a function of the ego, and the relevance of creative play for social interaction as summarized in the conclusion of this chapter.

As indicated by D. Lebo (1952), "the first person to advocate studying the play of children in order to understand and educate them was Jean-Jacques Rousseau (1758). He recognized the fact that childhood was a period of growth" (p. 418). Rousseau (1758) provides the first documented theory on childhood and play:

> Hold childhood in reverence, and do not be in any hurry to judge it for good or ill . . . Give nature time to work before you take over her business, lest you interfere with her dealings . . . childhood is the sleep of reason. (p. 71)

Rousseau found a natural progression from play to work stating that, "Work or play are all one to him (the growing child), his games are his work; he knows no difference. He brings to everything the cheerfulness of interest, the charm of freedom" (p. 126). Play as an avenue for freedom of expression has since become a basic premise for further theoretical developments of play.

It was not until 1901, with the publications by Karl Groos, that play began to receive a more scholarly examination. Groos (1901) stresses the importance of games in the process of social development in his statement, "how valuable is the cheering, and humanizing effect of play, both physical and mental, and especially of those games which are calculated to strengthen the social tie" (p. 395). The games in the play process serve as a link to socialization opportunities.

Shortly after the introduction of writings on play by Groos, Sigmund Freud (1905) referred to play as an avenue in which children experience pleasure:

> Play—let us keep to that name—appears in children while they are learning to make use of words to put thoughts together. This play probably obeys one of the instincts which compel children to practice their capacities (Groos [1899]). In doing so they become pleasurable effects, which arise from a repetition of what is similar, a rediscovery of what is familiar. (p. 128)

Freud (1908) expands on play and its pleasurable effects in his writings on creativity when asking the following question that assists in the linking of play and creativity:

> Should we not look for the traces of imaginative activity as early as in childhood? The child's best-loved and most intense occupation is with his play or games. . . . In spite of all the emotion with which he cathects his world of play, the child distinguishes it quite well from reality; and he likes to link his imagined objects and situations to the tangible and visible things of the real world. (pp. 144-5)

While Freud treated children using adult psychoanalytic methodology, he reinforces the importance of play and its functions as a bridge between the world of the imagination and the real world. Play and its creative capacities allow the child an opportunity to experiment with the outside world and approach the challenges of the environment around him or her.

The psychoanalytic interpretation of play by Melanie Klein (1932) expands on the close relationship between play and reality. She suggests that "early analysis has shown that in play the child not only overcomes painful reality, but at the same time uses it to master its instinctual fears and internal dangers by projecting them in the outer world" (p. 177). Klein recognizes the value of following the changes in the child's games for the purpose of gaining a better understanding of the "various currents in the child's mental life" (p. 105).

John Bowlby (1953) focuses on the symbolic function of play and the social development of the individual when stating "in a family a young child is within limits encouraged to express himself both socially and in play . . . he is learning to change his social environment to a shape more congenial to him. The same occurs in his play, where in a symbolic way he is creating and recreating new worlds for himself" (p. 64).

The symbolic function of play was expanded upon at length by Jean Piaget (1962), perhaps the most prolific writer and theorist on this subject. He postulates that in the child's cognitive development the symbolic function that play provides is extremely important. In an attempt to understand the aspect of play that contributes to socialization and the relationships with others, Piaget advanced several ideas about the symbolic function of play, especially focusing on the development of relations with others through game play.

Piaget (1962) recognizes three main categories of games in the process of play: practice games, symbolic games, and games with rules, with interest centered upon the symbolic or make-believe games. In an effort to decipher the main problems of the interpretation of play, Piaget orders the symbolic games of play into several stages reflecting on different stages in early development, the behavior, or the sensory-motor schema, and not the individual object or image. He believes that symbolism has considerable significance for the subsequent development of play in that the symbolic representation will enable the child to assimilate the external world. It is in this way that symbolic play begins to take shape. The child exercises individual powers "to reproduce his own actions for the pleasure of seeing himself do them and showing off to others, in a word to express himself" (p. 121). Each stage in the early development of symbolic game playing contributes to this discussion of play and its value in the socialization process.

Stage I of Piaget's theory is termed as "projection of symbolic schemas on to new objects" during which, through the mechanism of imitation and the relationships established between himself and others, "(the child) will apply the now familiar schema to other people and objects" (p. 121). This stage applies to the child during the first four years of life and is characterized by the imitation and the relationships established between him or herself and other individuals. Stage I is further characterized by "simple identification of one object with another and identification of the child's body with that of other people or with things" (p. 124). It is during this phase that the child creates fictitious characters in his or her play as companions that "acquire existence only insofar as they provide a sympathetic audience or a mirror of the ego" (p. 131). The assimilation of reality by means of symbolic make-believe takes place during this period giving the child the opportunity of creating an environment to which he/she can relate.

Stage II affects children from the age of four to seven and is termed as "simple identification of one object with another" is characterized by the loss of importance of the activity of symbolic games and the existence of more direct imitative representation of the real world. Instead, orderliness, the exact imitation of reality and the appearance of collective symbolism take precedence. Collective symbolism has been in existence in the previous stages with the child playing with one or more companions. After the age of four, however, roles are differentiated. The child develops more coherent thought processes from his or her progress in socialization. There is a transition from "initial egocentrism to reciprocity, as a result of double co-ordination in inter-individual relationships" (p. 138).

In stage III, termed "simple combinations" and affecting children between the ages of seven and twelve, socialization in general occurs where there is a definite decline in symbolism and an increase in games with rules. Symbolic constructions that are related to adapted work are evident. The rule replaces the symbol and integrates practice as soon as certain social relationships are discovered and formed.

In summary, Piaget has contributed significantly to the discussion of the association between play, socialization, and the development of relationships. He is criticized, however, for the limited aspect of his theories in that they are focused on cognitive and early developmental processes in children rather than on the effects of these in later life. Nevertheless, his contributions to the understanding of play have been profound in viewing play as a tool with which the child exercises his or her newly acquired powers in the act of game-playing. This acquisition is intensified through "fictitious control of the whole natural and social world" (p.146). The development of games with rules represents a "subtle equilibrium between assimilation to the ego—the principle of all play—and social life" (p. 168). In his view, play is an innate response to being born and through its development from practice to symbolism and eventually to work, the individual connects with the environment and the external forces.

Erikson (1963) refers to play in children and adults as an activity which the ego uses to find recreation and self-cure. He postulates further that "play is a function of the ego, an attempt to synchronize the bodily and the social processes with the self . . . when man plays he must intermingle with things and people in a similarly uninvolved and light fashion . . . he must feel entertained and free of any fear or hope of serious consequences . . . the playing adult steps sideward into another reality; the playing child advances forward to new stages of mastery" (p. 211-222). Erikson defines the ego as dwelling between the id and the superego which "keeps tuned to the reality of the historical day, testing perceptions, selecting memories, governing actions, and otherwise integrating the individual's capacities of orientation and planning. To safeguard itself, the ego employs 'defense mechanisms' " (p. 193). He uses the words of Anna Freud (1937) to further explain the ego and the defenses:

> the ego is victorious when its defensive measures . . . enable it to restrict the development of anxiety and so to transform the instincts that, even in difficult circumstances, some measure of gratification is secured, thereby establishing the most harmonious relations possible between the id, the super-ego, and the forces of the outside world. (p. 194)

This summary of Anna Freud's theory on the ego and the necessity of defenses, as presented by Erikson, suggests that strengths develop for the individual through the building of defenses that act against external threats. In summary, children develop self-protection in early life development through the process of play.

Winnicott's writings focus on play within a developmental perspective (Scarlett, 1994). He argues that play facilitates the development of the self in relation to others (Marans, Mayes, & Colonna, 1993). Winnicott (1971) develops the thesis that "an infant's employment of a transitional object . . . [is] the child's first use of a symbol and the first experience of play" (p. 96). He defines the transitional object as the symbol of the union of the baby and the mother (or parts of the mother). This symbol can be located. It is at the place in space and time where and when the mother is in transition from being (in the baby's mind) merged in with the infant and alternatively being experienced as an object (p. 96).

This interpretation of the origin of play was one of Winnicott's major contributions to the subject of play. He postulates that the psychoanalytic literature lacks any useful statement about play, taking issue with Melanie Klein who wrote about the difference between play, as most refer to it, and playing. In order to examine where playing belongs, Winnicott chooses to describe a sequence of relationships related to the developmental process. The sequence involves, first, the baby and object merged in one another which is presented as an early relationship. Second, Winnicott indicates that the object is "repudiated, re-accepted, and perceived objectively" (p. 47), thereby giving the baby the experience of control. He considers this "a playground because play starts here" (p. 47). Third, he stresses that the child is now playing on the basis of the assumption that the mother is reliable and to be trusted and the child is able to be alone in the presence of someone else. Eventually, the child and mother "play together in a relationship" (p. 48) each with his or her own wishes. The ability to form a relationship within the primitive bond of mother-child originates through the play process that provides an environment for experimentation, control and autonomy. Weininger (1989) summarizes Winnicott's study of play, indicating that "play is universal . . . playing facilitates growth [and] leads into group-relationships" (p. 158). In summary, play facilitates community connections.

Liederman et al. (1989), in the examination of social relationships within the life cycle, suggest that play performs a function in each of the developmental stages, infancy to adolescence, preschool to adulthood, school age to adulthood, and adolescence to adulthood. These theorists suggest that "play for the infant and young child provides an opportunity for the rehearsal of later social roles . . . play provides a relationship of non-purposive joyful interaction, enabling appreciation of 'the other' " (p. 171).

In all relationships within the life cycle, play serves as an important function (Liederman, 1989). The developmental period of infancy to adolescence, during which time care giving and care receiving are the evident types of relationships, is characterized by the parent/child engagement in complimentary relationships serving such functions as protection/survival, physiological need regulation, responsivity/security (attachment), psychosocial need regulation, teaching/learning, empathic intimacy, and play. Preschool to adulthood, the second relationship stage, involves peer affiliation as the type of relationship within which psychosocial need regulation is experienced and empathic intimacy, and play as the functions of the reciprocal process between peers. School age to adulthood, the third stage, provides a mentoring process with teaching/learning, empathic intimacy, and play as the major functions. Lastly, adolescence to adulthood, the romantic/marital relationship period, includes play, physiological and psychosocial need regulation, responsivity/security (attachment), and empathic intimacy as major functions (Liederman, 1989). Play is a function of all the developmental stages during the life cycle.

Scheuerl (1975), in his phenomenological analysis of play, comments on the relationship between play and the environment. He suggests that play serves as a dialogue between a person and his or her environment, each influencing the other. He stresses that play is always performed in relation to something or somebody. In contrast, Moran (1987) suggests that play is not always an activity that takes place in relation to others. He postulates that "every so-called normal child will develop his own unique style of tempering reality with pretense. The way in which different children do so varies greatly. Some children continue to prefer play enactments while others become humorous or witty, and still others alter more privately by indulging in daydreams" (p. 28). Children choose to play in relation to others or opt to play with toys, thereby metaphorically playing with other objects. Allowing the child the freedom to make this choice is essential in his or her development.

Play is conceptualized as providing the child opportunity for free or unimpeded motion (Merriam-Webster, 2012). The child is able to make the choice as to how play will be employed in his or her development, providing that opportune circumstances exist. Coleman and Skeen (1985) define play as free of space, time, and role limitations, self-directed and spontaneous, and involving internal rewards of self-expression and self-discovery of one's capabilities. The autonomous nature of play is essential to the child's ability to feel control over his or her environment so that with freedom and trust he or she is able to venture out if he or she chooses and to connect with objects that are in the surrounding region. Mook (1994) observes the existence of a connection between the autonomous function of play and relationship development in her statement that "play is an autonomous and an imaginative exploration of the child's relationships to him or herself, to others, and to his/her world" (p. 46). There is a common implication that play implies an activity in relation to another. The child's ability to control his or her environment and choose the nature of the play is an important aspect of play.

Pepler (1991) sets out to examine further the link between play and creativity or divergent thinking, which she considers an aspect of cognitive skill development. Her review of the research available on this topic addresses several questions, one of which concerns the effect of the durability and stability of play on the child's creativity. Two studies conducted by Pepler and a colleague focus on play and problem-solving. Their findings indicate that children who have divergent play experiences are imaginative in their responses to divergent thinking tasks, suggesting that it is not play per se, but play with unstructured play materials that contribute to creativity. Pepler postulates that there may be a generalized transfer of a playful attitude or a flexible response from the play to problem-solving situations. She reviews the study of Dansky and Silverman (1973) that recognizes that children with play experiences may be flexible, curious, spontaneous, and interested in the task. Pepler summarizes that the research of Johnson (1976) reinforces the links that play has with creativity and relations with others. One can conclude that the play experience involving social interaction affects subsequent divergent problem-solving performances.

Pepler (1991) concludes that "individual differences in the predisposition for creativity should be identified, examined and fostered for their potential in helping children face the divergent problems of everyday life" (p. 77). There is a link between play, creativity, and divergent thinking in that they collectively contribute to an increased potential in the child to deal with problem-solving in relation to the external conditions and influences affecting his or her life and development. Pepler recognizes the inconclusiveness of her findings but sees these as potentially important links between play and responsiveness to environmental situations.

SUMMARY OF PLAY AND ITS APPLICATION TO RELATIONSHIP DEVELOPMENT

This preceding chronological review of selected play theories has focused on both classic and contemporary theorists who have devoted some of their analyses of play to the subject of socialization and interpersonal relations with others. The following eight points synthesize this material with respect to play and its contributions to socialization and relationship development.

1. Play provides an avenue for freedom of movement within certain limits (Rousseau, 1758); one has the freedom of expression to play alone or with another (Coleman & Skeen, 1985).
2. Play allows the child the opportunity to have pleasurable experiences, to practice that which he or she is capable of and to gain mastery of the surrounding environment (Freud, 1905; Klein, 1932; Piaget, 1962).

3. Play is a link between the imagined world and the real world for the child, overcoming the pain of the real world through play (Freud, 1908; Klein, 1932).
4. Symbolic play helps children to assimilate to the ego, the principle of all social life, to imitate others, and to consolidate emotional experiences with the external world (Piaget, 1962; Erikson, 1963; A. Freud, 1937).
5. Play and playing with others results from a sequence of relationships that occurs during the developmental process (Piaget, 1962; Leiderman, 1989; Winnicott, 1971). Play provides the opportunity for experimentation, control, and autonomy for the child within his or her environment (Winnicott, 1971).
6. Play provides an opportunity for the child to express him or herself and to strengthen the child's abilities through socialization (Gross, 1901; Bowlby, 1953).
7. Play serves as a dialogue between the person and his or her environment, each influencing the other (Scheuerl, 1975).
8. Play contributes to creativity, divergent thinking, problem-solving, and the ability to develop and sustain relationships with others (Pepler, 1991).

PARENT AND SIBLING INFLUENCES IN PLAY[1]

There is no doubt that family members assume an important role in the development of children's play skills and participation. The longer and more advanced play sessions that have been found to occur when a mother or sibling joins, as compared to the child playing alone, suggest that these relationships have an influential nature when it comes to prompting self-expression and exploration through play (Dale, 1989). The context that is established through the presence of a parent or sibling facilitates expression and creativity while also influences the content and direction of children's play behaviors (Howe & Bruno, 2010). Dynamics of the real-life filial relationship may come forth in a play session, feelings may be expressed more freely through the disguise of an assumed character, and negotiation and communication skills may be enhanced to then be applied in problem-solving situations.

There are a number of reasons why the involvement of family members in a child's play, as well as the home setting in which this play often takes place, are important in children's social, emotional, and cognitive development. As children enter formal schooling, imagination and creativity through play continue to be important for expressing ideas, wishes, and feelings, yet the focus often turns to engaging in games. Thus the private context of the home offers toys and objects, along with family members as play partners, which allow for continued development and consolidation of pretense, theory of mind, and other social-cognitive skills (Howe & Bruno, 2010). This, in turn, contributes to healthy emotional expression and social relationships. Through the enactment of narrative scenarios, not only do children master reality through the exploration of ideas, thoughts, and emotions, but they also strengthen filial bonds through cooperation, collaboration, and communication with their parent or sibling play partner (Eckhoff & Urbach, 2008; Howe & Bruno, 2010).

Gil (1994) states that "the integration of play with family therapy" strengthens both the child's relationship with the therapist as well as with their family members (p. 33). The demonstrated effectiveness of this versatile incorporation of play techniques in clinical situations suggests that family members are key participants in a child's therapeutic process, as they can learn to effectively engage in and support play at home (Haslam & Harris, 2011). In filial play sessions we see "facilitation" by the play partner which differs in nature depending on the family member engaging with the child. Siblings facilitate cooperation, playfulness, and the acquisition of a social role whereas parents, particularly mothers, prompt consolidation of the play scenarios, enhanced complexity, and tutoring of the relations and regularities in the non-play world (Dale, 1989). Thus, play with different partners will consistently require the child to adopt a shared framework for play yet may lead to differential outcomes in terms of social cognition and emotional expression, depending on the family member with whom the play is shared (Youngblade & Dunn, 1995). Together, these results suggest that through play in a therapeutic setting, family members having the potential to enhance their facilitative role in the child's play, while also learning to draw on strengths, address weaknesses, and prompt the healthy expression of feelings in a play episode. This, in turn, will allow the struggling child to have access to a continuous and supportive imaginative world in which to work out his or her problems.

PLAY AND ITS APPLICATION TO THE THERAPEUTIC PROCESS

Play has many functions within the therapeutic process. A. Ornstein (1984) suggests that play "serves as a window through which the investigator or therapist can take a glimpse at the workings of the mind . . . in the case of play, the therapist can also respond, interact with the player, and thereby effect its outcome" (p. 349). Because of this quality, play can be a catalyst for change and, consequently, has become a major contributor to the methods of psychotherapy for children. One such method, play therapy, consists of different orientations and foci, each of which utilizes the play process in various ways. The generic label of play therapy "covers a variety of clinical theories and interventions that warrant careful elucidation" (Phillips, 1985, p. 758). Interest in the theoretical implications of play and its contribution to the psychotherapy process arose during the twentieth century as more was being discovered about the inner workings of the child. Psychoanalysis, as it was applied to the treatment of children, played an important part in these investigations as did academic psychology, especially following Piaget's pioneering research into cognitive development, establishing that play carries traits conducive for growth. As suggested by Frank (1955), it has become apparent that play provides the possibility and opportunity for children to live in a social order and a cultural world. Furthermore, theorists such as Herzka (1986) stress the importance of play as a catalyst for the development of social relationships and the development of individuality (Herzka, 1986). But as Chethick (1989) points out, it is not play per se that produces the changes for the child in the therapeutic context. The therapist's use of play creates a catalyst for change. Vandenberg (1986) proposes that therapy is accomplished by the particular themes of the play. He states that "the relationship is the vehicle that helps the children learn to trust, invest belief in, and create meaning in their lives" (p. 86). The therapist's understanding of the relationship development process is essential in the direction of the healing process.

Play and its many qualities that encourage relationship development within an environment of social interaction has been the subject of this chapter up to this point. The focus now turns to a more specific overview of the relationship between play and its functions within the relationship development process of play therapy. To this end, the techniques or procedures that specify how play can be utilized, namely, the therapeutic factors of play will be outlined. This will be followed by a history of the development of the various methods of play therapy, reinforcing the recognition that the relationship between the child and therapist contributes to the growth of the child. Particular focus within this discussion will be placed on those methods of play therapy that utilize the relationship as a vehicle for change and the inclusion of the family in this process.

In preparation for the theoretical review of the play therapy process, figure 2 illustrates the circular view of the general phases of the therapeutic process, both generally acceptable and applicable to play therapy. The needs of the child are understood, a plan which may be developed in collaboration with the child and family is prepared and the process takes place. The relationship that occurs between child, therapist, and family members needs to be trusted as taking the course that is natural and unimpeded.

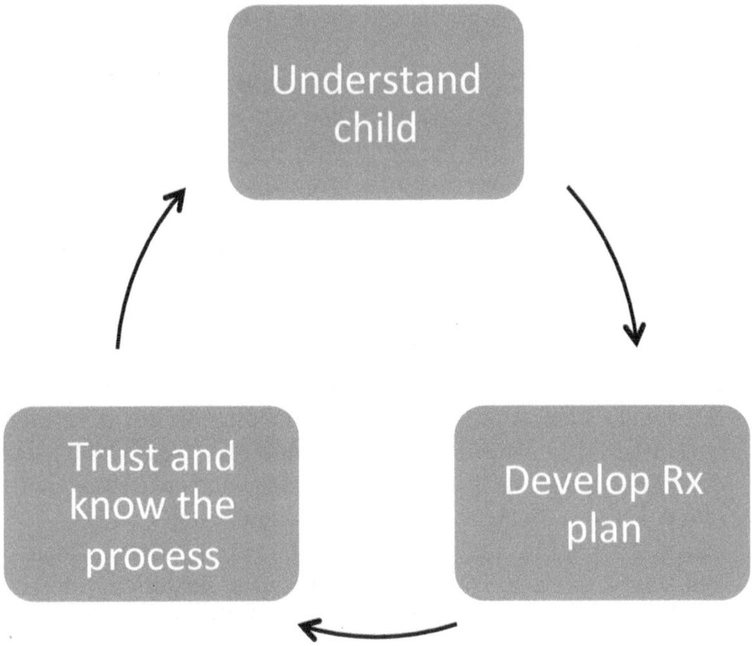

Figure 2.1. The Collaborative Process of Play Therapy

THERAPEUTIC FACTORS OF PLAY

Charles Schaefer, a prominent theorist of the play therapy process, defines play therapy as "an interpersonal process wherein a trained therapist systematically applies the curative powers of play that help clients to resolve their psychological difficulties" (Schaefer, 1993, p. 3). He recognizes that there are specific therapeutic factors or components of play that have different benefits, believing that "the play therapy process contains a limited number of elements that are differentiated from each other by their specific effects on a child" (p. 5). He suggests that if a factor results in a clinical improvement of some sort, it is deemed to be a therapeutic factor, defined as "an element of play that contributes to a positive outcome" (p. 5). A review of these established therapeutic factors provides at this point an overview of the ways in which play does contribute to the therapeutic process. Once reviewed, those specific components of play within the play therapy context will be highlighted in preparation for a review of play therapy methods that place importance on the relationship development process.

1. Overcoming Resistance: Play seems to assist in establishing rapport and alliance with a child. It encourages voluntary acceptance of thera-

py, a recognition that problems exist, and develops a wish to talk to a "strange" adult.

2. Communication: Play acts as the most natural medium of expression for self-expression or communication. As stressed by Piaget (1962), "fantasy play provides the child with the live, dynamic, individual language indispensable for the expression of his subjective feelings for which collective language alone is inadequate" (p. 166). This communication process through play functions on the conscious and unconscious levels and can provide an alternative to talk therapy for young children (Ebrahim, Steen, & Paradise, 2012, p. 203) in many settings including the home, school, community activities, etc.
3. Competence and Mastery: Play is a self-motivated activity that satisfies a child's innate need to explore and master his environment (Berlyne, 1960), and his activity in turn contributes to the child's sense of power and control. It is the child's sense of competence that motivates him or her to learn about the world and acquire skills.
4. Creative Thinking: Play encourages children to improve their problem-solving skills and promotes creativity and flexibility. Consequently, children are able to find alternative and effective solutions to real life social and emotional problems through play.
5. Catharsis: The safety of the playroom allows children the opportunity for emotional release without fear of retaliation or censure. The cathartic effect of play lies in the child's sense of freedom and comfort, allowing the discharge of strong emotions for therapeutic relief.
6. Abreaction: In play, children can slowly digest and assimilate traumatic experiences by reliving them with an appropriate release of affect. Piaget (1962) conceptualized this model of assimilation proposing that a traumatic experience must be gradually assimilated into a schema (frame of reference, script) that is developed by the therapist-child interaction. As a result, a sense of mastery is gained through this self-therapeutic process (Erikson, 1940).
7. Role-play: In play therapy, children are encouraged to try out alternative behaviors or roles. Garvey (1976) suggests that there are four major roles assumed by children in play: functional roles, relational roles, occupational roles, and fantasy roles. By playing the roles of others, children gain a reflected view of their own identity from the perspective of those identities whose roles they enact (Stone, 1971).
8. Fantasy: One of the major therapeutic functions of play is that it enhances the flexible and varied use of one's imagery capacities. In the process, the child is given the opportunity to experience power and control over the world as well as mastery over his/her environment (White, 1959; Saltz & Johnson, 1974).

9. Metaphoric Teaching: Children in play therapy can be provided with new myths that address the sources of conflicts, fears, and hostilities in their lives and offer more adaptive solutions for consideration. If these conflicts and feelings are repeatedly experienced in play without resolution, the therapist can replay the situation in a way that suggests new options or solutions.
10. Attachment Formation: Through the replication of positive child-parent interaction, the child has the potential of establishing a secure attachment experience.
11. Relationship Enhancement: The role of play in facilitating a positive relationship between child and therapist is related to the nature of playful interactions facilitated by the positive mutual feelings between the child and the therapist. The therapist-child relationship is seen as crucial for the child to gain a more adequate acceptance of him or herself.
12. Positive Emotion: Play is free from external demands, obligation, and serious intent. Research indicates that children do better work under the influence of a strong emotion, that enjoyment of a task enhances striving and persistence at it, and that joy provides motivation in unrelated activities (Reichenberg, 1939).
13. Mastering Development Fears: Play can reduce anxiety and fear through the process of systematic desensitization by exposing a child to a fearful situation through the relaxation of play. The pleasure of play can counteract and neutralize fearfulness so the child can perform the desired behavior.
14. Game Play: Games are a primary way for children to become socialized. Through interactive play and learning the rules of games children prepare for the rules of life. Game play prepares children for their roles in the social world, enhancing ego development.

(pp. 5-13)

The eleventh factor, relationship enhancement, as indicated in the aforementioned review, is singled out as it affects the occurrence and intensity of all other thirteen factors. For instance, the relationship that develops through the play process between the child and therapist allows a form of communication to develop with which a medium of expression is established. Consequently, with this encouragement and trust, role-playing, fantasy opportunities, creative thinking, positive emotions, and game play may ensue. As the therapy progresses, the child may grow to develop a sense of competence and mastery, may overcome resistance, assimilate traumatic experiences through the process of abreaction, and master developmental fears. The process of attachment formation between the child and therapist ultimately offers the child the ability to attach and develop self-growth within the overall therapeutic process. It is understood that a secure parent-child attachment is an essential foundation for the formation of a child's well-being (Darewych, 2013) with both art and play therapy processes providing an opportune environment for the attachment process to be fostered and developed. This phenomenon is relevant for all ages. It is noted that "some adolescents strive to cultivate a rich interior life in relation to their most significant relationships, including the play therapist" (Green, Myrick, & Crenshaw, 2013, p. 99). From early childhood to adolescence and adulthood play has a part to play in the development of relationships, attachments, and community participation.

In conclusion, "play therapy is a type of counselling that aims to meet the emotional needs of children in a developmentally appropriate way" (Ray, Lee, Meany-Walen, Carlson, Carnes-Hold, & Ware, 2013, p. 43). As we examine play and its link to the relationship development process between the child and therapist the healing power of the play therapy models is evident. It is suggested that play and the family therapy approaches could be integrated (Haslam & Harris, 2011), this being evident in the concluding part of this chapter.

THE HISTORY OF THE EMPHASIS ON RELATIONSHIP DEVELOPMENT IN THE PLAY THERAPY PROCESS

Clarification of the terminology, child therapy versus play therapy, is necessary for the task at hand. Child therapy is described by Sours (1980) as a "relationship between the child and the therapist, aimed primarily at symptom resolution and attaining adaptive stability" (p. 26). Eliana Gil (1991) states that the terms, child and play therapy, are often used interchangeably. For the purposes of this study, the terms will be distinguished and referred to within the contexts of their respective modalities.

The development of play therapy during the last 100 years has produced four distinctly different methods: (1) psychoanalytic play therapy; (2) structured play therapy; (3) relationship play therapy; and (4) non-directive play therapy. Each of these, along with contemporary play therapy models, will be overviewed in order to highlight aspects that focus on play and its effect on the relationship between play therapist and child. Several of the models of play therapy involve the family at different points and others include the family throughout.

1. Psychoanalytic Play Therapy

Child therapy, as a separate and distinct method, has been evolving since 1909, when Freud first attempted psychotherapy with the now historic patient Little Hans. Dell Lebo (1952) suggests that the case of Hans was the first recorded actual use of play in therapy. Historical records indicate that for years Sigmund Freud had been urging friends and pupils to collect observations on the expressions of children. The parents of the fearful child, Little Hans, collected data over a period of years and submitted them to Freud. In turn, Freud made his diagnosis from the reports and offered therapeutic advice. It was Freud's interpretation of Little Hans' play that became useful in the treatment which raised much reaction at the time. Although many believed that Hans had been made the victim of psychoanalysis, the success of the treatment which led to Freud's conceptualizations of play and child psychoanalysis has made the case noteworthy.

Charles Schaefer (1980), in his historical account of play therapy, states that play was not used directly in the therapy of children until 1920 when Hermine Von Hug-Hellmuth began using play for the diagnosis and treatment of childhood emotional problems. Von Hug-Hellmuth (1921) reports that play is essential in child analysis when treating children seven years or younger, in that play serves as a bridge to verbal communication for children. He stresses the first hour in treatment as being of utmost importance when indicating that "it is the opportunity for establishing rapport with the young creature . . . when dealing with children of seven or eight years of age, the analyst can often pave the way by sharing in the play activities, and thus he can recognize several symptoms, peculiar habits, and character traits; and in the case of these young patients, very often play will enact an important part throughout the whole treatment" (pp. 293-295). Hug-Hellmuth stresses the importance of play in the development of the rapport or relationship between the child and therapist as is illustrated in the use of the "peekaboo" game (Burton, 1986). In a personal conversation with Anni Bergman she also noted the importance of the peekaboo process for the early establishment of a child's sense of self and separateness from others.

Ten years later, in the early 1930s, the two psychoanalytic schools of Melanie Klein and Anna Freud were developing. They formulated the theory and practice of psychoanalytic play therapy. These two schools along with those of D. Winnicott/E. Erikson and M. Lowenfield constitute the four major approaches to play therapy in Britain during the past sixty years (McMahon, 1992). Each focuses on different aspects of play as a catalyst for therapeutic growth.

Anna Freud recognized the benefit of play as providing a nurturing relationship that, in turn, allows the child to develop a dependency on the therapist. In her words, "I took great pains to establish in the child a strong attachment to myself, and to bring it into a relationship of real dependence on me" (A. Freud in C. Schaefer, ed., 1976, p. 142) while being cognizant of parental reactions to this process. Lebo (1921) clarifies this aspect of Anna Freud's approach when writing that, "because the child's superego was regarded as undeveloped, the importance of the emotional relationship existing between the child and the analyst was emphasized" (p. 419). The writings of

Anna Freud suggest that play would aid in the relationship development and through this dependency the child will feel free to re-play real events or explore him or herself in the pure sense. She postulates that playing is a means of permitting children to talk about conscious feelings and thoughts and to act out unconscious conflicts and fantasies within a conducive environment, or relationship. Anna Freud stresses the importance of creating a transference relationship and opposes the use of quick and deep interpretations based on the symbolic meanings of the child's play actions, both in the playroom and outside of it. B. Mook (1994) summarizes Anna Freud's use of play suggesting that "she did not value play in its own right but saw it only as serving an intermediary means of expression when the child could not yet verbalize his or her thoughts and feelings" (p. 40). Nevertheless, it is clear that Anna Freud recognizes the importance of play in the establishment of a bond between the child and therapist as part of the beginning process of the therapy.

The writings of Melanie Klein deliberately focus on the child's anxieties rather than the development of the rapport with the child (M. Klein in C. Schaefer, ed., 1976). Klein would interpret the preconscious and conscious meaning of the play to the child in the hope that additional material would come up in the play. Klein recognizes that "through the changes which the child's games undergo, we can get to know the various currents of its mental life" (Klein, 1975, p. 105). In this way, play is utilized for the freeing of emotion, or free association, although she did not place a particular emphasis on the rapport between the child and therapist. It would appear that she understood the relationship to be implicit and a necessary tool for her task of interpretation. In the case of Egon, Klein resorts to encouraging the child to play with therapeutic toys as he did not respond to classical analysis on the couch. She recognizes that Egon "preferred playing games . . . I played with him for weeks in silence and made no interpretation, simply trying to establish rapport by playing with him" (p. 68). Her treatment resumed its interpretative style, but Klein recognized the value of the relationship through the "freeing" aspect of play.

Klein (1955), while criticized in terms of the extremity of her interpretive approach, is recognized as the first therapist to use a carefully planned playroom that included a large variety of miniature toys, drawing and painting materials, materials for cutting, and water. Materials were kept in their own separate drawers for each child with the children directing their own play, a concept that is used in more contemporary play therapy methods. These elements of the play process imply Klein's respect for the child and her recognition that play serves as a catalyst for the production of unconscious material. The actual relationship between the child and therapist was not a focus for Klein although she appears to recognize the relationship as an implicit component of her interpretative method of child psychotherapy. One would assume that there has to be a foundation and sense of trust based on which the child can be forthcoming with private and hidden material.

Winnicott and Erikson, following the middle of the twentieth century, began to stress the value of play in the self-exploration and the self-expression process of the child. Winnicott (1971) views play as having an innate therapeutic value suggesting that "play is being honest with oneself . . . playing is itself a therapy" (p. 50). As interpreted by Dasgupta (1999), Winnicott saw the therapist/child relationship as echoing the earlier mother/child relationship. He hoped that the therapeutic relationship would be able to repair what was lacking, or wrong, in the earlier one. Winnicott (1971) postulates that every therapist should "allow for the patient's capacity to play" (p. 57) and when playing is not possible then the therapist may bring the child from a state of not being able to play into a state of being able to play.

E. Erikson, a child psychoanalyst, started as a teacher in Anna Freud's school in Vienna before going to the United States and followed the basic belief that children are able to heal themselves through play (McMahon 1992, p. 34). He suggests that the therapist's task is to try to understand the meaning of the therapeutic play to gain insight into the child's sense of identity within his or her culture and environment. Erikson believes that play is only successful where there are social and cultural reinforcements, both in the family and beyond.

Lowenfield (1970), also of the British school of play therapy, stresses her use of sand play in her therapeutic work with children. She encourages the child to construct a series of miniature worlds in a sand tray and then asks them to explain this world to her. She believes that the role of the therapist is to encourage and help, using interpretations sparingly. Lowenfield notes some recurring themes in the sand play, such as a dam holding back water (feelings) to be eventually released or the building of a volcano, representing internal turmoil (McMahon, 1992, p. 36). The child is allowed to make suggestions about the meaning of the play when he or she chooses. Lowenfield, like Klein, believes that the relationship between the child and therapist within the British model of psychoanalytic play therapy is implicit but not recognized as an important component in its own right.

2. Structured Play Therapy

Structured play therapy, known also as release, directive, or active play therapy, emerged from a psychoanalytic framework. This model of play therapy was developed by Levy (1937), Solomon (1938), and Conn (1948) and emerged from a belief in the cathartic value of play and the active role of the therapist in determining the course and focus of therapy (Gil, 1991; Schaefer & O'Connor, 1983). Dell Lebo indicates that in the active play therapies of Conn and Levy there "is no need to build up a feeling of rapport between the child and the analyst" (p. 420). His approach resembles in many ways the method of M. Klein.

D. Levy developed release play therapy believing that there was no need for interpretation within the therapeutic process and based his approach primarily on a belief in the abreactive effect of play (Landreth, 1991). The child is encouraged to play freely to gain familiarity with the room and the therapist, and then the therapist intervenes shifting the play scenes in order to recreate the experience which precipitated the child's anxiety reaction. The re-enactment of the traumatic event allows the child to release the pain and tension that it caused. The therapist reflects the verbal and nonverbal feelings expressed by the child.

The method of Solomon, on the other hand, stresses the observation of the emotional relationship between the child and the therapist. He recognizes the diagnostic value of play with the therapist as indicative of the child's relationship with others outside of the play therapy situation. Solomon (1954) offers a conceptualization of how children respond to the therapeutic environment in terms of "primary" and "secondary" integration. As stated in his article, "Play Technique and the Integrative Process" (1954), the child comes to the early phase of the relationship with different emotions depending on the trauma that has been experienced and the ego development that the child possesses. The ability of the child to master the presenting problems, thereby crystallizing his or her ego process, is defined as "primary integration." If the child sets up defenses against the emotional reactions arising from the conflict situation, "secondary integration" is in process (p. 595). The therapist can assist in a reconciliation of the conflict by allowing the relationship to provide a learning process for the child. Through an analysis of the degrees of integrative capabilities of the client, the therapist can be aware of the child's capacities for growth in developing interpersonal relationships.

3. Relationship Play Therapy

At the same time, in the late 1930s and early 1940s, a more passive model of play therapy was developing. The Relationship Play Therapy model involved the play of the child as being non-restrictive. Within this model, the therapist observes as the child tests out the play environment to find out what is permitted and eventually the therapist becomes part of the play. The basic premise of this method is to allow the child to work out anxiety, hostility, or insecurity through the play at his or her own pace. This style resembles the method of relationship therapy, a method that was originated by Otto Rank.

Relationship therapy was developed by Otto Rank as a reaction to dynamic therapy which he felt failed to appreciate the actual therapeutic agents within the therapeutic process. Rank (1968) stresses the importance of understanding the role of the therapist which he states "is given through the patient, who functions as author; the task of the therapist is rather that of producer, who has to see to it that the performance runs successfully and undisturbed, and who must be always ready to take over any role that is demanded" (p. 168). Rank believes that the therapist is to understand the various roles that the patient may give to the therapist and to utilize these dynamics therapeutically. He validates the existence of the therapeutic relationship, its power in the change process and the mutuality in the process. Premises from this model have been widely used within the play therapy framework.

The emphasis that was placed by Otto Rank placed on the curative power of the emotional relationship between the therapist and the child prompted the emergence of relationship play therapy with the work of Jesse Taft (1933) and Frederick Allen (1934). Allen states that therapeutic relationships "form a pillar in the therapeutic foundation . . . as a present reality which affords the patient a clarifying milieu . . . of what he is experiencing with me at the moment" (p. 197). He suggests that younger children relate to the therapist on a basis of play for the purpose of bringing into the play "reactions and feelings common to his relations outside" (p. 199). Play is seen within this model to be a naturally forming phenomenon that allows the child to bring into the therapeutic situation certain aspects of him or herself from the surrounding environment.

Relationship play therapy emphasizes the importance of spontaneous play activity of the child which is substituted for free association in the psychoanalytic play therapy. Allan and Taft stress that children have the inner strength to alter their behavior in a constructive way, suggesting they be given the freedom to choose to play or not to play and to direct their own activity. Landreth (1991) summarizes this hypothesis of relationship play therapy when stating "that children gradually come to realize that they are separate persons with their own strivings and that they can exist in a relationship with other persons with their own qualities" (p. 32). The child takes responsibility for his or her own participation in the play therapy process. The realization that play can give autonomy and control has also been adapted to the non-directive play therapy model.

4. Non-Directive Play Therapy

By the mid-point of the twentieth century, the non-directive approach to play therapy was taking a prominent position. This method was based on Carl Rogers' client-centered therapy (Rogers, 1951) which is also known as person-centered therapy (Meador & Rogers, 1980). The non-directive approach is based on the assumption that human values are incorporated in the functioning of the individual and "promotes the full acceptance of the child as s/he is, and stresses the importance of the therapeutic relationship" (Gil,

1991, p. 31). This approach has come to be recognized as an important approach to understand behavior and focuses not so much on controlling or changing the client's way of living, but on the creation of a therapeutic situation which provides experiences that make changes possible within an environment of freedom (Lebo, 1955, p. 421). The client (adult or child) is left with the liberty of action to decide the nature and direction of the change. Meador and Rogers (1980) suggest that the central hypothesis of person-centered therapy is that "the growthful potential of any individual will tend to be released in a relationship in which the helping person is experiencing and communicating realness, caring, and a deeply sensitive nonjudgmental understanding" (p. 131).

Clark Moustakas recognizes that the child has the capacity to solve problems from within and to create change for him or herself. Moustakas (1959) derives his existential model of play therapy from both the relationship and non-directive methods, suggesting that "in relationship therapy the focus is always on the present, living experience . . . the therapist waits for the child to come to terms with himself, to express his difficulties, and to find new ways of relating and living" (p. 2). The therapist represents a new reality for the child and the relationship between the child and the therapist assists in the restoration of the individual powers of the child. The self is reaffirmed in this process. While Moustakas has changed his theoretical and methodological orientation from relationship play therapy to phenomenological play therapy during the past forty years, he maintains the emphasis on the honesty of the therapist as well as the patience that the therapist must have to move at the pace of the child. In a personal conversation with Dr. Moustakas, he indicated the importance of the play therapy relationship as it affects change within the school and community settings. The relationship between therapist and child is integral to the work of Moustakas.

Axline (1947) is credited with the creation of the non-directive method of play therapy, believing in the child's natural wish for growth and his or her capacity for self-direction. The child is capable of self-realization, self-awareness, and self-direction. For this reason the component of freedom is very important within this model. The child's discovery of the play therapy environment and of the self gives the child a sense of mastery. Axline (1950) summarizes her concept of play therapy by stating,

> A play experience is therapeutic because it provides a secure relationship between the child and the adult, so that the child has the freedom and room to state himself in his own terms, exactly as he is at that moment in his own way and in his own time. I am using the term "play" as "freedom or room to act" . . . The child enters into a relationship with an adult who becomes symbolic of the child's external world, the audience before which he plays out his innermost feelings and attitudes. (p. 68)

The theatrical analogy used by Otto Rank and Virginia Axline allows the reader to visualize the power of play in creating the parameters and the characteristics and conditions necessary for the roles to be played out in the play therapy process. A recognition that the relationship between the child and therapist is integral to growth in the therapeutic environment is paramount to relationship and non-directive play therapists.

CONTEMPORARY MODELS OF PLAY THERAPY

Since the writings and practice of Virginia Axline in the mid-twentieth century, the focus on the relationship as integral to the play therapy process has become a basis for other play therapy models which are widely applied for psychotherapeutic work with children. The complete overview of the theories behind and application of the various models of Play Therapy are very adequately described in *Play Therapy: Theory and Practice* (O'Connor & Braverman, 2009, 2nd Ed.). This book does not serve to review each model as the O'Connor & Braverman work does this quite adequately, but highlights of the models that incorporate the family and/or systems application within the healing process are noted at this point, some which are presented in more detail in following chapters.

The child-centered model of play therapy, not synonomous with "non-directive" but a type within this framework, focuses on intrapsychic changes within the child through his or her own ability to heal. Guerney (1980) and Landreth (1991) employ the client-centered model in their writings and practice of filial play therapy, whereby the parent becomes trained in a short-term model to play with the child and "to help them provide a consistent environment" for the child (Sweeney & Landreth in O'Connor & Braverman, 2009, p. 141).

Sand play, a model of play therapy devised by Dora Klaff (1980), focuses heavily on the interpretative aspect of the therapist's interventions. This method is based on the principles of Jungian therapy with the therapist interpreting the child's use of symbols and placement of objects in the sand tray. As with Kleinian play therapy, the interpretation is the main task of the therapist with the assumption that the relationship between the child and the therapist develops implicitly. There are several models of play therapy that include sand and other similar mediums for self-expression with families being part of the process as deemed appropriate.

The Jungian play therapy approach, a psychoanalytic approach, highlights the parents' participation at a designated point. With the direction of therapist and the analytic process "Jungians accentuate strengths of the child and the family and build on those assets in a strengths-based approach to psychic healing" (Green in O'Connor & Braverman, 2009, p. 92). Inclusion of the filial method within the treatment goals of this Jungian model speaks to the integrative aspect of play therapy.

In the 1960s, cognitive behavioural play therapy developed. Based on the principles of learning theory, this approach focuses on the problem behavior with a varying focus on affective release, cathartic or abreactive work, and expression of feelings. The development of the cognitive behavioural play therapy model continues to be understood and celebrated as an adaptable model employing creative tools for "homework" journals and life books that can act as "transitional objects" between therapy, home, and school. Families can be an integral part of this change process from the get-go, with the parents pivotal in the goal setting process in the introduction phase, included in the discussion about regressions and setbacks during later phases. Applying the collaborative approach, the child and family can develop a life book, journal, and celebration of goals accomplished as the termination phase takes place.

The Ericksonian play therapy model, with a "solution-focused" orientation, recognizes that the development of the relationship with the child is essential so that the child may utilize the therapist's image as a "wise" companion, a positive element in his or her life that may not have existed prior to the therapeutic relationship. This model provides a story telling component as seen in narrative play therapy which facilitates the opportunity of children and families to tell their stories, deconstructing and reconstructing new outcomes. Families may be invited into these healing processes according to the needs of the child. The narrative approach is presented in detail in chapter 4.

Adlerian play therapy focuses on the reduction of discouragement through play and facilitates conversations between the therapist and the parents. "In parent consultation sessions, the Adlerian play therapist teaches the parent(s) specific strategies for encouraging the child and for teaching the child how to connect with parents and with others (Kottman in O'Connor & Braverman, 2009, p.240). The relationship between child and therapist is based on the development of empathy during the first phase of treatment, so that the child's lifestyle can be explored in the second phase. Insight is offered in the third phase followed by a conversion of the insight gained in the fourth phase (Kottman, 1996). The parents are involved in ongoing consultations so that the strengths of the child can be noted and reframing and unique aspects of the child can be highlighted. The parents' own unique and subjective perspectives are included in this collaboration.

Gestalt play therapy, brought to prominence by V. Oaklander (1997), is described as a "humanistic, process-oriented form of therapy that is concerned with the integrated functioning of all aspects of the person: senses, body, emotions, and intellect" (p. 184). Of particular emphasis within this method is the child's interaction with the environment and making meaning during the process of development and, ultimately, differentiation. Perls (1948), the pioneer of Gestalt therapy, identifies the goal for treatment as the "achievement of integration which facilitates its own development" (in Carroll & Oaklander, 1997, p. 188). The therapeutic relationship focuses on the child's effort to support him or herself with the sense of self becoming clearer during the process. In the process of assisting the child with building life supports, family therapy, and education, school and medical consultations may be indicated. As with other models of play therapy, Gestalt play therapy may include the family within a filial therapy plan as part of the course of treatment.

The group therapy model has enjoyed a contemporary popularity due to its numerous "curative" (Yalom, 1975) effects. The development of relationships between individuals participating in a group requires the enhancement of socializing techniques. This model promotes group interaction and the reinforcement of cooperative efforts (Mandell, Damon, et al., 1989). Ginott (1961) suggests that "the presence of several children seems to facilitate the establishment of a desired relationship between the therapist and each child . . . [and that] the groups induce spontaneity in the children; they begin to relate to the therapist and to trust him more readily than they do in individual therapy" (p. 2-4). Ginott's model of group play therapy is, in fact, very similar to individual play therapy in respect to its persistent focus on the individual child rather than on group cohesion. In this way, Ginott's model resembles the client-centered or non-directive approach practiced widely today. Several models of play therapy are now conducted within a group therapy framework highlighting the importance of children who collaborate with each other in the healing process.

There are several play therapy models that work directly within the context of the family, all of which are theoretically summarized in *Play Therapy: Theory and Practice* (O'Connor, & Braverman, 1997; 2009) and within the following chapters of this book. Nevertheless, "because play therapy is often seen as a child-focused medium, this approach appears to be caught in this dialectic tension between child- versus family-based therapies" (Haslam and Harris, 2011, p. 52). Several models of play therapy, directly focused on inclusion of the family for the entire healing process, exemplifies the importance of family based models. In fact, the current focus on the prescriptive, integrative, and collaborative approaches suggest a turn in theoretical direction as the child, family, and systemic needs and collaborative treatment planning is currently relevant.

Family theraplay (described in a later chapter), dynamic family play therapy, strategic family play therapy, ecosystemic play therapy, and family play therapy (Gil, 1991) are such models. In each a different theoretical focus and healing process takes place, some with distinct steps and others with a more non-directive and creative approach. Attachment theory and improved relationships between children and parents are pivotal within the theraplay approaches to child therapy. The focus of the ecosystemic play therapy approach considers the ethnocultural identification that may be evident within the relationships and communication patterns of the family on a day-to-day basis. In this step-by-step approach, the family is included selectively for coaching and education purposes. Family play therapy, with varying applications depending on the individual therapist, is discussed as part of chapter 3.

This review summarizes those play therapy models that have, for the purpose of therapeutic growth, placed importance on the relationship that develops between child and therapist within the play environment. Furthermore, ways in which play is conceptualized within the development of the therapeutic relationship have been stressed.

Play can facilitate relationships that are within the context of the environment of the child, whether it be the nuclear or reconstituted family, a diverse family context, family within community, foster or kin family relationships, or adoptive family. How families facilitate a playful environment for relationship purposes and healing is as variable as the types of families around the world.

The following chapter will highlight the family, its development and models of healing that include play as a healing agent. Models of family therapy and family play therapy are presented along with creative family healing interventions of the last century throughout this and following chapters. There continues to be a movement toward psychotherapy integration (Corey, 2009) reinforcing the need for integration of theories and techniques into the healing process. Incorporation of play therapy within the family therapy framework provides this opportunity.

NOTE

1. Section contributed by Anna Riedel Bowers.

SELECTED REFERENCES

Allen, F. (1934). Therapeutic Work with Children. *American Journal of Orthopsychiatry*. 4(2), 193-202.

Axline, V. (1947). Nondirective Therapy for Poor Readers. *Journal of Consulting & Psychology*, 11, 61-69.

———. (1947). *Play Therapy*. New York: Ballantine Books.

———. (1950). Entering the Child's World via Play. *Progressive Education*. Vol. 27, 68-75.

Berlyne, D. (1960). *Conflict, Arousal and Curiosity*. New York: McGraw Hill.

Bowlby, J. (1953). *Child Care and the Growth of Love*. Baltimore: Pelican Books.

Bratton, S., Ceballos, P., Sheely-Moore, A., Meany-Walen, K.; Pronchenko, Y. & Jones, L. (2013). Head Start Early Mental Health Intervention Effects of Child-Centered Play Therapy on Disruptive Behaviors. *International Journal of Play Therapy*. 22 (1), 28-42.

Brown, S. (2010). *Play*. New York: Penquin Group.

Brumfield, K. & Christensen, T. (2011). Discovering African American Parents' Perceptions of Play Therapy: A Phenomenological Approach. *International Journal of Play Therapy*. 20 (4), 208-223.

Burton, C. (1986). Peekaboo to "All the all the Outs in Free"; Hide-and -Seek as a Creative Structure in Drama Therapy. *The Arts in Psychotherapy*, 13, 129-136.

Carroll, F. & Oaklander, V. (1997). Gestalt Play Therapy. In *Play Therapy: Theory and Practice*. O'Connor, K. & Braverman, L. (Eds.). New York: John Wiley & Sons.

Chethik, M. (1989). *Techniques of Child Therapy: Psychodynamic Strategies*. New York: Guilford Press.

Christian, K., Russ, S., & Short, E. (2011). Pretend Play Processes and Anxiety: Considerations for the Play Therapist. *International Journal of Play Therapy*. 20 (4), 179-192.

Coleman, D. & Skeen, E. (1973). Play, Games, and Sports: Their Use and Misuse. *Childhood Education*, 61, 192-198.

Conn, J. (1948). Play-interview as an Investigative and Therapeutic Procedure. *The Nervous Child*, 7, 257-286.

Corey, G. 8th Ed. (2009). *Theory and Practice of Counseling and Psychotherapy*. Belmont, CA: Brooks/Cole.

Dale, N. (1989). Pretend Play with Mothers and Siblings. *Journal of Child Psychol. Psychiatry*. 30 (5), 751-759.

Dansky, J. & Silverman, I. (1973). Effects of Play on Associative Fluency in Preschool Children. *Developmental Psychology*. 9, 38-43.

Darewych, O. (2013). Building Bridges with Institutionalized Orphans in Ukraine: An Art Therapy Pilot Study. *The Arts in Psychotherapy*. 40, 85-93.

Ebrahim, C. Steen, R. L. & Paradise, L. (2012). Overcoming School Counselors' Barrier to Play Therapy. *International Journal of Play Therapy*. 21 (4), 202-214.

Eckhoff, A., & Urbach, J. (2008). Understanding Imaginative Thinking During Childhood: Sociocultural Conceptions of Creativity and Imaginative Thought. *Early Childhood Education Journal*, 36, 179–185.

Ellis, M. J. (1973). *Why People Play*. Englewood Cliffs, NJ: Prentice-Hall.

Erikson, E. (1940). Studies in the Interpretation of Play. *Genetic Psychology Monographs*, 22, 559-671.

Frank, L. (1954). Play in Personality Development. *American Journal of Orthopsychiatry*. 25, 576-589.

Freud, S. (1905). Jokes and Their Relation to the Unconscious. S. E. 8. London: Hogarth Press.

———. (1906-1908). Creative Writers and Day-Dreaming. S. E. 9. London: Hogarth Press.

———. (1914). On the Beginning the Treatment. In Further Recommendations on Technique. SE. 14. London: Hogarth Press.

Garvey, C. (1976). Some Properties of Social Play. In *Play*, Bruner, J., Jolly, A. & Sylva, K. (Eds.) New York: Basic Books.

Gil, E. (1991). *The Healing Power of Play*. New York: The Guilford Press.

Ginott, H. (1961). Play Therapy: The Initial Session. *American Journal of Psychotherapy*. 15, 73-88.

Green, E., Myrick, A. & Crenshaw, D. (2013). Toward Secure Attachment in Adolescent Relational Development: Advancements From Sandplay and Expressive Play-Based Interventions. *International Journal of Play Therapy*. 22 (2), 90-102.

Gross, K. (1901). *The Play of Man*. New York: Arno Press.

Guerney, L. (1980). Client-centered (non-directive) Play Therapy. In *Handbook of Play Therapy*. Schaefer, C. & O'Connor, K. (Eds.). New York: Wiley.

Hart, T. (2003). *The Secret Spiritual World of Children*. Maui, Hawaii: Inner Ocean Pub.

Haslam, D. & Harris, S. (2011). Integrating Play and Family Therapy Methods: A Survey of Play Therapists' Attitudes in the Field. *International Journal of Play Therapy*. 20 (2), 51-65.

Herzka, H. (1986). On the Anthropology of Play: Play as a Way of Dialogical Development. In *Play-Play Therapy-Play Research*. van der Kooij, R. &

Hellendoorn, J. (Eds.). Netherlands: Swets & Zeitlinger and PAOS.

Howe, N. & A. Bruno (2010). Sibling Pretend Play in Early and Middle Childhood: Role of Creativity and Maternal Context. *Early Education and Development*. 21 (6), 940-962.

Johnson, J. (1976). Relations of Divergent Thinking and Intelligence Test Scores with and Nonsocial Make-believe Play of Preschool Children. *Child Development*. 47, 1200-1203.

Klaff, D. (1980). *Sand Play*. Santa Monical, CA: Sigo.

Klein, M. (1932). *The Psycho-analysis of Children*. London: Hogarth Press.

Kottman, T. (1996). Adlerian Play Therapy. In *Play Therapy: Theory and Practice*. O'Connor, K. & Braverman, L. (Eds.). New York: John Wiley & Sons.

Landreth, G. (1991). *Play Therapy: The Art of the Relationship*. Muncie, Indiana: Accelerated Development Inc.

Lebo, D. (1952). The Development of Play as a Form of Therapy: From Rosseau to Rogers. *American Journal of Psychiatry*. 112, 418-422.

———. (1952). The Relationship of Response Categories in Play Therapy to Chronological Age. *Child Psychiatry*, 2, 330-336.

Levy, D. (1937). *Studies in Sibling Rivalry*. Res. Monogr. American Orthopsychiatric Association. No. 2.

Lowenfield, M. (1970). *The Lowenfield Technique*. Oxford: Pergamon Press.

Mahon, E. (1993). Play: Its Role in Child Analysis, Its Fate in Adult Analysis. In *The Many Meanings of Play: A Psychoanalytic Perspective*. Solnit, A., Cohen, D. Neubauer, P. (Eds.) New Haven: Yale University Press.

Marans, S., Mayes, L., Cicchetti, D., Dahl, K., Marans, W., & Cohen, D. (1991). The Child-Psychoanalytic Play Interview: A Technique for Studying Thematic Content. *Journal of the American Psychoanalytic Association*, 4, 1015-36.

McMahon, L. (1992). *The Handbook of Play Therapy*. New York: Tavistock Routledge.

Meador, B. & Rogers, C. (1980). Person-Centered Therapy. In *Current Psychotherapies*. (Eds.) R. Corsini and Contributors. Itasca: R. E. Peacock.

Meares, R. (1993). *The Metaphor of Play*. Northvale: Jason Aronson Inc.

Merriam-Webster Online Dictionary (2012).

Mook, B. (1994). Therapeutic Play: From Interpretation to Intervention. In *Play and Intervention*, Hellendoorn, J., van der Kooij, R. & Sutton-Smith, B. (Eds.). Albany: State University of New York Press.

Moran, G. (1987). Some Functions of Play and Playfulness. *The Psychoanalytic Study of the Child*, 42, 11-30.

Moustakas, C. (1959). *Psychotherapy with Children*. New York: Harper & Row.

O'Connor, K. & Braverman, L. Eds. (2nd ed).(2009). *Play Therapy: Theory and Practice*. Hoboken, NJ: John Wiley & Sons.

Oaklander, V. (1978). *Windows to our Children*. Real People Press.

Ornstein, A. (1984). The Function of Play in the Process of Child Psychotherapy: A Contemporary Perspective. *Annual Journal of Psychoanalysis*, 12, 349-366.

Oxford English Dictionary, (2nd ed.). (1989). Vol. X1. Oxford: Clarendon Press.

Pepler, D. (1982). *Play and Divergent Thinking*. Contr. Hum. Dev., 6, 64-78.

Phillips, R. (1985). Whistling in the Dark?: A Review of Play Therapy Research. *Psychotherapy*, 22 (4), 752-760.

Piaget, J. (1962). *Play, Dreams and Imitations in Childhood*. New York: W. W. Norton Press.

Rank, O. (1968). *Will Therapy and Truth and Reality*. New York: Alfred A. Knopf.

Ray, D., Lee, K., Meany-Walen, Carlson, S., Carnes-Holt & Ware, J. (2013). Use of Toys in Child-Centered Play Therapy. *International Journal of Play Therapy*. 22 (1), 43-57.

Reichenberg, W. (1939). An Experimental Investigation of the Effect of Gratification Upon Effort and Orientation to Reality. *American Journal of Orthopsychiatry*, 9, 186-204.

Riedel Bowers, N. (2009). A Naturalistic Study of the Early Relationship Development Process of Non-Directive Play Therapy. *International Journal of Play Therapy*. 18 (3), 176-184.

Rogers, C. (1951). *Client-Centered Therapy*. Boston: Houghton-Mifflen.

Rubin, K. (1982). Early Play Theories Revisited: Contributions to Contemporary Research and Theory. *Contr. Hum. Dev.*, 6, 4-14.

Scarlett, W. (1994). Play, Cure, and Development: A Developmental Perspective on the Psychoanalytic Treatment of Young Children. In *Children at Play*, Slade, & Wolf, D. (Eds.). New York: Oxford University Press.

Schaefer, C. (Ed.). (1993). *The Therapeutic Powers of Play*. New Jersey: Aronson.

Schaefer, C. & O'Connor, K. (1983). *Handbook of Play Therapy*. New York: Wiley.
Scheuerl, H. (1975). *Theorien des Spiels*. Weinheim: Beltz.
Solomon, J. (1954). Therapeutic Play Techniques. *American Journal of Orthopsychiatry*. Vol. 25, Jan. 1955.
Sours, J. (1980). Preschool-age Children. In *Emotional Disorders in Children and Adolescents*, Sholevar, G., Benson, R. & Blinder, B. (Eds.). New York: Spectrum.
Stone, G. (1971). The Play of Little Children. In *Child's Play*, Herron, R. & Sutton-Smith, B. (Eds). New York: Wiley.
Taft, J. (1917). *The Dynamics of Therapy in a Controlled Relationship*. New York: MacMillan Co.
Vandenberg, B. (1986). Play, Myth and Hope. In *Play-Play Therapy-Play Research*. van der Kooij, R. & Hellendoorn, J. (Eds.). Netherlands: Swets and Zeitlinger and PAOS.
van der Kooij, R. & Hellendoorn, J. (1986). *Play-Play Therapy-Play Research*. Netherlands: Swets and Zeitlinger and PAOS.
Von Hug-Helllmuth, H. (1921). On the Technique of Child-Analysis. *International Journal of Psychoanalysis*, 2, 286-305.
Weininger, O. (1989). *Children's Fantasies*. London: Karnac Books.
White, R. W. (1959). Motivation Reconsidered: the Concept of Competence. *Psychological Review*, 96, 299-333.
Winnicott, D. (1971). *Playing and Reality*. London and New York: Routledge Press.
Yalom, I. (1975). *Theory and Practice of Group Psychotherapy*. New York: Basic Books.

Chapter Three

Family Therapy

Kristin Trotter

It's beautiful here with my family. The stunning raw beauty of the Canadian North is a fine backdrop to a week of holidaying together: My son just returning from kayaking to a small island across the lake; my partner on one side of me; my sister on the other; and my eighty-five-year-old father sitting on the deck under an umbrella blasting Opus I by Tommy Dorsey, followed by the classic In the Mood. Jersey Bounce by Benny Goodman doesn't interrupt my mother's afternoon nap. Her shoulder is bothering her and she is in pain and we are all worried. She is old and we all adore the matriarch.

Moonlight Serenade sounds so sweet.

My brother-in-law and his granddaughter are sitting on the lawn reading a book, his daughter joins them. She lights a cigarette. He sips his rum and Pepsi. The music builds to a crescendo and the wind picks up. Tiny little whitecaps form on the lake. Everybody slaps at the bugs and the conversation turns to annoying deerflies and how they are not that bright.

Everybody who wants one has a drink. It's all expressive activity, expressive of who we are as individuals and who we are as a family. It's perfect and perfectly imperfect all at once.

My grandsons are out in a boat in the lake bothering the fish. Boogie Woogie pumps out of the speakers . . . . family memories, family stories, and family history in the making.

The stories come from the life and history of the family as it wends its way through the tunnel of time, fielding joys and tragedies, love and hate, peace and war, and leaving legacies of generations lost and found. The ever changing face of the family is a product of its people, its time, its culture, and its heart, much like the discipline of family therapy itself. It has a history with stories and a dynamic changing face as it ages and matures and its grandfathers and grandmothers get old and die and new faces take their place.

A BRIEF HISTORY OF FAMILY THERAPY

It was the 1980s when I entered the field of family therapy. The tears were still drying on the faces of Virginia Satir's students following her death of pancreatic cancer. One of Satir's students taught at the center where I began my studies and where I sat rapt as she and others taught me about systems theory, survival stances, Erikson's uncommon therapy, and Haley and Madanas' wily application of it to the family. I marveled at their strategic moves and gobbled up Palazzolis' *Paradox and Counterparadox* (1978) like a hungry rabbit in a bin of lettuce. I found Minuchin and his structural family therapy fascinating. The full impact of the feminist critique was being absorbed and the discipline's inability to deal with even the most conspicuous and striking power inequities was being laid bare as the feminists broke the deafening silence about spousal abuse, child physical and sexual abuse, and racism and discrimination. The sharp turn toward the postmodern was well underway. The Mental Research Institute was alive and well in California and experts were now "emphasizing a rhetorical rather than etiological stance" with families (Hoffman, 2002, p. xv), and what was said, how it was said, what to do about it, and what it meant to family members became more important than dysfunctional labels and treatments.

But that was decades ago and family therapy can no longer rest on the sizable personalities of its founders, its grandmothers and grandfathers, and its radical departure from the traditional individual treatment approach. Big thinkers and personalities like Salvador Minuchin, Virginia Satir, Jay Haley, Cloe Madanes, Carl Whittaker, and Michael White are either aging or have "shuffled off this mortal coil." These innovative thinkers, along with the powerful and critical feminist voices of Rachel Hare Mustin, Bunny Duhl, Margaret Thaler Singer, and Florence Kaslow have morphed into a new breed of family therapy practitioner. A breed that is: (a) far more conscious of diversity of all kinds; (b) more aware of the radically changing role of women; (c) more respectful and tentative in talking to families; (d) more aware of the middle class, patriarchal, Caucasian values that infused family therapy in its nascent developmental stages; and, among other things, (e) more conscious of how language and diversity define reality. In short, a far more postmodern breed of practitioner now sits with family pain.

Satir said, "Family therapists deal with family pain" (Satir, 1983, p. 1) and regardless of the evolutionary shifts that have occurred in the field that fact has remained a constant and is as true today as it was in 1983 when the third edition of *Conjoint Family Therapy* was published. However, family therapists have had to evolve, adapt to, and absorb profound changes to the field in order to keep pace with the changing face of families and the cultures that sustain them.

The inception of family therapy is generally located in the 1950s and its evolution is usually tracked from there through the grand, radical, and free-thinking heyday of the 1970s, to the impact of the feminists and the postmodernists in the 1980s and 1990s, to the integrative and metamodels of today. In spite of a certain amount of confusion that exists in the literature both around the term "integrative" and precisely what an integrative model can and does accomplish, integration can be studied from the perspective of emergence and "as an expression of chaos and complexity science" (Smith & Southern, 2005, p. 394), as well as from the understanding that families have "meaning only in relation to larger groups, organizations, or society" (Smith & Southern, p. 494). Moreover, the three major categories across which therapeutic integration has been conceptualized are: theoretical integration, or the combining of principles and practices into a new approach to therapy; technical eclecticism, or the application of intervention techniques from a number of models as they fit the family without regard to a particular theory; and common factors, or identifying across models effective ingredients and principles in the therapeutic process (Smith & Southern, 2005).

As one of several combinatory models that have developed during the last several decades, *Metaframeworks* (Douglas Breunlin, Richard Swartz, and Betty Mac Kune-Karrer's, 2001), is an example of a model of family therapy that seeks to transcend the limitations of existing models. As a model in and of itself that invites the family therapist to draw on techniques and theories from all available practice models, it is, to some degree, theoretical, technical eclecticism, and common factor driven. In an attempt to tuck under its wing structural, strategic, intergenerational, narrative, and other postmodern forms of family therapy, it provides a way to think inclusively across all aspects of the field of family therapy, which currently appears to be sitting at a crossroads in North America.

According to Beels (2002) family therapy is facing an identity crisis where it is losing ground and definition as a distinct discipline. Although some models such as Minuchin's structural, White and Epston's narrative, and Satir's family therapy are managing to survive the crisis, others such as strategic, systemic, and Eriksonian have continued, but perhaps with less vigor and morphed into models such as brief solution focused family therapy.

In my own university faculty, the advanced study of family therapy has recently become an elective rather than a required course and this is echoed in the larger cultural reality, as family therapy training institutes close and systems thinking, once the very foundation of family therapy and that which set it apart, is not only questioned but apparently can be discarded for the more fluid theories of the narrative and postmodern persuasion.

This crisis of identity lies not only in the current theoretical tension between a systemic and a postmodern perspective, but also, according to Beels (2002), in not anchoring family therapy to its more deeply entrenched historical roots. Reaching beyond the commonly accepted origins of the 1950s into a "longer and larger history of both practice and thought about the family" (Beels, 2002, p. 67), one finds the influence of social work, psychology, and psychiatry. Some of the earliest practitioners, such as Nathan Ackerman and Murray Bowen, were psychiatrists and psychoanalysts. In the longer and larger history of working with families, one finds the theories and practices of the likes of Mary Richmond, the founder of social work, who was working with families as early as the 1930s. One finds the brilliance of William James, John Dewey's organic view of systems, and George Herbert Mead's symbolic interactionism. Edward Sapir, who taught that language shapes thought, and the trance work of Anton Mesmer, which was later used by Milton Erikson and infused into family therapy through the strategic work of people like Madanas, Haley, and Watzlawick, all define family therapy and reach much further down the tunnel of time than the pseudo-tidy world of the postwar 1950s family.

Kaslow (2000) chronicles family therapy through its generational development of "pioneers and renegades (pre-1969); innovators and expanders (1969-1980); challenges, refiners and researchers (1980-1989); and integrators and seekers of new horizons" (1990-1999). Where it has moved in the last decade would seem, at least in part, to be toward a loss of identity. How family therapy evolves in the decades to come means resolving this identity crisis through not only plumbing the depths of its history, as Beels suggests, but also in dreaming into its future.

As family therapy struggles in North America, it has gained ground internationally and has spread to parts of the globe as diverse as Latvia and China, where both Satir and Minuchin are popular. Internationally, patterns of the evolution and development of family therapy in diverse countries have followed courses similar to those in North America, as well as reflect the "different cultural, political, and social contexts" (Kaslow, 2000, p. 2) of the country in which it developed. Argentina, Germany, Brazil, Mexico, the Scandinavian countries, South Africa, and the former Yugoslavia, where family therapy was well established by the end of the 1980s, have developed historical and practice roots and a set of precise interventions unique to those countries.

However, in spite of the fact that, as Kaslow (2000) says, "the field now exhibits a multihued patchwork quilt of many different, though interconnected schools of thought that undergird clinical practice and research" (Kaslow, 2000, p. 1). Consistent with culturally syntonic application, family therapy training and practice has not corrected its historically abysmal record of not including young children in therapy and further developing family play therapy as integral to the process. Training institutions do not include or teach family play therapy as readily as other models and it is a well-accepted fact in the field that young children have traditionally been poorly served by family therapists. Less than one-third of all family therapists include children in their family sessions (Korner & Brown, 1990; Lund, Zimmerman, & Haddock, 2002). This is a rather appalling figure when one considers the relevance, impact, and importance of children in a family. Even when children attend or are invited to sessions it is often the case that, at best, they are not actively included in the session and are left to play on their own or, at worst, are considered an annoyance and an interruption.

Personal discomfort and inadequacies, along with lack of training, are not the only reasons why family therapists are reluctant to include children. The family therapist who wants to be inclusive of the child faces rather formidable barriers, such as: (a) developmental divides between adults and children that make it difficult to engage in therapy that is simultaneously age-appropriate for all; (b) the child's tendency to interrupt adult conversation and be "disruptive" along with developmental needs to touch and explore and interrupt the flow of discourse; (c) inadequate and unsafe room arrangements; (d) discussion of sensitive topics that may not be appropriate for children; and (e) a lack of appropriate techniques (Lund, Zimmerman, & Haddock, 2002).

Systematically infusing play therapy into family therapy, under the rubric of a meta-theoretical stance that can include techniques from all models of family therapy, could give the field a needed nudge in terms of future directions, definition, and scope of practice. Hence, this chapter will not only briefly discuss the history of family therapy and explore the metadomains of *Metaframeworks*, it will also focus on being inclusive of the world of play and family play therapy which is both a model as well as something that might be infused into every aspect of the family therapist's work.

FAMILY THERAPY

Theoretical Foundations in Cybernetics, General Systems Theory, Dynamical Systems Theory, and Postmodern Thought

Family therapists use many metaphors when talking about the history and practice of their craft. Kaslow's multihued patchwork quilt becomes Hoffman's (2002) strands of braided bread or a river with many currents, eddies, tributaries, and branches. When exploring the history of family therapy one is struck by the amazing capacity of the family therapy movement, as Hoffman puts it, "to fold back upon itself and change" (p. xiv). The movement's history reflects its capacity to iteratively enfold, absorb, and reabsorb information and then fold back into itself in such a way that it constantly creates and recreates itself through its metaphors, metatheories, models, and practices.

Our metatheories and theories, to a large extent, determine not only how we know the world but what we can know about the world. The language we use to describe these theories and the reality they purport to reflect constitute, confine, and dictate our understanding. Hence, with the advent of general systems theory and cybernetics, which became popular in the 1950s and 1960s "mostly through the contributions of family therapy and the community mental health movement" (Hudson, 2010, p. 9), it became possible to explore the relational and interdependent dynamics of the family. Along with a host of other factors such as the reuniting of families following World War II, the growth of couples and pre-marital counseling, the growth of the child guidance movement, and advances in group dynamics, the stage was set for a radical shift away from working with the individual and seeing the family as the enemy, to not only including the family (Nichols & Schwartz, 1998), but seeing the family as a meaningful part of the solution.

From a metatheoretical perspective, the field of family therapy has evolved and been informed and profoundly impacted by diverse ideas from disciplines such as mathematics, physics, biophysics, biology, engineering, anthropology, computer engineering, psychology, and sociology, to name a few. Ideas that range from the cybernetics of Norbert Wiener, to Ludwig von Bertalanffy's general systems theory, to the intricacies of complexity and chaos theory, to the open-ended self-reflexive processes of the postmodern and feminist thinkers, have been channeled into the mosaic that constitutes family therapy theory and practice.

Central to connecting family therapy's more recent theoretical history to its longer and more informal theoretical history, as outlined by Beels (2002), are the Macy Conferences, which ran from 1946 to 1953. At these highly significant interdisciplinary conferences, simulated neural networks emulating the calculus of propositional logic, child psychology, communication, memory, and, of course, the study of cybernetics were just some of the shared intellectual fare. As a result of that series of learned and erudite exchanges the early cybernetic work of Wiener, a brilliant mathematician who had undergone his own psychoanalysis (Wiener, 1961), emerged as a guiding principle to the earliest family therapists. In attendance at the Macy Conferences was anthropologist and social scientist Gregory Bateson, who applied Wiener's mathematical brilliance and observations to the family. Words and ideas such as homeostasis, or the tendency of a system to maintain a stable state, positive and negative feedback loops, which either oppose or encourage systemic change, circular causality and recursivity all took on profound meaning when applied to the family and helped make sense of the complex webs of connectedness that are inherent in family dynamics. The therapeutic task became one of looking for and modifying complex and patterned sequences of interactions in communication rather than simple linear chains of cause and effect.

Interconnectedness, mutuality, relationality, interdependence, and contextual ways of thinking constitute some of the main characteristics of systemic thinking and represented a revolutionary shift in the history of Western philosophical and scientific thought (Capra, 1996). Instead of focusing on autonomous parts as independent and isolated, the emphasis could now be on the relationship between the parts. The nonlinear, patterned, and systemic way of thinking that is adopted by many family therapists when sitting in the midst of a family is an essential ingredient to efficacious practice and is precisely what advanced and fostered the field as well as encouraged its growth and maturation. Individuals live through the death of spouses, children, parents, grandparents, extended family members, and close friends, all in the context of the family. Family members create and grieve estrangements from each other, and fight and love and win and lose with passionate abandon.

Systemic thought is intricate, complex, and bound only by one's lack of ability to fathom the complexity of systemic interaction, because systemic thought, when applied to families, concerns itself with the functioning of open, not closed, systems. Hence, the family and its individual members are always seen as interacting not just within what Bronfenbrenner (2005) called the micro and meso systems, but also within much larger, more complex and dynamic exo and macro systems. The material world is seen as a dynamic web of interrelated events where multileveled realities are perceived as networks nested within networks, which are nested within other networks. The couple, community, and political systems that impact upon the family can be addressed within systems theory and interventions can be designed for and aimed at all levels. Systemic thinking helps to guide the family therapist into the heart of the family and the relationships that sustain it.

Hence, along with the influence and welcomed contributions of postmodern thought to the more recent developments within family therapy, understanding and appreciating systemic thought is foundational to working with families. Steadfastly refusing to attribute responsibility for the problems of the family to one member of the family, provided the problem is not violence, is precisely what takes family therapy out of the realm of blame and into the realm of systemically congruent thought.

The family is a system with permeable boundaries and, as Austrian-born biologist and founder of general systems theory Ludwig von Bertalanffy (1968) said, each variable within a system affects itself and all other variables, and interacts with and affects variables in other systems. His ideas, which were popularized in psychology in the 1950s and in the 1960s in social work (Hudson, 2010), saw a dynamic system as consisting of a set of interacting component parts or elements and the relationships which organize those elements. Mutuality, he held, is a distinctive property of all open systems and the property of the parts can only be understood from the organization of the whole (von Bertalanffy, 1968). He argued that concepts like wholeness and organization sprang up everywhere in the world of the biological and behavioral, and the social sciences, and were therefore indispensable for dealing with organized wholes such as living organisms or social groups (von Bertalanffy, 1968, p. 34) like the family. Although both general systems theory and cybernetics are influential in forming the metatheoretical foundations of family therapy and the two are often used interchangeably, von Bertalanffy distinguished between them.

Although closely related, it is commonly accepted that cybernetics focuses more on how systems function and communicate and general systems theory focuses on how systems are structured. Function and structure cannot, however, be understood in isolation, so it is with a certain amount of relief that they have all been gathered under the umbrella of the sciences of complexity. What have remained constant throughout the development of systemic thought are the cardinal principles of relationality, interdependence, and shifting attention from the parts to the whole. Due to breakthroughs in mathematics, physics, and the study of complex living systems, along with the advent of the computer, the horizons of systemic thought arising from cybernetics and general systems theory have expanded in the past several decades such that by the 1980s "a coherent theory of living systems, together with the proper mathematical language" (Capra, 1996, p. 79) to describe and model those systems finally emerged.

More recently, developments within the science of complexity include the idea that the nature of change within a complex, far-from-equilibrium system is nonproportional and nonlinear, and chaotic and self-organizing. Family therapists have drawn on these scientific concepts and have in a genuine and unfortunate way divorced them from their grounding in physics and mathematics. The work of Wiener and von Bertalanffy, and the more recent application of complexity theory, all emerged from the so-called hard sciences. For example, feedback, like many of the ideas recruited by the early family therapists, is a central construct in family therapy, biology, and physics, as are the more recent innovations of complex ideas such as chaos, nonproportionality, and self-organization. With the advent of what has been referred to as dynamical systems theory, or the study of complex systems, that which had hitherto been implicit in dynamic systems theory became explicit in dynamical systems theory and the disconnection between the original mathematics in which systemic thought is grounded and the practice of family therapy became even greater. However, in spite of the protestations of some of those in the hard sciences, who see the application of these ideas to relationships by those in the social sciences as a gross misunderstanding, even if only applied metaphorically, they are meaningful and helpful in practice as well as analogously applicable to the complex workings of the family.

The developments that have revolutionized systemic thought during the last several decades concern the constructs of nonlinearity and chaos theory, which emphasizes sensitivity to initial conditions, or the new mathematics of complexity, and the powerful novel concept of self-organization. As stated, the study of interdependent self-organizing behaviors represents a furtherance of dynamic systems theory and these refinements have occurred between earlier conceptualizations of what is referred to as dynamic systems (von Bertalanffy, 1968; Wiener, 1961) and what is currently being referred to as dynamical systems (Van Geert, 1994; Vallacher et al., 1993; Albert, 1995).

In a dynamic system there is a direct and predictable linear relationship between input into the system and system output (Vallacher et al., 1993; Albert, 1995). Change in such a system is linear and proportional, and a change in A creates proportional changes in B. In a dynamical system, change is nonlinear and nonproportional and there is no proportional relationship between input into a system and output, hence a small and insignificant change in system input can create unpredictable and/or large and significant changes in output. Change in such a system is nonlinear and nonproportional. Whereas linear models preclude the notion that fundamental to all organic and inorganic processes is the ability to spontaneously self-organize, nonlinear models suggest that, given the right circumstances, systems, including human systems, will self-organize and structure and restructure themselves in novel and unexpected ways.

The central organizing principle of dynamical systems theory pertains to the study of self-organization, and when a system self organizes it increases in size, and/or complexity, and/or organization. Moreover, it does so as a result of a coherent systemic behavior or pattern occurring without being explicitly imposed by the outside environment (Schiepek et al., 1992). Self-organization is something a system engages in because it has to and because internal and/or external perturbations have caused the system to pass the point of period doubling, which is defined as that place where it can no longer avoid tumbling into chaos. Beyond that, the construct of self-organization predisposes one not just to look for the possibility of rapid and novel change, which is seen to be especially rich at points of crisis, but upholds what Minuchin has long professed: that the family is responsible for solving its own problems. The family therapist's job is to facilitate the creations of the conditions within which that can happen.

Closely linked to that central organizing principle of self-organization is the notion of the strange attractor which, "when it exists, is truly the heart of a chaotic dynamical system" (Lorenz, 1993, p. 50). Strange attractors are exquisitely complex configurations that represent the system's tendency to get pulled into or move toward an underlying pattern, and patterned systemic behavior is generated by the underlying system attractor or attractors. Theories of chaos and strange attractors, complexity and dynamical systems, self similarity and fractals, and nonlinearity and sensitivity to initial conditions all entered the lexicon of family therapists as systemic thinking about families struggled to move beyond homeostasis and positive and negative feedback loops. For those who adhered to the systemic foundations of family therapy, discussions of chaos and complexity theory were welcomed and absorbed into the theoretical discourse around family change.

Synonyms for chaos, like bedlam, anarchy, disarray, and pandemonium could not be further from the notion of chaos as a mathematical construct, where it is construed as ultimately leading toward death or a new and more functional order. In the context of the science of chaos theory, it has been referred to as "orderly disorder" where the system, or in this case the family, enters chaos and must either die to its original structure and form or spontaneously self-organize by developing an order of greater complexity, organization, and/or pattern (Werbos, 1994). Chaos shatters old structures so new and more complex ones can emerge and therefore plays a critical role in self-organization. In order for a system to self-organize it must go through periods of chaos where chaos is simultaneously a constructive and destructive force that leads systems along pathways to change. It cannot and should not be avoided. Rather, all nonlinear systems, as they evolve and change and die or self-organize must invoke transitions to chaos. Chaos is not only a harbinger of change; without it any system stagnates and/or dies (Wieland-Burston, 1992).

As such, dynamical systems theory provides a theoretical basis for a strengths based approach to family therapy, where the possibility of rapid, novel and unpredictable change always exists (Warren et al., 1998). It is a way of thinking that allows for and encourages evolutionary systemic change. In this context, the experience of chaos can be normalized and contextualized as purposeful and meaningful.

Such a metaphor resonates with the family therapist who, for example, is working with a family where a death occurs or a divorce takes place. The family enters chaos and dies to the old way of being. The metaphor helps to make sense of shifts within a relationship and a family when a marital infidelity is exposed. The relationship cannot exist in the same way it once did. A rupture has occurred that the system must deal with or die, and it is not enough or even possible to return to the established homeostasis which existed prior to the affair. The couple, the family, the system must self-organize into something vastly different in terms of complexity and organization and the homeostasis that once served the family is no longer viable. A new and more intricate "normal" must evolve.

The demand that a system self-organize can also be evident in a family that is struggling with the developmental shift of a child or children from preadolescence to adolescence. Metaphorically, the family is moving into chaos. Parents can no longer relate to their children in the same way. Negotiation skills must increase. Trust and truth telling are highlighted as the teen moves into a circle of peers and away from the influence of the family. Adolescent experimentation with sex, substances, relationships, religion, and identity constitute different developmental tasks and require much more sophisticated parenting skills than the developmental tasks of the latency age child.

Take, for example, this nuclear family of four: heterosexual parents and two boys, fifteen and thirteen, who came to therapy because the boys were "out of control." For years, as the two boys were growing up, father was the unchallenged head of the household and mother, for the most part, did what she was told, rarely protected the boys from father's anger, and secretly cleaned the toilet with his toothbrush as an act of defiance. As the boys grew older and needed her less and less, she took her love of fashion and sewing and trained at a local college to be a designer. Her natural flair blossomed into a mature, chic, and urbane style of design that ultimately got her noticed by teachers and potential employers. As the boys moved into adolescence she moved into the work force and began earning a living wage. When the family entered therapy, father's mantra was, "I wish everything could be like it was five years ago." In one form or another, this was his refrain throughout therapy.

Father was refusing to relinquish any authority and mother, along with her sons, was refusing to do what she was told, and profound changes related to power structures within the family were being challenged in a way that previously had not been possible. Therapy was progressing nicely and subtle but very real shifts in the family structure were becoming evident.

The boys commented in a therapy session that this was working and things were beginning to change around the household. From the boys' perspective there was less fighting, fewer boundary violations, and things just seemed more peaceful. Shortly after this announcement, however, father terminated therapy in the same way he had run his household for more than a decade, in that he announced in mid-session, much to his sons' dismay that the family would no longer be coming to therapy, no discussion and no negotiation. Characteristically, the mother was absent from this session.

Shortly thereafter, however, at his wife's and sons' insistence, he moved out of the family home.

The family system entered chaos as a result of fundamental shifts in power and developmental realities. It died to what it once had been, and failed to self-organize into something more systemically and relationally complex. From a dynamical systems perspective, this kind of chaos in a family is a primary force in self-organization, where points of deep instability or perturbations act as central organizers of the change process. They are an inevitable occurrence in all evolving, far-from-equilibrium systems such as the family. These kinds of persistent encounters with chaos can and do create considerable movement toward self-organization, where critical choice points might, if dealt with effectively, actively encourage the emergence of a new order of complexity.

From a systemic perspective the question, however, is not what father, mother, or the boys are doing, or what motivates them to do what they do, or even how their collective and individual pasts impact their present. The more pertinent question is, "How are members interacting in a way that keeps the family stuck in unworkable interactions?" As Minuchin states, "this question shifts the focus to a transactional perspective" (Minuchin, Nichols, & Lee, 2007, p. 17) in that we are no longer dealing with an autocratic father or the presenting problem of two rebellious adolescent boys or a passive but very angry mother. Rather, we are dealing with a system nested within systems, nested within systems. Raising two adolescent boys requires a new, more adaptive family structure of much greater complexity, where the relationship between system levels and the interdependence and interconnectedness that is a foundational idea in systemic thought necessitates that attention shift from one level to another, thereby contextualizing the individuals within the family within systems of their world.

This family is an organized and patterned whole and working with this family, like any other, requires some way to enter into the space between family members. Complexity theory provides such a metatheory and, as such, a powerful inquiry into and questioning of the modernist notions that the world is governed by knowable mechanistic principles and predictable chains of causes and effects can be instigated.

No dash through the history of the theoretical foundations of family therapy, no matter how record breaking, could cross the finish line without at least some mention of postmodern influences and feminist influences. Michael White is credited with ushering family therapy into the postmodern world and with it the advent of the dominant trends that include social constructionism, narrative therapy, and solution-focused therapy. Without the feminist writers and critiques, the field would never have progressed from its early male dominated, patriarchal perspective to the richly diverse, self-reflexive, and thoughtful and critical consideration of dominant social discourse that it now supports. Deconstructing modernist discourse by asking questions about who is defining what reality and querying the motivation behind knowledge production has served the profession in such a way that discourse can open up possibilities rather than close them down through pathologizing family dynamics.

Postmodern thought questions uncritical loyalty to any mode of thought, including postmodernism, and insists upon deconstructing all modernist notions of truth, power, knowledge, history, language, and, by extension, ideas about the family. For the postmodernist a subjective rather than objective reality reigns. Truth is a matter of perspective, and deconstructing dominant discourses is a therapeutic mandate.

Deconstructing the therapeutic discourses that pervade family therapy means the therapist must recognize that there are multiple realities and truths that guide family functioning, that powerful meanings are apparent as well as hidden in discourse, and that diverse perspectives are valid and important. Postmodern discourse allows the family therapist to engage in what has been referred to as positioning theory (Winslade, 2005). "A vision of the self that is multiply located in competing stories" (p. 1) can direct and encourage the family therapist to "notice the active resistance" of family members to "oppressive discourses" and facilitate family members in relocating themselves in a new and alternative narrative (Dickerson, 2007, p. 27). Moreover, the family therapist cannot sit outside the family and act upon it, but rather is acknowledged as an actor who functions within the family system and is instantly co-opted by the system. The family therapist challenges, or collaborates, or colludes with family members to construct meaning that either expands or constricts the family's existing narrative and the larger cultural narratives within which the family lives, loves, hates, destroys, and creates.

Power differentials at the intersection of race, class, sex, gender orientation, age, and disability have become part of the discussions around diversity within the theory and practice of family therapy. However, during intense work with a group of families who had fled Bosnia-Herzegovina during the war, it became painfully clear to me that as a middle-class, middle-aged, Canadian-born Caucasian, I could not and never would, have any real understanding of their struggles with war, trauma, flight, and resettlement in a host country. And if the most recent family therapy conference I attended is any indicator, there is still a powerful predominant presence of western Caucasian family therapists. This means that the prevailing social constructions that inform family therapy, and the way in which meaning is assigned, come through the perceptions of those who understand and adhere to the dominant discourse. Like the fish that attempts to study the water in which it exists, the family therapist struggles to explore and deconstruct the meanings inherent in the profession separate from the cultural context in which it is embedded and from which it arose, while simultaneously trying to reach into the subjective reality of the culturally diverse family: hence the myth of the culturally competent therapist.

Social constructionism, or the position that perceived reality as dynamically socially and culturally constructed, and constructivisim, which argues that reality is personally constructed and we are, indeed, the authors of our own fortunes and misfortunes, along with poststructuralism, in part "asserts that all phenomena including the self and the mind are themselves nothing but texts" (Xu, 2010, p. 67). Because therapy is essentially linguistically constructed, it follows that such a postmodernist metatheoretical position would usher narrative family therapy into being and use narrative and language to deconstruct and help to understanding power and discourse in the therapy room. The dominant discourses around power, perspective, sex, race, culture, disability, and sexual orientation, that provide the taken-for-granted norms against which therapeutic conversations are measured and interventions weighed, give space to marginalized discourses that help to contextualize families.

For example, a father brought his eighteen-year-old son to therapy because his son has been diagnosed with schizoaffective disorder and the family was at a loss as to how to deal with him. His wife, the young man's mother, had died a painful death ten years earlier of stomach cancer. Dad's new girlfriend accompanied them and his older sister had elected not to come as she "was not the problem." The young man, who was a junior in college, had been hallucinating three government agents and a large black dog at the back of his classrooms. These agents and the dog had followed him on the bus, he had seen them in the back yard at his home, and they often followed him from classroom to classroom.

Without a context and without some way to deconstruct this therapeutic conversation there is little question that the young man needed antipsychotics and should, at the very least, lower his career expectations around working in the stressful world of politics. However, exploring the diagnosis within the context of the family revealed that the young man had been with his mother when she died and he had cared for her in the best way he could for at least six months prior to her death. He had few memories of her or her illness and had no memories of being with her when she died. Following her death, his sister was accorded the onerous job of raising him while father drowned his grief in alcohol. At the time of therapy he was still actively alcoholic. Moreover, it was quite clear that the patriarch of the family had very strict and traditional notions around sex and gender roles and may well have projected onto his daughter some of the adoration he had felt for his beloved spouse. The young man's sister had been supported financially and physically and had been driven all over the city to dance classes and special events while the young man, whose job it was to become a man, had lugged heavy bags of sports equipment to and from practice each morning and received little to no supervision or support. He was offered little help physically and financially and so afraid was he of asking for assistance that he had once sat alone in his room with a broken limb for most of the day, too terrified to ask for help.

Given this kind of contextual detail, as well as some acknowledgment on the young man's part that he had been using recreational drugs and alcohol to excess since school began, the therapeutic discourse can be opened up in such a way that dominant narratives around mental illness can be explored and possible new meanings can emerge. Working with the family to create greater supports for the young man and helping him and the family remember and mourn the death of his beloved mother as well as working with the family's addictive behavior, allowed this young man to heal to the point where he is no longer on antipsychotics or medication of any kind, has graduated with honors, and has been able to work consistently at something he is trained to do and thoroughly enjoys.

Understanding and integrating the postmodern perspective is precisely how the family therapist challenges rather than supports dominant socio-cultural meanings around disability and gendered narratives that uphold patriarchal values concerning sex roles and sexual orientation, as well as recognizes the profound distortion of meanings about race and class. When diverse perspectives and marginalized discourse are consciously valued and enfolded into the complex iterations of the therapeutic conversation, then all knowledge can be viewed as relativistic and situational rather than legitimately true as dictated by prevailing privilege and power. Reality can be seen as socially and personally constructed.

Postmodernism has also been described as chaotic, fragmented and ephemeral, the shadow side of modernity (Peters, 2009), and useful only in its power to deconstruct rather than construct except through the power of the text. In Derrida's (1995) words, "there is nothing outside the text" (p. 89). However, to paraphrase Martin and Sugarman (2000), it is important to resist an either/or stance when it comes to modernism and postmodernism and take a both/and position where there is a dual understanding of the family as a kind of context dependent, "nonessentialist yet real and understanding-capable" (p. 398) meaning making system. As family therapists, it is important to retain an understanding of families as unique creations while simultaneously understanding them as systemic entities and contextualizing them as part of an infinite web of connectedness.

The beauty of family therapy is that by its very nature, and deeply embedded in its historical roots, is the insistence that the family be viewed through constantly evolving multiple lenses. Metatheoretically, it can be viewed through modern and postmodern as well as systemic and cultural lenses. Theoretically, the family can be seen through feminist and social constructionist, psychoanalytic and behavioral, and/or neurobiological and humanistic (Dickerson, 2007) lenses.

Single model therapeutic styles simply will not do justice to the intricate and complex world of today's families. Multinational realities, along with wildly varying family structures, dictate the need for creative and innovative assessment and intervention techniques. Integrative and transcendent models, under which can be gathered traditional as well as postmodern theories of the family and how it operates, are as necessary and relevant today to family therapy as systemic thinking was at its inception.

METAFRAMEWORKS: A METAMODEL

One O'clock Jump, *Benny Goodman keeps it all so entertaining and fun. The dogs, asleep in the shade of lawn chairs, are oblivious to it all. There have*

> *always been dogs in this family, but these two are particularly wonderful creatures.*
>
> *Ahhh Sinatra . . .* New York, New York *. . . My father's voice croons along with Frank. He loves to sing. He has a beautiful set of pipes and has sung all his life—everything from opera to well, Frank.*
>
> *Everybody now. And the folks on the deck erupt in song . . . and hoooold that final note.*
>
> *We all go home tomorrow so there is an undertone of sadness. It's been a fine, fine week and we have truly enjoyed each other's company. We have come together and will go apart taking with us all that it means to be a family. We'll go home and we'll be fragmented once again. We'll get caught up in our separate lives, phoning occasionally, getting together on birthdays and holidays but, for the most part, living our separate lives in our separate houses connected by the silver threads of the family kinship system where the connections are deep and lasting—an intricate web of relationality and intense interdependence. One part of the web vibrates and it is felt throughout.*
>
> *Like my family of origin, family therapy is grounded in Western ideas and experiences, but it has found in its grandchildren a wonderful mixed race identity where cultural difference is woven in and absorbed. When considered as a whole, we are a blended family, a mixed-race family, a nuclear family and just about every other configuration of family the literature deals with and somewhere, all of those threads, like the threads that make up the rich and varied tapestry of family therapy, have to come together and make a whole and integrated picture.*

Integrative and transcendent models strive for inclusivity. Because there is so much rich tradition in the theory and technique of family therapy, abandoning it at this stage of the field's evolution would constitute folly, indeed. Sacrificing the wealth of theoretical and experiential wisdom that, for example, Satir and Madanes brought to the field in the interests of culturally contextualizing the family in the postmodern and narrative sense is neither wise nor practical. Understanding and using its short but diverse history as well as its capacity to fold back on itself and recreate itself is central to whether or not, let alone how, the profession will evolve as a method of practice distinct from work with the individual.

Being able to see and utilize the family as part of the solution means knowing family members, not only in the way a client describes them but meeting them in the context of the therapy room. It means embracing a distinctly systemic way of thinking while simultaneously using the best of the postmodern world to create a respectful and egalitarian surround, recognize multiple realities, adopt a nonjudgmental philosophy, and contextualize the family in its socio-cultural and socio-political reality. An inclusive model brings to bear all that family therapy has to offer in terms of what its foremothers and fathers created along with its more recent incarnations.

Breunlin, Schwartz, and Mac Kune-Karrer's, *Metaframeworks: Transcending the Models of Family Therapy* (2001), provides such a model and although they are clear to define it as transcendent rather than integrative, it appears to have aspects of both. In many ways, it is somewhat awkward if not impossible to plug all that has gone before into the six core metaframeworks these authors discuss, and as such it is not an integrative model. As the authors argue, "model integration requires both an in-depth understanding of each of the models and a set of guidelines for combining them in a systematic way" (Breunlin et al., 2001, p. 286), neither of which they provide. However, using the six metaframeworks of internal family systems or mind, sequences, organization, development, gender, and culture that this model proposes, does allow seasoned family therapists to organize thoughts and hypotheses derived from various models of family therapy. Treatment is matched "to one or more metaframework rather than a model so interventions drawn from a number of different models can be used" (Breunlin et al., 2001, p. 286). Within these six metadomains the therapist is free to use as much or as little knowledge as is available to her or him, and because the authors have "distilled core ideas" from different models of family therapy into a brew they have called "metaframeworks" everything from Bowen's emphasis on intergenerational work to Satir's emphasis on self-esteem to Minuchin's emphasis on family hierarchy and structure can be utilized and organized into work with families. Although in the metaframeworks model words and constructs such as hierarchy have softened to become words like leadership, balance, and harmony, the metadomains, the blueprint for therapy, and the four cornerstones of the model allow the underlying patterns that connect various approaches to shine through. For example, the four cornerstones of the model are highly consistent with family therapy and its historical context and are as follow:

a. The systemic view, where systems theory refers to all the widely accepted notions of systemic thought such as pattern and self-organization;
b. A set of presuppositions concerning the human condition;
c. Six core domains or metaframeworks: internal processes or internal family systems (IFS), interactional sequences or patterns of interaction, organization, development, gender, and culture;
d. The blueprint for therapy which consists of: hypothesizing, the basis of which is the presuppositions and the six metaframeworks; planning, or the process of selecting a course of action for conducting therapy at any point; conversing, which is deciding what to say to the family on a moment-by-moment basis; and reading feedback, or watching and attributing meaning to the family's interactions in the context of therapy.

And because it is a model where theories and techniques from existing models can be incorporated and applied, thereby transcending the limits of particular models, family play therapy and appropriate techniques can be infused into all six of the metadomains.

Family work is intricate, complicated, challenging, and, as previously mentioned, is made up of human systems nested within systems nested within more systems, much like the Russian matryoshka dolls, so metaframeworks must rely on core systemic concepts such as pattern, relationship, context, multilevel realities, feedback, circularity, and recursiveness (Breunlin et al., 2001). The metaframeworks definition of a system is quite simply stated as "a set of objects, together with the interaction between the objects and their attributes" (Hall and Fagan, as cited in Breunlin et al., 2001, p. 24).

The presuppositions include the following:

a. A concept of multiplicity of mind, borrowed from psychosynthesis which is the work of Italian psychiatrist, Roberto Assagioli (1965). His work relies on the construction of parts or subpersonalities which can take extreme and destructive positions when there is no leadership from the Self. This concept of multiplicity of mind becomes the basis for the core domain of internal family processes;
b. A concept of Self, which has the capacity to lead these internal subsystems or subpersonalities;
c. A construct of "constraints," which can exist at any or all levels of a human system and block people's access to their own healing potential and resources. Moreover, the more entrenched these systems are the harder it is to solve the inherent problems;
d. A more postmodern construction of the structural and strategic notions of hierarchy, and power and control, which become leadership and balance and harmony;
e. An understanding that the goal of effective leadership is to create balance and harmony through mediating conflict, meeting the needs of and encouraging growth in all family members while simultaneously honoring the needs of the family as a unit, allocating resources and providing reasonable limits, anticipating and preparing for the system's or family's future, and positioning the family within the larger socio-cultural reality;
f. A belief that people will mobilize their power and resources to solve their problems (Breunlin et al., 2001).

These presuppositions are what upholds the six core domains and allows the practitioner to adopt what the authors call a metaframework perspective. The overarching therapeutic goal of "removing constraints" is accomplished through drawing from techniques across family therapy models and across the six metadomains. The focus is not on a particular model but, rather, the metadomains act as a kind of motherboard into which all models, techniques, and understandings of family therapy can be plugged, so that within these metadomains and the flexible blueprint for therapy the practitioner has at his or her disposal the whole of the extant body of knowledge that makes up the theory and practice of family therapy. The six core metadomains classify ideas and organize them into metapatterns (Breunlin et al., 2001) that allow for the systematic use of all available techniques, models, and theories of family therapy. Hence, this metamodel has integrative properties, that although not organized around or inclusive of other methods and models in any formal way, does provide the family therapist with a model that has both integrative and transcendent capabilities.

In a later incarnation (Pinsof, Breunlin, Russell, & Lebow, 2011) the metaframework model, the Integrative Problem-Centered Metaframeworks Therapy (IPCM), appears to be more declaratively integrative and "solution constraint" focused (p. 295). "Constraint Theory" is derived from Bateson's work, where therapy is seen as the "identification and removal of constraints that prevent problem solving and instead of asking, "Why a family is stuck" one's query becomes, "What prevents this family from changing and using its strengths?" and "What would happen if the family did change?" (p. 295).

Moreover, it is worth noting that the IPCM model has added two metadomains to the original six. Biology and spirituality have been added to culture, gender, internal family systems or mind, sequences, organization, and development. In effect, biology has been elevated in this revision of the model, from a system constraint to a metadomain, and spirituality has been added in an effort to acknowledge its role in healing from addiction and working cross-culturally where it can play a large role in healing processes (p. 303).

THE SIX METAPATTERNS OR METADOMAINS

The Internal Family System or Mind: The IFS/Mind Metaframework

This particular metadomain involves connecting people to their inner resources as a way of releasing constraints and reconnecting to self and others in a more authentic and fulfilling way. The metaframeworks model, particularly due to this metapattern, helps to highlight and correct some of the early pundits' original rejection of the intrapsychic. Within the metaframeworks model all discourse, from the intrapsychic to the familial to the societal, is available for exploration.

IFS uses techniques from Bowenian family therapy, including ideas of differentiating from the more destructive aspects of the self, and structural and strategic ideas around boundaries and metaphor, respectively. Further, along with borrowing from many forms of individual therapies, IFS adopts Satir's thinking and techniques on empathic, open-hearted connection, and her Parts Parties which are designed to integrate different aspects of the personality, as well as borrowing from narrative therapy where notions such as externalizing the problem are used to release constraints.

Theoretically, solutions within the IFS domain are found as the synthesizing, unifying, conscious sense of "I" or Self, at the center of our being, begins to take conscious control of the parts within. The IFS concept of the Self is key to healing both the individual and the family system. As a core concept and a foundation for IFS therapy, the Self, which is conceptualized as a healing force, is differentiated from the conflicted and disparate parts. As internal constraints are brought into consciousness and released, the Self can be accessed and its energy used to direct the internal family system. Schwartz (1995, p. 138) uses the metaphor of an orchestra where the parts are the musicians and the Self is the conductor. Without the direction of the conductor, the orchestra can be a cacophony of disharmony, lacking leadership and a vision of the whole. When the energy of the Self is brought into focus and the Self or conductor is actually encouraged and allowed to conduct, then the Self can lead in healing the client's inner system of parts.

It is in this metaframework that multiplicity of mind combines with systems thinking to foster family therapy moving inward. In the tradition of Assagioli's multiplicity of mind and subpersonalities, individuals in family systems are conceptualized as having parts that are interconnected but operate mostly autonomously. Hence, rather than being viewed as a single entity, the individual family member is seen as, in part, consisting of a multidimensional complex array of unintegrated subminds where these subminds not only take on different roles, feelings, and behaviors, but also carry substantial and extreme burdens, beliefs, or emotions that have been absorbed as a result of immersion into the family. These burdens act as internal directives that set the script and agenda for particular subpersonalities. Moreover, these subpersonalities can carry intergenerational or "legacy burdens" which echo down the tunnel of time, connecting the generations in painful patterns of dysfunction. Assagioli (1976) puts forward a psychological model of the human being as composed of:

a. The lower unconscious, or fundamental drives and primitive impulses and complexes charged with intense emotion;
b. The middle unconscious, or those psychological elements similar to our waking consciousness and easily accessible to it;
c. The higher unconscious, or superconscious, which is a region from which we receive our higher intuitions and inspiration;

d. The field of consciousness, or that part of our personality that we are directly aware of;
e. The conscious Self or "I" at the center of our being;
f. The higher self, or that part of us that is connected to the Divine;
g. The collective unconscious or that part of us that is open to the collective aspects of humanity.

It is within the lower unconscious that the subpersonalities or unintegrated psychological traits, which are often fueled by anger, worthlessness, and fear, are to be found. Because these subpersonalities are forced into extreme roles and operate without the unifying consciousness of the Self or the "I" at the center of our being, they are seen to be at the root of problematic external and internal relationships.

Consciously synthesizing these parts around the healing energy of the Self as well as facilitating expression of these parts through the Self, is the work of therapy, and if intrapersonal harmony can be established then it becomes much easier to establish interpersonal harmony. Using notions from structural family therapy, family members are encouraged to place boundaries around these troublesome parts and, as a result, start to distinguish those interfering parts from the Self. The central relational problem is that parts do not trust the Self and will continually attempt to highjack the process. As in all models of family therapy, however, the therapist watches for the patterned ways in which this "highjacking" occurs, not just within the family and its members but between parts of the individual. Intra sequences are tracked with the same care and doggedness that the therapist tracks sequences between family members. Discussing with family members what changes can be made in their relationships so these parts will interfere less, along with facilitating family members' capacity to differentiate activated parts from the Self, can help in restructuring both the intra and interpersonal landscape.

These parts are categorized into a "three-group system" of managers, exiles, and firefighters (Schwartz, 1995). Using a process called "in-sight," clients are encouraged to identify these manager, firefighter, and exiled parts through working with something akin to Eugene Gendlin's (1981) felt-sense, body sensations, images, sounds, and memories. Managers are protective, strategic, and invested in controlling the environment and keeping the world safe. They can, for example, be critical, pleasing, performing, and perfectionist. Exiles, who are often wounded and want nothing more than to be cared for and loved, are always highly sensitive and, therefore, will be corralled and imprisoned by the managers for the safety of both the internal and external systems. They carry the pain, hurt, humiliation, shame, vulnerability, and worthlessness and are often conceptualized as young, needy, and afraid. Firefighters act swiftly, unconsciously, and automatically to douse, distract, soothe, or stifle the expressions of need and pain carried by the exiles. Their methods are harsh, sometimes deadly, and never effective in the long term. Addictions of all kinds, self-harming behavior, overwork, rage, and suicide are all examples of the how the firefighters put out the blazing pain of the exiles.

Eighteen-year-old Louisa, for example, has been living with her older brother and father since her mother abandoned the family four years ago. Louisa says she is her father's slave. He openly disapproves of everything about her from the way she dresses to the way she packs his lunchbox each morning before work. She cooks for both her father and brother, cleans, works part time, and tries to attend classes at a local college. She takes Ritalin for her diagnosis of ADHD, Clonazepam for her panic attacks, and is secretly addicted to morphine. She has vivid memories of the night her mother left and describes herself as an angry adolescent who would physically attack other children. The night her mother left she went into the kitchen to ask her mother for a ride to a local shopping center. She noticed a suitcase at the door and asked her mother where she was going. Her mother replied that she was on her way to a friend's. Louisa was furious at her mother for refusing to give her a ride and stormed out, slamming the kitchen door behind her. Louisa got a phone call from her father that evening telling her that the marriage was over and that her mother had left and was never returning. She never saw her mother again.

Her exiled parts are in agony and riddled with anger and guilt, while her managers keep her, her father, her brother, and the household going. Her firefighters keep her addicted and numb to the excruciating pain of the exiles. This house of cards cannot stand much more or much longer. Because exiles bear the internal pain they are kept out of awareness. They are burdened with unbearable feelings of unworthiness, hopelessness, and powerlessness and can become "receptacles" for feelings that other parts, such as managers, do not want to carry (Schwartz, 1995, p. 47).

Louisa describes her father, who steadfastly refused to attend a family therapy session, as an "old-school male chauvinist when it comes to how to act with women" and although she hates her mother for it, she understands now why her mother left. Beliefs around gender roles, power, sacrifice, and escape, and feelings of guilt and shame, along with behaviors around protection and abandonment, have been passed from one generation to the next. The legacy burden lives on as Louisa struggles in therapy to give her exiles a voice, calm her firefighters, and express the managers' exhaustion and frustration.

Managers fear the exiles' escape and work diligently at controlling any and all situations that could potentially release or unleash the pain of the exiles. According to Schwartz (1995), they are, like Louisa, akin to parentified children in a dysfunctional family in their attempts to fix, direct, control, and supervise all situations. Although their methods are diverse, both managers and firefighters have one primary purpose: to keep exiles in exile. Once an exile is born, the managers and firefighters are a certainty, as binding the pain and shame of the exile becomes paramount.

Inherent within and between these three groups and how they function are polarized positions, so once an exile has been brought to consciousness, the managers are politely requested to withdraw while the exiles, possibly for the first time, are given an opportunity to tell their pain filled stories. However, when an individual differentiates from an interfering part and the Self assumes leadership of the internal family, then the pain of the exile can be expressed through the Self. Hence, much of the work is getting people to speak for, rather than from, their parts.

Not unlike Bowen's construct of differentiation, giving the exile a voice can result in the individual understanding and resolving internal conflicts more readily, separating thoughts from feelings, creating boundaries between Self and parts, and bringing people into Self-to-Self relationship with each other.

When individuals are encouraged to differentiate from the interfering part, a shift can occur both in terms of how the individual relates to him or herself and how family members relate to each other. When systemic principles and techniques are applied to Louisa's internal process, changes can be made in her relationships so that these parts will interfere less. The caretaking/manager part that is both valued and abused by her father can find expression through determining what that part needs and wants and whether or not those needs and wants can be met in the current context. She can also explore what would be different if the Self were able to remain in charge. Because she has organized her internal family system around survival she has identified with the part of her that her father values, silenced and medicated her exiles, distanced herself from the pain through her addictions, and unconsciously shifts from one polarized subpersonality to another.

Sorting through this maze of conflicted parts, working carefully with a physician and Louisa's exiles to clear the addiction, listening closely as she describes the traits around which various roles are organized, positioning those traits and roles within the context of her internal and external family, and helping her to synthesize her parts while retaining their useful and positive characteristics, are essential ingredients of working with Louisa's IFS. Without emphasizing the reality of the Self and helping her discern and value its leadership, however, it would not be possible to facilitate the creation of the balance and harmony that is needed for her to reorganize her inner community, a community born out of the experience in her family of origin. Only by accounting for the whole system will the changes remain viable.

IFS therapy involves creating trust between parts, between parts and the Self, and among the Selves within the family. However, when that is not possible the task is to create that trust within. As boundary-making improves between the internal parts, so too will Louisa's capacity to make boundaries within the family, boundaries that serve her, rather than exploit her. Just as in Minuchin's enactments between polarized family members, where they are encouraged to push beyond where things always break down, other members of the family are kept from interrupting, and clear and direct communication is encouraged. Once internal parts communicate without the influence of other parts, the conflict which has kept the parts polarized can dissipate.

All models of family therapy can be used to work with individual family members' internal family systems, including narrative, in as much as the language of IFS allows the therapist to talk not about an anxious individual but about a part that feels scared. In this way the person becomes more than his or her problem, and because people are more than their problematic part they can learn to calm their anxious and fearful parts within to deal more effectively with the outer reality. By tracking problematic interactions and translating what the family says into "parts language," the therapist can use language in a way that heals rather than pathologizes.

It is the task of the family therapist to stay in the Self-leadership position as well as exercise respectful collaboration along with unwavering faith in family members' ability to connect with their own inner resources and healing wisdom. The therapist works first with individual family members' internal systems and the goals are to facilitate the release of "legacy burdens" along with the retrieval and repair of parts that have been exiled. The family therapist's compassionate witnessing of the pain that family members are in facilitates family members leading with the Self. Once the energy and leadership of the Self is accessible then productive discussion of problematic issues becomes possible.

PATTERNS OF INTERACTIONS: THE SEQUENCES METAFRAMEWORK

Patterns of communication have been a mainstay of how family therapists understand their work with families, and different models of family therapy emphasize different interactional sequences. Structural family therapy, for example, emphasizes in-session, face-to-face interactions as being of primary importance, whereas Bowenian family therapy looks at intergenerational patterns and sequences. What metaframeworks provides is a way to elevate all interactional sequences and examine a family's problems in such a way that both productive and unproductive interactions can be dealt with across all intervals of time. The fundamental task of the therapist is to collaborate with the family in replacing key problem interactional sequences with adaptive sequences that eliminate or reduce the problem (Breunlin et al., 2011, p. 295).

The second metaframework, patterns of interactions, provides the all important function of bringing into focus the long-acknowledged importance in family therapy of the components of interactional sequences and the patterns they create. An essential systemic ingredient to successful family therapy from its earliest to most recent incarnations is the tracking and highlighting of these highly patterned sequences. From a metaframeworks perspective, these sequences involve action, meaning, and emotions which recursively weave in and out of one another to create a context in which both functional and dysfunctional patterns survive and thrive.

Through continually making decisions about precisely how to work with these sequences of interactions, family therapists create some understanding of how sequences repeat in such a way that the presenting problem is either maintained or ameliorated. Sequences can be short and therefore contained within sequences of longer duration, and they can indicate a communication that pertains to the moment or one that contains intergenerational content. Metaframeworks does a rather brilliant job of categorizing these sequences into periodicities from short S1 sequences through to longer S2, S3, S4, and S5 sequences which constitute historical generational sequences and will be discussed as a function of the multicultural metaframework. Sequences can be both productive and unproductive.

The first class of sequences, S1, represents momentary face-to-face interactions. In such sequences the action component may be more apparent than the meaning or emotion component because, in effect, what you see is what you get. S1 interactions define the couple's or family members' style of relating. They are used by structural and strategic family therapists when working with in-session enactments and include both verbal and nonverbal behavior. There is an immediacy to S1 interactions that, although useful and heuristically valuable in sessions, are often not enough to solve the problem, as they are embedded within longer sequences.

These longer, or S2 sequences, constitute the family's daily routines and consist of patterns that are necessary for the family's existence. Temporally, they usually span a twenty-four-hour to one-week period. In the tradition of the ethnographer, gathering this kind of information can be invaluable for understanding a family and the challenges members face. Failure at this level creates huge constraints for the family. For example, chatting with a child about S2 interactions can reveal the extent to which the child is left unattended for various reasons. Were it not for inquiring into S2 interactions it would be more difficult to discover that your nine-year-old client's single mother leaves for work before he gets home from school and does not get home from her two part-time jobs until 5:00 a.m. and is asleep when he gets up to go to school.

The third class of interactional sequences, S3, represents the ebb and flow of family life which takes place over periods of time that range from several weeks to a year. These interactional sequences not only range over a longer period of time than S1 or S2 interactions, but they connect the family to its social environment and may, therefore, involve all manner of people from previous marriages to legal officials. S3 patterns become important as problems within families often ebb and flow over time.

For example, both David and Hilary, who have been coming for marital therapy intermittently for two years, are clear that Hilary is "normal" for one week of the month. She is a survivor of childhood sexual abuse, suffers from severe endometriosis, and has excruciating menstrual cycles where her mood is highly labile a week before and a week after menses. She is in great pain the week of menses. At twenty eight and childless, both are seriously considering a partial hysterectomy as a possible solution to the problem. This is complicated, however, by the fact that both want children and neither is clear that this is the desired solution to the problem.

Because S3 interactions ebb and flow over months, they contribute to expectations and the "affective tone" (Breunlin et al., 2001, p. 110) of the family's lived experience. Somewhere during the course of their six-year marriage, no matter what the reality of Hilary's experience, David has come to expect and brace himself against certain behaviors. At times in the past, Hilary's behaviors have included rejection of sexual advances and as a result David no longer makes such advances and eschews all gestures of affection as he is never sure how they will be received, and Hilary has stopped asking for any form of comfort during times of extreme need. S3 interactional sequences may, therefore, contain what Breunlin et al. (2001) characterize as "a crucial intermittent event which also includes the buildup and aftermath of the event . . . (and) may reflect the ebb and flow of a significant emotional or interpersonal variable" (p. 109).

The final class of interactions, S4 interactions, represents transgenerational sequences where events repeat over generations (Breunlin et al., 2001). S4 patterns are family of origin work and can be seen in themes and rules and behavior that operate and, in some way, repeat over generations. Long-term sequences are less easily recognized than short-term ones, but short-term sequences are generally embedded in longer term ones, which are "encoded as values, rules, and beliefs and may derive from the family's culture, or they may be idiosyncratic to a particular family" (p. 112). Rules, meanings, and behaviors that persist throughout generations are evidenced in patterns of pregnancy, divorce, addiction, and childrearing practices, as well as patterns of differentiation or lack thereof.

Models of family therapy that conceptualize emotional pain as arising out of one's family of origin, such as the work of Murray Bowen and Virginia Satir and their powerful understanding of legacy and legacy burdens that both bind people together and help them determine how they separate, and come into focus in this class of interactional sequences. Historical information is valuable, as is the understanding that the past influences the present and the future.

Rooted in any one of these sequences, S1, S2, S3, or S4, are complex patterns of action and meaning. For example, Rick and Suzanna have been married for six years. Rick is a widower with three boys, fifteen years old, eighteen years old, and twenty-two years old. Suzanna, who is seven years younger than Rick, also comes to the relationship with three children from a previous marriage. Millie is six, Jason eight, and Julia thirteen. The couple is lost as to how to pull together the disparate pieces of their families and, like any reconstituted family, faces an uphill struggle as they try to blend two very different family cultures. Within moments of the session getting underway an argument breaks out between Rick and Suzanna (S1) about how much driving Rick has done over the last few days for Suzanna's children (S2) and he is worried that this is going to become a habit (S3). As Suzanna's voice starts to rise (S1) and she energetically picks up momentum and becomes more and more forceful, Rick gets a tight but blank look on his face and remains withdrawn for the rest of the session and possible the entire day (S2), and unless something happens that creates a shift in how the couple is functioning, the fighting will go on until the next session (S3). By then a number of other issues will have been tossed into the mix, including the fact that Suzanna's ideas about raising children are far more lax and unstructured than Rick's, who hails from a harsher, more disciplinarian Portuguese family, where expectations of children are much higher in terms of manners, chores, respectful treatment of adults, and consequences (S4).

Examining any one of these sequences can lead a therapist to a deeper understanding of a family's problems, and how these sequences are related can be examined and explored through the five characteristics of sequences: recursiveness; constraints; embeddedness; calibration; and resilience.

a. Recursiveness, or the understanding that each event in a sequence influences and is influenced by other events in that sequence (i.e., one contextualizes the other), thereby increasing the probability that certain events will occur and new ones will be precluded;
b. Constraints, which can exist at all levels of sequences and prevent the family from talking and behaving in less constricting and constraining ways. Words like "always" and "never," which occur often during a therapy session, generally indicate a constraint in the system;
c. Embeddedness is captured in the notion that sequences of shorter duration are embedded and contained within longer sequences. An example is the fight that Rick and Suzanne get into every time Rick believes he has over extended himself with her children, in that the fight is an S1 embedded in Rick's fear of it becoming an expectation,

an S3, which is embedded in his gendered notions of who takes care of the children, an S4;

d. Calibration, which can occur when an embedded sequence generates or calibrates another sequence where the original sequence is affected by another variable that is ebbing and flowing in yet another sequence. An example in the above case study occurs in the relationship between Suzanna's son, Jason, and Rick. There is an increasingly close bond between the two as they both love hockey and Jason is a gifted player with a powerful drive and ambition to someday become a professional. The closer Rick and Jason become the more concerned Rick becomes about being co-opted into Suzanne's children's lives;
e. Resilience, or the ebb and flow of recursive sequences such as job loss or repeated patterns around addictive behavior, take a toll on family members and it becomes more and more difficult to rebound. Like a rubber band that has been snapped and stretched too often, family members lose their capacity to bounce back, which can account for the exhaustion and hopelessness family members express about anything ever changing.

All of these characteristics of sequences, as well as the sequences themselves, are interrelated and when carefully explored during a session can help the family therapist navigate his or her way through the perplexing, confusing, often hostile and tangled web of family members' communications. The more classes of sequences involved in a problem, or the degree of embeddedness, is directly proportional to the intractability of the problem. In addition, similar to working with internal family systems, addressing a problematic interactional sequence with one member of the family may do nothing to alleviate the stress on another member of the family. For example, bringing to light Rick's fear of getting too close to Jason does little to alleviate Suzanne's resentment toward him for his lack of help and involvement with her two girls and his previous lack of involvement with Jason.

Listening for information from S1, S2, S3, and S4 sequences and building on adaptive sequences which support leadership, balance, and harmony, while simultaneously defusing and gently exposing and exploring the constraints imposed by nonadaptive sequences, decreases the survival mentality of family members.

What Breunlin, Schwartz, and Mac Kune-Karrier suggest is for therapists to "attune their listening to information relevant to all four classes of sequences" (2001, p. 115) and plan how sequences will be addressed to achieve the all-important singular goal of removing constraints through altering sequences. Changing an S1 or S2 interaction may impact S3 and S4 interactions but if cultivating such changes proves fruitless then assume that an S3 or S4 pattern may be involved. If beliefs at that level are not explored then the constraint(s) will prevail. It is at this stage that drawing on the wisdom of other metadomains such as gender and culture may be useful. Moreover, it may be useful to move deftly back and forth between classes of sequences, making shifts in one in the hope that small and incremental shifts will take place in others.

Proponents of different models of family therapy emphasize and have developed techniques to alter different sequences. When working with sequences under the rubric of metaframeworks, the family therapist is not limited to structural enactments, Satir's survival stances, strategic paradoxes, or Bowenian techniques to establish differentiation. According to Breunlin et al., if the family therapist maintains a collaborative relationship with all family members as well as upholds the presuppositions, then mixing and matching from different models does not result in confusion but rather provides the family therapist with a key that opens the gate to the riches inherent in the entire field.

LEADERSHIP, BALANCE, AND HARMONY: THE ORGANIZATIONAL METAFRAMEWORK

This third of the six metaframeworks concerns itself with the structure and organization of the family, but unlike earlier conceptualizations, ideas about hierarchy have been replaced with notions of leadership, balance, and harmony. As in all of the metadomains, systemic thought informs at a basic level such that the family is more than the sum of its individuals and comes together in its organization and structure. Maturana and Varela (1980) called this organizing force "autopoiesis," a Greek word for self-creation. Like any system, there are rules guiding how the parts structure themselves in relationship to one another and to the system as a whole, and from a metaframeworks perspective, the whole can include not just the family but all the systems and cultural nuances in which the family is embedded.

Breunlin, Schwartz, and Mac Kune-Karrer quite accurately accuse the field of family therapy of decontextualizing the family and paying only lip service to the fact that families are impacted by multiple educational, legal, medical, political, financial, religious, and cultural systems. All of which can place considerable constraints on the functioning of a family and its individual members. The family is a subsystem of a powerfully interconnected global community and is embedded in massive systems over which family members, for the most part, have no control and often little understanding. Family is merely one aspect and, in some cases, not the most important aspect to explore in order to facilitate change. In broadening the concept of systems nested within systems, family therapists can consider the entire range of systems involved in a family's presenting problem. In collaboration with the family, the therapist can assess for the most effective place within the family and within the larger cultural context to begin creating desired goals and changes.

The goal is to remove the constraints that are unbalancing the family and creating and maintaining disharmony, where harmony is defined as just that, harmonious relating created through caring, healthy sacrifice, cooperation, and clarity of boundaries and belonging. Through collaborative exploration of how the family might improve leadership and boundaries, thereby eliminating polarizations and creating balance at whatever levels of the total system that seem the most constraining, the family might be empowered to strike more harmonious notes and chords among its individual members and the system as a whole.

Problems in communication occur when the organization of a system is confused and how a family system is organized is a crucial aspect of healthy family functioning. In fact, Haley was of the opinion that the majority of family problems derived from a poorly defined and dysfunctional hierarchy and the number of dysfunctional hierarchies a family member was involved in was directly proportional to the degree of disturbance the individual suffered. Hence, one of Haley's main therapeutic goals was to restructure a family's intergenerational hierarchies and augment and improve generational boundaries. In order for a family to feel valued, effectively problem solve, and regulate such things as responsibility, conflict, planning for and coordinating future goals, along with meeting individual and group needs, it must have efficacious leadership. Caring and control are balanced when harmony exists and leadership is effective. Nurturing, caring, encouraging, being fair and flexible, and balancing autonomy and connectedness, are all aspects of effective leadership (Breunlin et al., 2001).

Inextricably connected to leadership, harmony, and balance is the concept of organizational structure which has long been important in family therapy. So central are ideas of structure or patterns of organization to the theoretical foundations of family therapy that early structural family therapists believed that by studying and aggressively altering isomorphs, or short interactional S1 sequences, the family therapist could begin to change the more dysfunctional patterns of interaction. As with many beliefs and practices from those early days of family therapy, however, clinically disappointing results proved to be an impetus to rethink constructs of structure and how to work with them.

First of all, structure and organization are not static. Rather, they are dynamic and what is captured in the short in-session S1 interaction provides but a small piece of a much larger structure that evolves over time and across contexts. Second, although important information can be gleaned from S1 interactions in an in-session context, they are fodder for exploring the complex world of the family that unfolds within a contextualized acculturated reality that has and is moving through time. Third, the process of assessing structure is collaborative and takes place not just within the S1 face-to-face interactions of a family but also through a mutual investigation of the S2, S3, and S4 patterns within which the family is embedded, as well as across all other metadomains such as culture, gender, internal family systems or mind, and development.

As problems become more entrenched and severe, from a structural and organizational perspective the family organizes around the problem and the problem organizes the family. The goal of therapy with respect to the organization metaframework is "to remove the constraints impeding the balance and harmony of the family and the individuals within it" through collaborating with the family to enhance leadership and boundaries, and remove polarization at any and all levels of the system (Breunlin et al., 2001, p. 147). Moreover, unlike previous incarnations of structural and strategic work with families, there is no "normative map" of how a family should be organized. Models of family organization that are heavily weighted in terms of the individualistic capitalistic North American culture, as well as notions such as dysfunctional cross-generational coalitions and alliances, have given way to a wide variety of structures that honor differing cultural and historical realities where normative primary coalition may well be between mother and son, or father and son, or intergenerational.

Removing constraints at the organization and structural level may mean attending to polarizations at the following levels: intrapersonal or internal family systems; interpersonal or within family members; extrafamilial or people from external agencies such as schools and justice systems; and/or intracultural, which would include such elements as racism, poverty, or disability. However, in the best structural family therapy tradition, nothing can be achieved in terms of removing constraints at any level until the therapist has joined authentically and genuinely with every member of the family. Joining, or connecting to each individual family member, involving them and making them feel like a welcome guest in your office through empathetic listening, careful observation, and deepening and broadening an understanding of the family's viewpoint through reflecting back, is the first step toward creating a therapeutic environment. It is highly dependent upon the therapist's capacity for use of self, self-awareness and self-reflexivity, and is key to creating a collaborative working environment.

Kelly, forty-two, and her husband Bill, forty-four, have been married twenty-two years. They have come to therapy because Bill's brother and sister-in-law have both died within two years of each other of different but equally rare and virulent forms of cancer leaving Bill and Kelly to care for their two orphaned children, fourteen-year-old Rebecca, and seventeen-year-old Robert. Bill and Kelly have four grown children of their own, and all but one are living independently. The structure and organization of the family is in abject chaos. Polarizations are replete within all levels of the family as members struggle with intra, inter, and extrafamilial, and intracultural constraints. Bill, who is of Asian descent, and Kelly, who is Irish, have adopted polarized positions in terms of the children and what each believes the children need in order to recover from the trauma of their parents' deaths. Bill is taking a "hard line" in suggesting the adolescents must "pull themselves together" and carry on and Kelly is devastated both at the loss of her much loved sister-in-law and the suffering her nephew and niece have witnessed. She is advocating therapy, grief counseling, being lenient with school attendance and allowing the children pretty much anything they want to help them feel better. Bill accuses Kelly of infantilizing the children and Kelly accuses Bill of being "hard-hearted, insensitive, and downright mean and cold" in his treatment of the children. Moreover, Bill is furious at his brother for dying and both children are regressing and alternately withdrawing and acting out in terms of school attendance and behavior in general.

Exploring these polarizations from a multisystemic perspective and bringing some awareness to the fact that balance, harmony, and leadership have been profoundly impacted by events which have been outside both Bill's and Kelly's and the children's control is a first step to co-creating with the family some semblance of structural organization. Balance within this family system has been devastated as neither Bill nor Kelly or either of these adolescent children feel like they have any influence in terms of decision-making and outcome.

The magnitude and severity of the events that have occurred have left the couple and the adolescent children feeling virtually helpless and, therefore, unbalanced. Balance within a family's organizational structure is a function of the degree of influence an individual has in: (a) the family's decision making process; (b) accessing a system's resources; and (c) responsibility within that system, all of which have been impacted due to events beyond anyone's control. Moreover, events which are now unfolding, such as symptoms of traumatic bereavement in the children, have further polarized and unbalanced the couple and now the family. Both Bill and Kelly rigidly insist on maintaining his or her position in relation to what the children need. There is little capacity to cooperate and the opportunity for a new family system to form is blocked and profoundly compromised. Sandwiched between the couple's lack of balance and harmony, the children, who now have little to no leadership, have been left to manage their traumatic bereavement the best they can. The eldest has increased his marijuana smoking significantly and the youngest has created a much needed distraction by fighting bitterly with her uncle and grieving deeply with her aunt, thereby creating a dysfunctional triangle and unbalancing and polarizing the relationship further. In order to restore some form of leadership in this system the couple and therapist decided that work needed to occur first with the couple subsystem while simultaneously engaging the children in separate grief counseling. Once some form of leadership, balance, and harmony was restored in the context of the couple, family therapy would resume.

Harmony is about the quality of relationships among family members. In a system where balance and leadership exist, individuals can relate harmoniously. Beyond that, once the couple subsystem is balanced, more equitable boundaries can be created for the children, thus improving the potential for harmony and balance within the system as a whole.

The polarization that the couple is experiencing is an attempt to restore, or in this case, create some structure and leadership within the new family but, unfortunately, it is simultaneously making it impossible to achieve. When leadership is effective and the system is balanced then members of a family have an appropriate degree of influence, access to resources, and a level of responsibility that is appropriate to needs and to one's position in the system which is equal to that of other individuals at the same level (Breunlin et al., 2001, p. 136).

By taking a collaborative stance with the family and working diligently to join with each member by honoring the tragedy and pain, confusion and anger, and deep and abiding sadness that lies at the heart of this new configuration of family, the therapist can attempt to reach the organizational goals that mark this metadomain. By setting goals and facilitating balanced and harmonious as well as meaningful and efficacious leadership, along with exploring constraints and polarizations that are blocking the family's path to those goals, this family may be able to create a structure that will open possibilities for healing the formidable grief all members are experiencing. This, along with defining both intra and interpersonal polarizations, using internal and external resources such as adolescent grief groups, helping family members negotiate new responsibilities, and improving boundaries within and around polarized members, will help the family to reopen relationships, detriangulate, and differentiate from each other and the children's horrifically painful past.

THE DEVELOPMENT METAFRAMEWORK

The development metaframework and the cultural metaframework are intimately connected because development at all levels is defined by the dynamic cultural and societal beliefs and values that inform child rearing norms, relationship rules and realities, and adaptive and nonadaptive adult behaviors and development. Moreover, development in the metaframeworks model includes not only traditional conceptualizations of the family life cycle as it moves through time (Carter, McGoldrick, & Garcia-Preto, 2011), but also has been expanded to include biological, individual, subsystemic or relational, familial, and societal levels. At each of these five levels, development occurs and is affected by and affects development at all levels.

Life cycle change or nodal transitions, as they are called in the metaframeworks model, like marriage, birth, entering adolescence, leaving home, maybe divorce and remarriage, retirement, and death all signal a need for adaptation and change. Any change, even welcomed change, is stressful but unwanted change is especially stressful. Problems tend to constellate around times of family life cycle transitions, so nodal transitions are inherently anxiety provoking and how a family moves through the family life cycle in its traditional "moving through time" incarnation is heavily influenced by the rapidly changing social and cultural realities that families today are dealing with. Myriad influences from the micro to the macro affect how a family traverses life cycle changes, and the once relatively clear life cycle trajectory of starting a family to finding oneself in the midst of an empty nest is now far less linear and sixty year-old grandparents may find themselves struggling to raise an adolescent grandchild who has been unable to adjust to a reconstituted family configuration. As Breunlin et al. (2001) state, "the rapid social evolution of the past two generations has confused the developmental picture at all levels" (163) and families find themselves facing wide-ranging constraints. Because so many expectations about family life cycle development are in disarray in today's technology-driven Western world, the above example leaves a family facing the once disparate nodal transitions of adolescence and retirement simultaneously.

A family therapist today is more likely to be sitting with a family whose members are facing nonlinear, multiple nodal transitions than she or he is likely to be sitting with a nuclear family facing linear and expected ones. Consequently, a model of family development that encompasses nodal transitions as well as microtransitions allows the family therapist to create a more comprehensive developmental hypothesis. Understanding how development through nodal transitions affects a family and each of its members requires understanding development within other levels of the system and vice versa. Individual transitions, such as a child becoming potty trained as opposed to being in diapers, tend to be more incremental and are distinguished from nodal transitions and are referred to as microtransitions. From the perspective of metaframeworks, each developmental change in an individual family member necessitates an important and associated change in the family as a whole. "A recursive relationship exists among individual, family, and relational development" (Breunlin et al. 2001, p. 171).

This intricate recursivity is a function of the family's systemic reality in that as individual family members develop, their "potential for competence increases, and this new competence in turn can increase the flexibility and complexity of the family, which in turn can then foster further individual competence" (p. 171). Fostering an individual member's development, while attending to the needs and health of the family as a whole, is a juggling act worthy of any circus performer and necessitates that the family therapist have more than a working knowledge of appropriate child and adolescent development.

As developmental shifts occur, so too do shifts in family members' competence, and in the metaframeworks model development and competence are closely linked. Moreover, as in any complex system, small changes in input can produce significantly larger systemic shifts. Input is not equal to output. Such is the case with microtransitions. The family system must respond to microtransitions in individual members, so potty training a child changes many things as does a child's acquisition of language or learning to walk. Breunlin has suggested that families negotiate microtransitions through a process of oscillation (Breunlin et al., 2001, p. 172).

As the family responds to incremental developmental shifts, such as a child learning to crawl and beginning to engage in self-propelled movement, the change and the response to it exist concurrently with the old behavior. It is not a question of "out with the old and in with the new." Rather, the old and the new exist simultaneously and behavior oscillates between old and new and new and old until, eventually, the new replaces the old. "Oscillations represent the family's attempts to accommodate to individual development while remaining stable" (Breunlin et al., 2001, p. 173). In functional families, oscillations appear and then disappear or dampen as the new behavior takes over and individual developmental competence and mastery increases.

Promoting and nurturing developmental competence is critical to dampening oscillations and restoring family harmony. New sequences are developed in order to accommodate age-appropriate changes in behavior for both individuals and the family as a whole. This occurs in the interests of supporting microtransitions and emergent competence which are constantly taking place.

Given that oscillations dampen and microtransitions are successfully negotiated when family members' developmental competence is encouraged and occurs in predictable ways, it follows that symptomatic families are not able to dampen oscillations associated with mircrotransitions. Family problems can be located in a child or a parent's acting out in ways that are too young or too old. If oscillations are not dampened during a period of developmental shifts, then emerging competence is also discouraged. According to Bruelin et al. (2001) "symptoms are often a metaphorical expression of an oscillation: a child may be enuretic but also verbally precocious and the symptoms recursively interact with the system so that the child oscillates between competencies that are both less than and greater than expected" (p. 175).

As age appropriate competence is encouraged and oscillations weaken and new behavior becomes the norm, a child concomitantly develops a sense of self. Moreover, development at one level supports development at other levels and development, in a metaframeworks model, is assumed to involve the biological, individual, relational, and family level. The therapeutic task is to facilitate the family moving to an appropriate stage of the family life cycle. Constraints appear at the individual level when oscillations associated with microtransitions are not dampened through age-appropriate development of competence. Biological development, which is often ignored by family therapists, entails relieving constraints and restrictions at the biological level and can often include loosening the constraints associated with learning and physically challenged children and adults. Constraints can also appear at the relational level.

The relational level, in a metaframeworks model, involves six recursive processes: attraction or being drawn to another; liking, which entails an appreciation for and valuing another's attributes; nurturing, or the ability to give and receive care as well as create security in a relationship; coordinating meaning, which necessitates creating a consensual reality in the relationship through attributing similar meaning to speech, behavior, and events, thus coordinating meaning in a shared setting; setting rules that define relationships and the conditions under which they operate; and, finally, making metarules, or "rules for changing the rules of the relationship as it encounters new demands" (p. 184-185).

Patricia and Erik had been married for thirty years and for most of those thirty years Erik had been engaged in extramarital affairs. While Patricia was actively parenting their four children she had overlooked Erik's infidelities as he had created a multimillion dollar business and provided well for Patricia and the children. They had a traditional marriage where Patricia did the lion's share of the parenting and household duties and Erik ran the business and grudgingly doled out money. Although Patricia was aware of these affairs she had been preoccupied for twenty-five of those thirty years raising her four rambunctious children. She had the art of running a household down to a science and was an exquisite cook and caterer as well as seamstress and interior designer. She had also taught herself to weave and make pottery and for years had made all of the children's clothing and many of the household goods. On the surface the couple could not have appeared to be happier. However, as Patricia's role as mother receded and the children left home she was left with the role of wife and the couple found themselves with no capacity for development on a relational level. Although there was some small measure of attraction to each other there was no liking, no real nurturing from one to the other, no consensual reality or coordinated meaning, and no capacity for changing the rules of the relationship as it entered this new nodal transition. In spite of months of therapy and a deep willingness on

Patricia's part to keep the relationship intact, the couple simply could not salvage enough from the relational remnants to survive the family life cycle (FLC) transition and rebuild in the face of a totally new stage of the life cycle.

THE CULTURAL METAFRAMEWORK

By including culture as a metadomain in the metaframeworks model, its enormous importance as a basis for practice in family therapy is underscored. Culture has been a consideration for family therapists since the early work of Murray Bowen, Nathan Ackerman, and Don Jackson, who used "culture as a category of analysis" (Weinstein, 2004, p. 23) during family therapy's formative years. Moreover, due to the work of people like Celia Falicov (2003, 2005) and Monica McGoldrick (2005), transnational and cultural issues currently share center stage with other issues of diversity. Cultural competence on the part of the family therapist is highly valued and from a metaframeworks perspective diversity is seen as "a valuable resource" (Bruelin et al, 2001, p. 195). Culture is viewed broadly as consisting of a host of sociocultural contexts and encompasses race, gender, education, ethnicity, class, sexual preference, geographic region, economic status, religion, and age. And, in as much as culture influences values across all levels of a system (individual, family, community, institutional) and provides opportunities, it also can be responsible for considerable constraints.

Although myriad definitions of culture are adopted, discussed, and endorsed in a metaframeworks model, Falicov's definition of culture "as shared world-views and adaptive behaviors derived from simultaneous location in a variety of contexts" is viewed as an excellent systemic definition, and Karrer's expansion of this includes the anthropological perspective by considering the role of the observer and the multiplicity of values that is present in any cultural context (Breunlin et al., 2001, p. 197).

Immigration, for whatever reason, is a decision that "begins a process of cultural transition" (Breunlin et al., 2001, p. 206) that reverberates throughout the immediate and extended family for generations as the family struggles to sustain itself and achieve some semblance of balance in the host country. Achieving balance, however, is a far different process for the family that decided to immigrate to a new country than it is for the refugee family in that the former makes a choice to leave and the refugee is forced out. Understanding this difference as well as concepts such as: acculturation processes; kinship structures; power relations in the family and the therapeutic encounter; the use of family mapping and cultural genograms, where functional rather than only biological kin relationships are considered significant; family organization including understanding the dominant dyad; and consciousness concerning privileged discourses around the construction of "family," are all aspects of a cultural sensitivity and awareness that the family therapist needs in order to practice in a culturally competent way. The following case is riddled with cultural complexities that differ significantly from the value system of the middle-aged Caucasian therapist who worked with the family.

Newar is fifteen years of age and was six months old when his father, mother, older brother, Fuad, and paternal grandparents immigrated to the West. Fuad is ten years older than Newar and lives with his parents, grandparents, and Newar. On the whole, family members are well educated, wealthy (both in Egypt and in their current setting), and have struggled to retain as much of their Egyptian culture as possible in the host country. They were mandated to attend family therapy due to the fact that Newar ran afoul of the law and was caught smoking and trafficking marijuana in his local high school.

Because coffee is considered part of a traditional welcome in Egypt it was served at the first session in the traditional kanakah or small coffee pot and Sa'idi or small coffee cup. And, although mistakes were made, the family appeared appreciative of the therapist's attempts to make them feel comfortable and welcome. The hope was that through this gesture the family would be assured that every effort would be made to acknowledge and work with the powerful cultural divide that was present in the therapeutic environment as well as the potential therapeutic discourse. This was also intended as a strong message to the family that mistakes would happen but the therapist was open to learning about and respecting the cultural differences.

Shortly into the first session it was clear that the traditional values of a patriarchal society were honored by all members of the family and authority was exercised according to the hierarchy which went from father to eldest son, with grandfather sometimes being consulted, but only rarely due to his age, constant fatigue, and respiratory difficulties. It also became clear that Fuad experienced both auditory and visual hallucinations and complex behavior patterns that in Western medicine would be diagnosed as schizophrenia. Consistent with a tendency in Egyptian culture to experience shame around the type of symptoms that Fuad displayed and either ignore or hide them, the family refused to acknowledge any anomalies in the eldest son's behavior. Paradoxically, however, Fuad's problems were precisely why the family had immigrated to Canada.

Conscription is a duty in Egypt and young males are exempt from this duty only under very special circumstance, one being as an only son. With the birth of Newar, Fuad's conscription was a given. The patriarch of the family was well aware that his eldest son would not survive conscription, thus a move out of Egypt to a foreign land would be the most effective way to ensure his survival. As the family had relatives in Canada, the decision was made to emigrate.

Even more problematic, however, was the discovery that Fuad was physically and emotionally torturing Newar through beatings and threats. From the cultural perspective of the therapist, Newar had become the focus of a preponderance of positive symptoms and was a central figure in many of Fuad's hallucinations and delusions. As part of a strengths based assessment, along with an assessment of the various sources of family stress, Newar was seen alone and disclosed this information at that time. In this same session, he expressed his complete inability to protect himself due to the size and age difference as well as the fact that Fuad was his older brother and, therefore, demanded respect. Newar did not believe he could talk to his father about what was occurring between himself and his brother and he believed that his father already knew but refused to take action.

The therapist hypothesized that if she was going to facilitate cooperative exchanges then a common-sense, family-centered, non-labeling, externalizing, and task-oriented method of working was warranted. Honoring the family's cultural need to deny Fuad's problematic behavior while simultaneously acknowledging and understanding that this problem had organized the family's existence and was placing Newar in genuine danger, was central to working in a culturally syntonic way.

As family-based treatment for schizophrenia has been developed primarily in the United States and British Commonwealth countries (Miklowitz & Tompson, 2003, p. 612) cross cultural interventions present the therapist with myriad difficult overall, and in-the-moment challenges and decisions. Further, because schizophrenia is, in some sense, the quintessential madness and explanations of the disorder have ranged from possession to brain dysfunction, the decision was made to take a combined narrative, solution-focused, and strengths based approach to working with this family rather than a Western, medicalized, individual treatment approach.

Because Newar was being terrorized, immediate steps had to be taken to protect him and stop the physical abuse. To this end the therapist began by using a psychoeducational approach, not so much to help the family understand schizophrenia but, rather, to help family members understand the implications of this kind of family violence in their host country. In the interests of giving behaviors another name rather than speaking in terms of hallucinations, schizophrenia, and mental illness, as this immediately activated family members' shame and defensiveness, language was carefully constructed to be more solution focused and words such as imagination were used instead of hallucination. The beatings that Fuad was perpetrating were discussed as violence rather than as resulting from his delusions of persecution and paranoia and part of the psychoeducational process entailed outlining to family members the consequences of assault charges. It was also outlined to the family that all marriage and family therapists are under a legal obligation to report child abuse and should Fuad's violent behavior toward Newar be allowed to continue such a report would, by law, need to be made. It was noted that because the family was already under scrutiny from the courts this could be serious for Fuad. The need to exercise authority in the interests of protecting Newar, especially paternal authority as, ultimately, familial authority rested with him, was emphasized and the fact that he had moved his family to a new country in order to protect Fuad from certain death was used as an illustration of how incredibly capable he was of keeping family members safe. He was to generate a safety plan for Newar that was as foolproof as the one he had generated for Fuad, and all family members, including Fuad, were to be present in the next session and made aware of the plan and the consequences for violating the plan should the violence continue. In that session input would also be invited from the therapist and other family members. It was also decided that while the safety plan was being created and implemented, Newar could visit his uncle who lived in a nearby city.

Language and constructs which emphasized the fact that "tricks of the imagination" could cause people to do things that could hurt other people as well as make up things that others did not hear or see were used. In this way the problem of major mental illness was reframed and externalized but not minimized. This allowed the family's defensive structure to soften and at one point the patriarch asked how these kinds of tricks were explained from a neurological perspective. The therapist offered an explanation and this conversation lead quite naturally to a discussion of how medication impacted the brain and could help perhaps to modify these "tricks of the imagination." Once the problem of violence in the family had been addressed it became possible to address the presenting problem of Newar smoking and distributing marijuana at his high school.

A working knowledge is necessary, not only of what is similar and what is different across ethnocultural divides, but also what is meaningful and relevant to specific families within those diverse groups. For example, not all Egyptian families would react and respond like this family and these microcosmic differences are as important to understand as are the macrocosmic ones. However, a constructivist, solution focused approach assumes "family competence, orients the family toward a future when they will manage the problem, and builds on family strengths by highlighting previous successes in coping with and managing presenting difficulties" (Eakes, Walsh, Markowski, Cain, & Swanson, 1997, p. 146).

From a metaframeworks perspective, all models of family therapy can be commandeered into service under any one of the six metadomains and in the cultural domain the two levels of sociocultural context that contribute to diversity are cultural transition and sociocultural contexts such as race, age, socioeconomic status, education, ethnicity, religion, gender, minority/majority status, and geographical location. Cultural transition encompasses two temporal dimensions: historical/generational sequences or cultural evolution;

and immigration/acculturation, both of which evolve over time and are impacted by and intersect with sociocultural contexts such as age, race, ethnicity, and economics.

Refugees often struggle with several levels of cultural transition in that they are forced out of their homeland and often take a circuitous route to what ends up being their final destination. Unlike an immigrant who plans the move to a foreign land, the refugee will often hear in the morning that the Canadian or Australian embassies are taking applications and that afternoon will be filling out an application to emigrate. Further, this move has usually been preceded by a number of other moves to other foreign countries that became part of the flight path as they fled their homeland. One family from Bosnia/Herzegovina, for example, fled from Sarajevo to Croatia at the height of the war, where they lived in a refugee camp for a year before emigrating to Greece where they remained for a short time, and finally emigrated to Canada where they settled in Montreal. Here, they made an attempt to learn yet another totally new language and acclimatize to a new culture but found the acculturation process difficult and made the decision to move to Toronto, where they had to learn to function in English. Finally, they made connections within a culturally syntonic community and found work, which although certainly lacking the status of their careers in former Yugoslavia, was vaguely meaningful and fulfilling. Migration from one country to another and one region to another can quite literally go on for years before the refugee finds a place to settle. Such a historical/generational or S5 sequence defines and redefines in an ongoing way, beliefs which unfold during cultural evolution and allow people and families to draw on experiences from the past, consider the way these experiences fit the present, and use them to plan for the future through times of stability and times of transformation (Breunlin et al., 2001, p. 203).

Each generation garners meaning, belief, values, and behavior from the historical/generational sequence within which that generation is embedded and both therapist and family members are part of this historical context and, therefore, influenced by those meanings which are sometimes shared and sometimes not. Within a multicultural framework a series of questions helps to guide the therapist and the family in understanding what precisely is and is not shared in this particular sequence.

From a metaframeworks perspective, a series of questions concerning historical/generational sequences guides the therapist and the family through this aspect of this metadomain. Questions such as the following are designed to explore aspects of interactional sequences: "Are family members respectful of their generational differences?"; "Is there potential for expansion of beliefs through the understanding of generational historical sequences?"; "Are all family members familiar with the prevalent historical themes for their generations?"

Questions designed to explore immigration and acculturation might include: "Are members of the family at all phases of acculturation?"; "Do some members of the family always defend the country of origin's values?"; "Do some members of the family always defend the host country's values?"; "Has the family been able to mourn the loss of family and friends?"; "How much can family members discuss these differences among them?"; "Can the therapist examine both the constraints and the opportunities in the country of origin?" Moreover, the therapist must determine how willing the family is to discuss their immigration stories. Although it may be the case that immigrants love to tell their stories, for the most part, refugees do not, as their story may be rife with unbearable memories of flight, trauma, loss, and pain.

The patriarch of another refugee family from Bosnia/Herzegovina, for example, when asked about the family's migratory history, looked the therapist in the eye and in almost indiscernible English said, "So, you want to hear about our nightmares, do you? Well, I won't tell you and I won't tell them." He motioned to his two children and said, "They are too young to remember and that is right. No one should remember and I cannot forget."

Further, there can be huge differences in many instances between refugees and immigrants when it comes to sociocultural contexts such as economics, education, ethnicity, and religion. As well, resistance to or tolerance of the host country's attitudes toward gender can vary significantly according to ethnicity, race, and regional background. Each one of these sociocultural contexts comes with a series of pertinent questions that the therapist can use to explore familial history and current context as well as the fit between the therapist's experiences and the family's.

Goodness-of-fit in the metaframeworks model is about "congruence of sociocultural background between the minority and majority family, between the immigrant and the non-immigrant (or refugee and non-refugee) family, and between the family and the therapist" (Breunlin et al., 2001, p. 231). There is also an intersection at all of these sociocultural contexts which may not be apparent to the therapist until a thorough assessment of these factors is completed and/or more time has been spent with the family. Determining what beliefs the family and the therapist share and do not share is an outcome of exploring these sociocultural contexts. "Each context provides opportunities for expansion but also constrains the meanings that are attributed to experiences" (p. 232).

For a family to enter therapy its members are obviously experiencing constraints in at least one and possibly a number of different contexts. Satir called it a perceived lack of choice. The process of first focusing on what the family considers constraining and then facilitating the opening to possibilities and choices is the trajectory of therapy. Within a multicultural metadomain, self-reflexivity concerning the therapist's own sociocultural context and the family's, as well as expanding one's own cultural views, again through answering a series of questions, will allow the therapist to function within this metadomain in a conscious and fluid way.

THE GENDER METAFRAMEWORK

All of family therapy owes a great debt to the feminist critique. As Breunlin et al. (2001) point out, it is ironic indeed that in its infancy the field of family therapy, which emerged as an alternative to traditional therapies, actually decontextualized the family from the sociocultural context in which it was embedded and supported traditional social beliefs about the family and the roles within the family. The issue of power, power differences, and violence within the family were rendered invisible by the Batesonian view of power as an illusion. Women's lived experience within the family and the sociocultural context was disregarded and the field was replete with mother bashing and mother blaming. The idea that mothers were enmeshed with their children simply ignored the contradictory notions that families were far healthier places for men and children than for woman and that women were more symptomatic and unhappier than other family members.

In keeping with the feminist critique and the tremendous service feminist family therapists like Judith Myers Avis, Peggy Papp, Froma Walsh, Betty Carter, Deborah Leupnitz, and a host of others have performed for family therapy, the gender metaframework acknowledges that family members do not have the same opportunities, the same influence, and the same amount of power. Feminist family therapists created an awareness of power, hierarchy, and gender inequality and brought to life the notion that the personal is political and what goes on in the larger culture is reflected within the family and the therapeutic discourse. Feminist family therapy is not a method of family therapy as much as it is a way to analyze and question how we avoid thinking, or think, or do not think about women in families. In many cases, the feminist family therapist is faced with an impossible dilemma and that is that she is committed to working within the confines of the family while simultaneously understanding that the very notion of family is detrimental to woman.

From a gendered metadomain and a feminist perspective, therapy is not apolitical. It is a deeply political act and never value free. The gender metadomain consists of five gender evolution positions around which families are assessed: traditional, where families are organized around a patriarch and patriarchal values and men are seen as the primary breadwinner and women as the primary caregiver; gender-aware, where families are at different stages of awareness of gender inequities and family members are experiencing constraints and restrictions as a direct result of traditional gender role expectations, with women expressing and experiencing more discomfort than men;

polarized, where families are openly fighting about gender issues and challenging one another through interactions that are replete with blaming, demands for change, and divisive exchanges; in transition, where families are still arguing about gender roles and expectations but there is some hope that new and more balanced role definitions will emerge and family members are moving in the direction of greater equality in life and decision making; and balanced, where mutuality and collaboration exists in that balance is felt both externally within the family in terms of gendered awareness and role expectations and internally within members of the family.

The gender metadomain forces practitioners to think, as opposed to not think or avoid thinking, about women in the context of the family, and along with fostering an awareness within the self, family members are encouraged to consider how much gender-related constraints impact their everyday lives. In so doing, the therapist must find a way to question a family's gendered beliefs without being impertinent or rude or even presumptuous and this becomes more complicated in the context of cross cultural family therapy where the family might adhere to strict and extreme traditional gender roles and expectations.

Gender sensitive goals need to be initiated by the family, not the therapist. However, from a feminist perspective, declaring one's commitment to relational awareness and an exploration of power and oppression is critical to authenticity in relationship. Within the gender metadomain, the therapist might hypothesize and plan to introduce ideas one step beyond where the family is currently functioning. For example, within the context of the traditional family, the plan might be to support awareness of gender imbalances by "exploring each member's position and promoting dialogue among family members" (Breunlin et al., 2001, p. 258). Within gender aware families the task is to "validate everyone's experience while expanding descriptions and explanations" (p. 258). Decreasing polarization, while validating family members' experience, is the therapeutic task within the polarized family, as is diffusing blaming stances while simultaneously supporting family members' negotiating capacity. Because in-transition family members are working toward finding a new sense of harmony and mutuality, the therapist intensifies existing concerns and questions and then helps to solidify emerging descriptions and explanations. In balanced families the concern lies not so much within the family, but rather in exploring the family's lack of fit within the culture.

Movement within the gender metadomain is away from imbalance and toward balance, and away from inequality and toward relationships that are supportive of egalitarian roles. As such, promoting gender awareness as opposed to rigid traditional ideologies through expanding ideas on narrow gender role expectations, questioning areas of accepted male privilege, and validating internal experiences and struggles becomes fodder for therapeutic discourse. Promoting and supporting growth and changes in awareness, challenging and questioning gender-driven constraints, and exploring new roles and opportunities along with cultural and historical themes of oppression, will help to raise consciousness around issues of inequality. Promoting transition instead of polarization through validating experiences of oppression as well as the desire to change, airing injuries, exploring polarized parts, and encouraging empathetic understanding of one another's respective roles will help to clarify new roles and enhance changing roles. Promoting egalitarian roles and exploring depth and breadth of gendered experiences, as well as advocacy for change within the larger sociocultural arena through reinforcing mutual decision making, increasing intimacy, and improving capacity for authentic relationship, brings not just a feminist perspective to therapy but a fully human perspective.

Introducing complexity into the system, expanding experiences and promoting descriptions and explanations of gender inequality is a therapeutic responsibility as families struggle to attain new levels of balance and harmony in the midst of gender imbalances that constrain functioning. For example, Patricia and Erik, a case mentioned earlier in this chapter, have been married for thirty years and during that time Erik has had many extramarital affairs which Patricia has overlooked due to her involvement with the children and the home. In spite of the fact that Erik had created a multimillion dollar business the entire family operated under tacit and unspoken but precise and widely understood rules: Erik controls all the money all the time; don't ruin the lifestyle Erik is entitled to; everything of value is Erik's and everything that is not of value is everyone else's; Erik is the most important person in the family; Erik is head of the family and he should be happy even if he is the only one who is happy; Erik is always right and always needs to win and the family must support that; nobody in the family can be more successful than Erik; and the family is nothing without Erik.

It was not until the marriage disintegrated, however, and Erik left, that Patricia was able to identify any of these rules. She had spent all her married life creating a façade of the perfect family and the perfect marriage. Protecting Erik from being exposed and judged harshly by friends and family for his affairs and his abusive treatment of her and the children in the area of finances had become another of her many priorities and concerns. For the most part, she struggled to make ends meet. The house carried a hefty mortgage as it was considered her domain and she drove a small economy car while Erik drove the latest model Mercedes Benz. He traveled extensively throughout the year and she cared for the children. They belonged to a religious tradition where the male's right to head the household and female submissiveness was sanctioned through reference to divine authority. At church functions woman were segregated from men and sometimes made to face the wall. With minor variations patriarchy dominated and the family rules that Erik and Patricia adhered to were similar to what most members of her community adhered to.

The therapeutic task of questioning the family's organization around traditional patriarchal values, and introducing more gender-awareness in the context of this family and the community that supported it, was a Sisyphus like job. From Erik's perspective there was much to lose and little to gain by changing his oppressive behavior toward his wife and family and, in fact, he refused to even consider that his behavior could be construed by anyone as oppressive and an abuse of power. Surprisingly, however, the therapist's sometimes gentle and sometimes not so gentle questioning and observations supported Patricia's refusal to continue in the marriage if Erik was going to continue to evade her emotionally, ignore her physically, and deny her financially. Throughout the work of therapy Patricia continually expressed a desire for more and deeper connection now that her children no longer needed her in the same way. As she moved into the second half of her life she began to make demands on Erik for greater mutuality, authenticity, empowerment, and growth fostering interactions, and in so doing hastened the demise of the relationship. Both children supported her at the time and continued to support her through a long and protracted court battle for support and matrimonial assets. During the process Patricia struggled with massive amounts of guilt and deep feelings of wrong-doing. She lost her church, her community, her husband, and her friends but finally was awarded by the courts her share of the matrimonial assets. In the interim she started her own small business, cultivated new friends, and began to volunteer at a local shelter for women who experienced abuse.

Work within the gender metaframework is often messy, painful, and fraught with pitfalls for both the therapist and the family. Power dynamics within the culture are often mirrored within the family and, like many women, Patricia over-personalized the established political and cultural themes that informed her life and held herself personally accountable for the demise of the marriage and the pain she was "causing" her children and her expartner. Rather than challenging the social conditions, Patricia saw herself as culpable and it was not until she accidentally overheard Erik's male lawyer discussing with another lawyer what a "nasty client" he had that she was able to truly begin to endorse and sanction her own perceptions and let go of her guilt, self-blame, and shame around not only the loss of the marriage but also the fact that she was legally pursuing her rightful portion of the marital assets.

FLEXIBLE BLUEPRINT FOR THERAPY

Within the context of the metaframework perspective, the blueprint for therapy is what systematizes the six metadomains and provides the family therapist with a way to operationalize the model. From such a perspective the therapist can extract the best from all practice models while avoiding the limitations and constraints and, as previously stated, the goal within the metaframework model is to remove constraints. The pragmatic constraints the family is dealing with are envisaged as systemic and existing at the level of biology, the person, relationships, family, community, and society and as such are "referred to as a web of constraints" and can exist in any or all of the metadomains (Breunlin et al. p. 367). Constraints can be of a primarily biological nature, for example, and exist within the gender, multicultural, internal family systems or mind, sequences, developmental, and organization metaframeworks. A child born with cerebral palsy can develop differently in areas of locomotion, leave a primary caregiver, usually the mother, exhausted and worn out, stress the family financially and relationally, be the topic of severe fighting between parents and other family members, and create a situation where mother stops working in order to care for her child. Hence, this predominantly biological constraint involves person, relationship, family, community, and society constraints and is experienced across all metadomains.

Therapy varies according to the number of constraints, how they interact, and the metadomain(s) within which they are located. Locating and successfully shifting significant constraints within various metadomains is a co-created and co-constructed endeavor between therapist and family members and is the nucleus within which meaningful change takes form and shape. Metadomains are embedded one within the other and levels of constraints are equally interconnected with each other and within the six metadomains, creating a systemically organized model where interconnections are varied, rich, and complex. Moreover, not only is it possible within metaframeworks to discern information about how the human system called "the family" functions within larger systems, but it informs both the family and the therapist as to where "to look for and identify the constraints that limit functioning and maintain problems" (Breunlin et al., 2001, p. 282). The creators of the model conceptualize the constraints and the metadomains as a spider web, hence the term "web of constraints" and like any spider web when one part of the web is constrained or perturbed the entire web is impacted and the reverberations are felt throughout.

The components of therapy in the metaframework model are organized in the form of a blueprint for therapy and consist of the following:

- Co-Hypothesizing, which gives the session and the therapy direction, involves the therapist and family selecting, synthesizing, and organizing ideas and information that the family has provided into a coherent and understandable form which will ultimately evolve from a working but very general idea to a hypothesis that corresponds to each of the metaframeworks. Hence, one has a developmental hypothesis (HD), an interactional sequence hypothesis (HS), a gender hypothesis (HG), an organizational hypothesis (HO), a cultural hypothesis (HC), and a hypothesis concerning internal actions (HI). Hypothesizing makes sense of feedback offered by the family and is co-created with the family. However, all hypothesizing must be approached with openness, curiosity, and a willingness to radically reconfigure one's theorizing as required. From the perspective of Integrative Problem-Centered Metaframeworks Therapy (IPCM), "hypothesizing refers to the process whereby the therapist works with the family to identify the set of constraints, and the relationships between them, that prevents the family from implementing adaptive solutions" (Breunlin et al., 2011, p. 298). Further, from this perspective, problem sequences are integral to hypothesizing in that they form the "eyes and ears" of hypothesizing and are the "manifestations of the presenting problems and provide the most concrete, accessible, and ultimately changeable aspects of the problems. . . . IPCM hypothesizes that the clients' capacity to implement the adaptive solution sequence as an alternative to the presenting problem sequences is blocked by the Web of Constraints" (p. 298). In as much as hypothesizing organizes "theories of problem formation and maintenance, planning metaframeworks organize theories of problem resolution (Pinsof et al., 2011, p. 317);
- Co-Planning involves intervening, giving directives, and using techniques or strategizing in collaboration with the family to solve the presenting problems. Planning is about "selecting a course of action for conducting therapy at any point" (Breunlin et al., 2001, p. 287) and entails using techniques and interventions, but attempts to circumvent that kind of language and replace it with a softer and more inherently collaborative and participatory process. In planning, the therapist borrows from the postmodern and narrative traditions in that she or he works in conjunction with the family and must attend to the three components of relating, staging, and creating events. Relating, like Minuchin's joining, means establishing a relationship with each member of the family and maintaining that relationship through empathy and understanding as well as discerning each member's strengths and positive qualities and then accessing and evoking those strengths and qualities in a way that they can be used to loosen or remove constraints. Moreover, it is incumbent upon the therapist to trust the family's ability to self-organize and find the solutions to the presenting problems. In the art of relating the therapist takes a collaborative leader-

ship role in the interest of evoking the family's capacity to overcome the challenges that brought them to therapy. Staging is about knowing precisely where one is in the process in its moment-to-moment unfolding, the conversation in general, the session as a whole, and therapy as a whole (i.e., middle, beginning, or terminating). Creating events or engaging in therapeutic interventions means that the therapist works across models with the family using such techniques as circular questioning, modeling congruence and challenging survival stances, or creating an intervention in order to generate a plan that is either action or meaning oriented. All interventions and techniques are referred to as an "event" to invoke the idea that a family is not being acted upon but, rather, is being acted with. An event connotes that something of significance is taking place but it is a collaborative and co-planned occurrence.

- Conversing is about "deciding what to say to the family on a moment-to-moment basis" (Breunlin et al., 2001, p. 287) and concerns the conversations that therapist and family generate to find and clear constraints as well as create movement toward health and growth for all family members. It consists of questions, statements, and directives and rather than limit oneself to one of these forms of conversing, in a metaframeworks model the therapist uses all of the above in a way that is consistent with his or her personal style (Breunlin et al., 2001, p. 305).
- Feedback and reading feedback, which is closely related to hypothesizing in that it bridges the therapist's ideas and the family's shared information, guides what happens in the moment, in the session, and in therapy as a whole. "Reading feedback from a family and from members of a family is not about grasping the reality of the family, rather, it is about understanding the therapist's own attribution of meaning to the family's responses to one another" (Breunlin et al., 2001, p. 307) and only when meaning has been agreed upon and checked with the family can that feedback then become part of planning and hypothesizing. Reading feedback requires that the therapist call upon theoretical ideas and concepts and then translate them to the family in a way that meaning is created through the lens of the six metaframeworks.

These four elements of hypothesizing, planning, conversing, and reading feedback are recursively related and in the end form a Uroborus-like configuration where it is difficult to determine where one stops and another begins. Using the flexible blueprint for therapy requires that the family therapist focus on all components of the blueprint at all stages of therapy and move nimbly and deftly between the components and the metadomains. Returning to the blueprint and acknowledging the recursive nature of its elements at all times, and eschewing attachment to any one hypothesis or metadomain, no matter how seemingly brilliant or insightful, creates the necessary flow between family and therapist and the acts of co-hypothesizing, co-planning, conversing, and interpreting feedback. Feedback is constantly read by the therapist and fed back to the family so that hypotheses can be co-created and either confirmed or disconfirmed or discarded or modified. This iterative process is what moves therapy forward as is the co-constructing of hypotheses from all relevant metadomains.

The blueprint itself constitutes a complex flow between hypothesizing within the six metaframeworks and creating, where relevant, a hypothesis around internal processes (HI), gender (HG), development (HD), sequences (HS), organization (HO), and culture (HC), using conversing through statements, questions, and directives, planning through relating, staging, and creating events, and finally, reading feedback. During a therapy session this "blueprint" is replete with meaning, emotion, and therapeutic action and planning. Family systems can be both constrained and changed by focusing on action, meaning, and emotion and so a balance must exist in the focus of the session between the three (Breunlin et al., 2001, p. 357).

REFERENCES

Albert, A. (Ed.) (1995). *Chaos and Society*. Oxford, England: IOS Press.

Assagioli, R. (1965). *Psychosynthesis: A Manual of Principles and Techniques*. New York, NY: Viking Press.

Beels, C. (2002). Notes for a cultural history of family therapy. *Family Process*, 41(1), 67- 82.

Breunlin, D., Pinsof, W., Russell, W., Lebow, J. (2011). Integrative problem-centered Metaframeworks therapy I: Core concepts and hypothesizing. *Family Process*, 50(3), 293-313.

Breunlin, D., Schwartz, R., & Mac Kune-Karrer, B. (2001). *Metaframeworks: Transcending the Models of Family Therapy*. San Francisco, CA: Jossey-Bass Publishers.

Bronfenbrenner, U. (2005). *Making Human Beings Human*. Thousand Oaks, CA: Sage Publications Inc.

Capra, F. (1996). *The Web of Life: A New Scientific Understanding of Living Systems*. New York, NY: Anchor Books, Doubleday.

Carter, B., McGoldrick, M., & Garcia-Preto, N. (2011). The Expanded Family Life Cycle: Individual, Family, and Social Perspectives (Ed.) (4th Ed). Boston, MA, Allyn and Bacon.

Derrida, J. (1995). The play of substitution. In W. Anderson (Ed.), *The truth about the truth: De- confusing and re-constructing the postmodern world* (pp. 86-95). New York: Putnam.

Dickerson, V. (2007). Remembering the future: Situating oneself in a constantly evolving field. *Journal of Systemic Therapies*, 26(1), 23-37.

Eakes, G., Walsh, S., Markowski, M., Cain, H., & Swanson, M. (1997). Family centred brief solution-focused therapy with chronic schizophrenia: A pilot study. *Journal of Family Therapy*, 19, 145-158.

Falicov, C. (2003). Culture in family therapy: New variations on a fundamental theme. In T. Sexton, G. Weeks, & M. Robbins (Eds). *Handbook of Family Therapy: Theory, Research and Practice*. New York, NY: Brunner-Rutledge.

Falicov, C. (2005). Emotional transnationalism and family identity. *Family Process*, 44, 399-406.

Gendlin, E. (1981). *Focusing*. New York, NY: Random House, Inc.

Hoffman, L. (2002). *Family Therapy: An Intimate History*. New York, NY: W.W. Norton.

Hudson, C. (2010). *Complex systems and human behavior*. Chicago, IL. Lyceum Books.

Kaslow, F. (2000). Continued evolution of family therapy: The last twenty years. *Contemporary Family Therapy*. 22(4),357-386.

Kaslow, F. (2000). History of family therapy: Evolution outside of the U.S.A., *Journal of Family Psychotherapy*, 11(4), 1-35.

Korner, S. & Brown, G. (1990). Exclusion of children from family psychotherapy: Family therapists' beliefs and practices. *Journal of Family Psychology*, 3, 420-430.

Lorenz, Edward (1993). *The Essence of Chaos*. Seattle, WA: University of Washington Press.

Lund, L., Zimmerman, T., Haddock, S. (2002). The theory, structure, and techniques for the inclusion of children in family therapy: A literature review. *Journal of Marital and Family Therapy*, 28(4), 445-454.

Lyotard, J.F. (1984). *The Post-modern Condition*. Minneapolis: University of Minneapolis Press.

Martin, J. & Sugarman, J. (2000). Between the modern and the postmodern: The possibility of self and progressive understanding in psychology. *American Psychologist*, 55(4), 397- 406.

Maturana, H. & Varela, F. (1980). *Autopoiesis and Cognition: The Realization of the Living*. Dordrecht, Holland: D. Reidel Publishing Co.

McGoldrick, M. (2005). *Ethnicity and Family Therapy* (3rd Ed). New York, NY: The Guilford Press.

Miklowitz D. & Tompson, M. (2003). Family variables and interventions in schizophrenia. In G. Sholevar & L. Schwoeri (Eds). *Textbook of Family and Couples Therapy: Clinical Applications*. Washington, DC: American Psychiatric Publishing, Inc.

Minuchin, S., Nichols, M., Lee, W. (2007). *Assessing Families and Couples: From Symptom to System*. New York, NY: Pearson Education, Inc.

Nobel, C. (2004). Postmodern thinking: Where is it taking social work? *Journal of Social Work*, 4(3), 289-304.

Nichols, M. & Schwartz, R. (1998). *Family therapy: Concepts and methods* (4th Ed.). London, England: Allyn and Bacon.

Nims, D. (2007). Integrating play therapy techniques into Solution-Focused Brief Therapy. *International Journal of Play Therapy*, 16(1), 54-68.

Papp, P. (1983). *The Process of Change*. New York, NY: The Guilford Press.

Peters, H. (2009). Navigating the shifting sands of social work terrain: Social work practice in postmodern conditions. *Journal of Progressive Human Services*, 20(1), 45-58.

Pinsof, W., Breunlin, D., Russell, W., & Lebow, J. (2011). Integrative problem-centered Meta-frameworks therapy II: Planning, Conversing, and Reading Feedback. *Family Process*, 50 (3), 314-336.

Satir, V. (1983). *Conjoint Family Therapy* (3rd Ed). Palo Alto, CA: Science and Behavior Books, Inc.

Selvini Palazzoli, M. (1978). Paradox and Counterparadox: A New Model in the *Therapy of the Family in Schizophrenic Transaction*. New York, NY: J. Aronson.

Schiepek, G.; Fricke, B.; Kaimer, P. (1992). Synergetics of psychotherapy. In Tschacher, Schiepek, Brunner (Eds). *Self-organization and Clinical Psychology: Empirical Approaches to Synergetics in Psychology*. London, England: Springer-Verlag.

Schwartz, R. (1995). *Internal Family Systems Therapy*. New York, NY: The Guilford Press.

Selvini Palazzoli, M. (1978). Paradox and Counterparadox : A New Model in the *Therapy of the Family in Schizophrenic Transaction*. New York, NY: J. Aronson

Smith, R. & Southern, S. (2005). Integrative confusion: An examination of integrative models in couple and family therapy. *The Family Journal: Counseling and Therapy for Couples and Families*, 13(4), 392-399.

Swearer, S. (2006). Problem-solving play therapy. In H. Gerard Kaduson (Ed.), *101 Favourite Play Therapy Techniques: Volume III*. Northvale, NJ: Jason Aronson, Inc.

Vallacher, R.& Nowak, A. (Eds.) (1993). *Dynamical Systems in Social Psychology*. New York, New York: Academic Press, Inc.

Van Geert, P. (1994). *Dynamic Systems of Development: Change Between Complexity and Chaos*. New York, NY: Harvester Wheatsheaf.

von Bertalanffy, L. (1968). The meaning of general systems theory. In L. von Bertalanffy *General Systems Theory: Foundations, development and application*. New York: George Braziller, Inc.

Warren, K.; Franklin, C.; & Streeter, C. (1998). *New directions in systems theory: Chaos and complexity. Social Work*, 43 (4), 357-372.

Wieland-Burston, J. (1992). *Chaos and order in the world of the psyche*. New York, NY: Routledge, Chapman & Hall, Inc.

Weinstein, D. (2004). Culture at work: Family therapy and the culture concept in Post-World War II America. *Journal of the History of the Behavioral Sciences*, 40(1), 23-46

Werbos, P. (1994). Self-Organization: Reexamining the basics and an alternative to the big bang. In Pribram (Ed). Origins: *Brain and Self-organization*. Hillsdale, New Jersey: Lawrence Erlbaum Associates, Publishers.

Wiener, N. (1961). *Cybernetics: Or Control and Communication in the Animal and the Machine* (2nd Ed). Cambridge: MIT Press.

Winslade, J. M. (2005). Utilising discursive positioning in counselling. *British Journal of Guidance & Counseling*, 34, 1-14.

Xu, J. (2010). The impact of Postmodernism on counseling: Boom or Bane? *International Journal of Advanced Counselling*, 32, 66-74.

Chapter Four

Family Play Therapy

Kristin Trotter

There are deep rifts in the family and there are problems, people missing from this holiday, but nothing changes the beauty of the moment in the sun with people who I know and love more than any others on the planet and who love me the same way. I take solace in the fact that we got that part right. The rest, well . . . that's the challenge of family.

We are all a little worried about Mom but in the time it takes to throw in, dry, and fold a load of laundry she's up and has joined us all on the lakefront. And the music has changed. Now, it's Pat Boon crooning, different time, different crooner, different generation served.

"Mom, can I have a towel please?" Three generations of moms look in the direction of the voice and someone tosses a towel in that general direction.

And the music has changed again. Now it's CCR.

My father joins us and says, "I got tricked into doing a puzzle." We laugh. And, from my partner who notices I've been reading and typing: "And now we all have to read a chapter of Family Play Therapy." More laughter. "We can read it after we go swimming tonight and if that doesn't put us all to sleep . . . . ."

Someone has turned the music down but it's still audible . . .

The sun is hanging lower over the horizon like a gigantic red ball . . . Follow that bouncing ball . . . . somebody sings along with Bob Seger. Mom is sitting very still, maybe sleeping. But then she moves and I ask her what she is thinking about. She smiles, "Oddly enough, my dad. I had a dream about him the other night. It was odd to dream about him." Generations lost, generations found.

"Love hurts" . . . plays softly in the background . . . .

Supper is a hodgepodge of leftovers. Last night at the lodge.

The cottage door opens. "Supper is served." It's my sister, self appointed chief cook and bottle washer. Hates the job but takes it on because she does it well and certainly would never trust it to me. She wants a vacation where she does nothing—no cooking, no laundry, no work. She wants a vacation where she orders a beer in a foreign language.

We talk about how she is feeling and we all sympathize and we are genuinely sorry. "I know it's me," she says. "I know I can't let it be. I know my crew and I know when they need to eat and I might as well throw something in for the rest of you." A float plane from the neighboring lodge takes off. "Oh God. I've always wanted my pilot's license . . . just the freedom to fly away like that." She gets teary. She talks about the fact that her husband stayed up late one night watching the movie, "Bridges of Madison County." "He sat me down a few nights later and said, "I don't ever want to block you from fulfilling your dreams. Get your pilot's license."

The music keeps the beat alive . . . It's easy. It's relaxed and it's home, home inside the heart of the family. Family play therapy at its best.

When working with families and children, meaning is embedded in action and behavior, and play is a significantly ingenious and creative way to illuminate meaning through an action that constitutes the child's preferred way of communicating. In spite of the fact that play extends the family therapist's "holding capacity" (Scharff, 1989, p. 172), Cederborg (1997) found that in family therapy, where talking represents the primary mode of communication, young children between four and seven years of age "do not participate in the therapeutic process to any great extent," (p. 36). They do not achieve "full membership status" (p. 36) and may in fact be "accorded the status of a nonperson" (p. 28). The antidote is to include play in family sessions. "When play is included in family sessions, clinicians treat children as equally important family members, with valuable information to provide and to assimilate." Moreover, ". . . play is inherently valuable because it lowers defenses and elicits and unlocks a deeper level of interaction, in which fantasy, metaphor, and symbol can emerge" (Gil, 1994, p. 41).

Play is a powerful medium within which to work with families and offers therapist and family members alike myriad wonderful techniques that range from family art therapy to family puppet interviews to spontaneous and meaning saturated storytelling. Big stories, stories with thick and rich plots and subplots tumble out of a family at play. Apart from directing therapy away from the analytical and toward the metaphorical and fantastic, play has many benefits. It creates feelings of well-being between players, helps to release emotions, is a natural way to express the self, facilitates positive interactions between parent and child, creatively and symbolically deals with concerns, allows processing to take place on a number of different levels, and allows family members to step outside the confines of well-rehearsed and problem-saturated narratives. In addition, family play therapy increases the potential for family members to laugh and have fun together and engenders creative expression in both problem formulation and solving. Make believe helps family members retain self-esteem while expressing problematic feelings and family pain, encourages and facilitates contact and relatedness between family members, promotes attachment, creates a new lens through which to view family members and issues, promotes a lack of inhibition, and exposes underlying thoughts and feelings in a non-threatening way.

"Play provides an opportunity to experience what has been denied or ignored, in the safe, benign, fun world of pretend. The play experience lives in the twilight zone between cognition and emotion, where the defenses are not on the alert" (Ariel, 2005, pp. 6-7) and because family members are both themselves and the character they play they are afforded an opportunity to observe as the puppet, the story teller, the doll, or the drawing tells the tale. The exploration of possible worlds is facilitated through make believe and is therefore less threatening, however "play in therapy must be facilitated by an involved clinician in a meaningful way" (Gil, 1994, p. 4). In family play therapy, as in play therapy in general, play serves as a vehicle for the expression of conscious and subconscious thoughts and feelings. And for children, the nonlinear, spontaneous nature of play is the natural medium through which they explore themselves and their world.

However, therapists' attitudes toward play and working with young children range from downright uncomfortable and ill at ease, to comfortable but ineffective, to both at ease and effective, with the latter category apparently being sparse indeed. As the family therapist moves from family therapy to family play therapy, however, modifications are necessary not only in the more esoteric and indeterminate shift to the fluid, symbolic, nonlinear, and nonverbal world of a child's play but also in the concrete space, which has to be child-friendly and come complete with readily available props, puppets, toys, and craft material. With the exception of role play, which needs no props and has been described as the "most flexible, revealing and impactful play techniques in the therapist's treasure chest" (Chasin, 1989, p. 16), children need help to communicate and express themselves and the metaphor of the puppet, the toy, the craft material, is a perfect vehicle for expression. The art and act of playing is a perfect vehicle for directly and indirectly teaching language and behavior and cognitive and emotional skills. The simple game of hot potato/cold potato, where a ball is tossed between family members and is at first a hot potato and therefore must be gotten rid of quickly, or a cold potato and therefore slows the toss down considerably, can teach rudimentary emotion regulation. One can heat up and one can cool down. And, because all of this must occur while retaining adult interest and curiosity, such a shift is neither obvious nor easy for the family therapist in spite of the fact that, in some respects, they are already doing much of what is required to work with young children, such as being patient, flexible, receptive, present, and open to what is happening in the session and in the therapy as a whole, as well as open to letting events and encounters unfold contrary to one's agenda.

Effective family therapy strives to heal relationships so that all family members can engage with each other in a way that encourages safe, positive, and creative relating. In family play therapy, play is the vehicle for change and it is a vehicle for engagement. It provides a context for both assessment and intervention and is the crux of therapeutic communication. And, although the therapist may use the play metaphors, it is not the therapist who initiates them; rather they are initiated by the family (Ariel, 2005).

In family play therapy, goals must be simply stated, relevant, meaningful, and specific to the family's situation. Goals need to be concrete, focused on the positive expression of behavior rather than the absence of a negative one, and on some specific behavior that the family has a desire to experience. From a solution-focused family therapy perspective, for example, a detailed description of goals for therapy is critical and identifying a clear goal(s) is the best predictor of a desired therapeutic outcome (Sklare, 2005). Family play therapy as a theory and a practice model fits well under the metaframeworks umbrella in that family play therapy techniques are instrumental in creating the conditions necessary for the family to begin to see some way to loosen and possibly release the constraints that are keeping its members stuck in painful behavior and interactions.

The six metadomains, as well as various aspects of family functioning and more globally accepted aspects of therapy such as goal setting, or model specific techniques such as the miracle question in brief solution-focused family therapy, and searching for exceptions, a critical aspect of narrative family therapy, can be explored through art-based therapy, sandtrays, and puppets in an effort to map how the family might loosen the constraints that bind it. It is unfortunate that most family therapists do not receive training in how to play with children, in the various models and techniques of play therapy, and in combining those with a metamodel with integrative properties such as metaframeworks. Integrating play in theories of family therapy flows quite naturally. Doing a Satir family sculpt, for example, where each individual family member is asked to use other family members to make a sculpture of how they see the family, is a wonderful assessment and prescriptive technique that children, parents, and therapists often enjoy. Such a technique in the latter half of the first session leaves a family not only with a nonverbal, visual, and visceral understanding of where everyone is at the moment, but also where everyone would like to be and how they would like to see the family responding to one another. A good sculpt involves not just sculpting how members of a family perceive themselves and others in terms of the problem but also how members of a family would like to be relating to one another in spite of what brought them to therapy. Generally, the work of therapy is to figure out how to get from what they are doing to what they would like to be doing together and the parts language of the metadomain of internal family systems is one way to work at bridging this gap and is both child, adult, and family play therapy friendly. The language of parts can be talked about and it can be "played" out using miniatures, puppets, or expressive art and role play.

Developmentally, preadolescent children are unable to engage in abstract thought (Piaget, 1962) and they lack the cognitive and verbal skills to articulate what they are thinking and feeling. The very modality that therapy relies on, talking, cannot work for young children and their families. The mind of the child is a concrete one where the symbolic world of language must give way first, to behavior and second, to the creative metaphor of play. Moreover, as is the case with traumatized children who can be paralyzed with anxiety and riddled with problematic physical and emotional symptoms such as irritability and digestive problems, hyperarousal and night terrors, and avoidance and numbing, repetitive posttraumatic play is a symbolic reenactment of the traumatic event and affords the child a way to "talk" about the experience. Provided the child can move beyond this repetitive reenactment of the trauma the contents of the experience can also be explored, as can the feelings and reactions to that experience, along with what is needed to heal.

Jill, Rachel, Amanda, and Henry would be a case in point. Jill and Rachel have been married for two years. As a same sex couple who had lived together for ten years prior to marrying, they had married specifically because Rachel's daughter, Elizabeth, and her two children, nine-year-old Henry and thirteen-year-old Amanda, had come to live with them. The abrupt transformation in the family structure had stressed the relationship to the point where the couple was fighting constantly and the equilibrium had disappeared along with the idyllic existence of work, play, and travel. In an effort to mitigate the relational jeopardy the couple married. Shortly after the wedding, Elizabeth, who is a recovering cocaine addict, abandoned the family and returned to a life of using and prostitution which she had been battling since mid-adolescence. Following her leaving, Jill and Rachel made the decision to raise the children and filed for custody.

Due to Elizabeth's lifestyle and intermittent drug use prior to moving in with Jill and Rachel, both children had been neglected and sexually and physically abused by at least one of Elizabeth's many partners. Elizabeth moved in with her mother and Jill after being charged with possession of cocaine, and following a decision by the courts to remove the children from her care if substantial changes were not made in terms of Elizabeth's drug use, lifestyle, and living conditions. Amanda has no memories of the abuse she suffered but Henry remembers being punched in the stomach by one of his mom's "friends" and that his "bum was all black and blue" from being hit by another of Elizabeth's short-term live-in companions, who also acted as her pimp. He also remembers witnessing Amanda being beaten on numerous occasions by a man who was living with his mother. Further, Amanda is extremely dissociative and Henry suffers from night terrors where he appears to be awake but is suffering an intrusive, highly dissociative reliving of the traumatic wounding, and screaming that he cannot "talk" and he cannot "tell" about what has happened because "it is too horrible."

Elizabeth herself had been a victim of childhood sexual abuse and Rachel's ex-husband, Don, Elizabeth's biological father, had been charged and convicted of possession and distribution of child pornography. Elizabeth disclosed the abuse to Rachel and although Don was never charged with sexually abusing his daughter, Rachel did report him to police and he was eventually charged and convicted of possession and distribution of child pornography. The intergenerational trauma also reaches back into Rachel's childhood as she was physically abused by both her mother and her alcoholic father who abused both her and her mother. Home was a violent place and over the years Rachel spent a great deal of time and energy working toward healing herself and her ability to be in relationship with others.

Jill appears angry at everyone and "has reached the end of her patience with the chaos." She is also fantasizing about leaving Rachel and the children. She yells and screams and is, according to Rachel, "nagging, bitchy, and rigid." The solidarity that led them to marry has disintegrated and they are polarized in terms of their positions, each adopting an extreme position on almost every issue the couple faces. They both find that the kids are more relaxed and manageable when each member of the couple is alone with them. Together, Jill and Rachel "yell and scream at each other and at the kids or Jill yells at the kids and Rachel yells at Jill." Rachel believes that Jill is too strict and that she needs to protect the children from Jill who can be verbally quite cruel and "mean." Rachel says she gets "stuck in Jill's rigidity" and the relationship has become highly verbally abusive.

For months after Elizabeth's departure more than a year ago, Rachel spent her evenings driving through the "red light" district of the city in search of her daughter, leaving Jill to care for the children. The children's behavior deteriorated and temper-tantrums and fighting increased. Henry regressed to bed wetting and Amanda withdrew into herself and spent much of her time in her room reading or talking online with friends. With no sign of her daughter after several months of searching, Rachel gave up but has been depressed, angry, and despondent as well as highly protective of her grandchildren.

Although there was no overt physical violence in Jill's family of origin, Jill was afraid of her alcoholic father who was verbally abusive to both her and her mother. Jill's only brother was the favored child in the family and as the oldest of five siblings Jill describes her childhood as nonexistent and her life, until she left home at sixteen, as "an extension of Mother" in that she spent much of her childhood caring for her siblings and cooking and cleaning while her parents worked.

The first session included only Jill and Rachel, at their insistence. They felt they needed to talk about what had been happening since the marriage and they wanted a chance to talk about facts they had been withholding from the children concerning Elizabeth's drug use. Following this session a very general hypothesis was formulated and, simply stated, that although the couple had in the past been generally deeply committed to one another, the dramatic and substantial shifts in the couple's lives during the last three years, along with the frustrations of parenting and step parenting one needy adult child, currently lost to addiction and a life of pain on the streets, and two traumatized grandchildren, had strained the relationship and increased relational tension to beyond tolerable levels. From an internal family systems perspective, already overloaded pain filled exiles had been further activated by the loss of Elizabeth and the inevitable managers and firefighters had mobilized to manage and douse the pain (HI); among other communication challenges, trauma driven intergenerational S1, S2, S3, and S4 interactional sequences were exacerbating day-to-day and week-to-week stressors (HS); leadership, harmony, and balance were constrained as a result of societal, community, relational, family, and personal tensions (HO); the family was experiencing microtransitions as well as nodal ones as Jill and Rachel had been preparing to retire and were now raising a young family. In both children, new behaviors and competencies that had been emerging prior to Elizabeth's leaving disappeared, oscillations did not dampen, and old behaviors reasserted themselves (HD). Powerful misogynistic and cultural discourses around a female-headed, lesbian household shaped by relations of knowledge and power as well as ignorance, strained the family socially, relationally, and culturally within the community and society. The social privilege afforded a professional heterosexual couple would not be something either Jill or Rachel could enjoy, although both are professional women with more than adequate salaries (HC). Further, many of the same cultural constraints that plague this couple/family would spill into the gender hypothesis. It has been noted (Golding, 2006) that same-sex parents who defy culturally transmitted stereotypes must not only have "a deep, passionate desire to raise a child, love a child, and fully live the profound interdependency that only a child-parent relationship can embody" (p. 45) but must also possess "incredible personal strength, a strong sense of self, ability not only to protect and make sense of an unacceptable world for themselves, but for their children as well" (p. 45), none of which were available to Jill and Rachel in the current state of their union (HG).

One way to explore the disconnections and constraints within the couple and the family from a biological, relational, cultural, personal, societal, and community perspective, along with the feelings of helpless overwhelm in the face of the current multifaceted, complex problems is through a play genogram. Based on the assumption that because toys are symbols and the suppressed comes forward in the symbols that people choose, a play genogram could engage the family in a creative and nonverbal way through:

a. Acting as an assessment tool to help articulate the problem and problem areas;
b. Identifying areas of distress, conflict, and things left unresolved;
c. Identifying perceptions of the self in relationship to others in problematic and functional ways;
d. Helping to externalize the problem and deal with the issues as metaphor and within the metaphor of the toys;
e. Identifying the first small steps that will take the family in the direction of healing;
f. Identifying resources and what works and what doesn't work;
g. Creating goals through the metaphor of the miniature toys;
h. Advancing issues that have been identified in the assessment.

When the entire family, minus Elizabeth, came to the first session it was striking how much they resembled one another and looked like they belonged together. In spite of the dissent between members everyone moved the chairs into a closer and more tightly knit circle than the original setting. Both children appeared to be struggling developmentally in that Amanda looked and acted more like a typical ten-year-old than a thirteen-year-old, and Henry talked readily and often about his struggles at school with reading and math. Henry's psychoeducational assessment had uncovered two forms of dyslexia which he summed up as "jumbled up letters in my head." The first several family sessions were spent defining problems and goals, determining how family members wanted to be addressed, drawing family genograms for everyone who currently lived in the household, and finding figures to represent family members on those genograms as well as the relationships between them.

Balancing, conversing, hypothesizing, feedback, and planning and spontaneity is the work of any session while simultaneously joining with each family member in an open and respectful way which begins immediately and on first contact with the family. A modified version of Chasin's (1989) five-step protocol for whole-family sessions was applied and provided an overarching structure to the assessment phase while still allowing genuine and spontaneous encounters. The therapist explained to Jill, Rachel, and the children her limited understanding of the problems and why the family was meeting, as well as invited family members to add to, correct, or disagree with this as well as state their own version of the problem. The therapist also explained that there were some very important rules that needed to be adhered to about coercion or being forced to say or do something, safety, discipline, and use of space and equipment. The most important rule was that no one was to be coerced into doing something he or she did not want to do and as a result people did not have to answer any questions they did not want to and should say "pass" or "not now" and the same applied to any activity.

Connected to that rule was another rule that included the notion that everyone was obliged to do his or her best to keep everyone safe and if something was happening that felt unsafe then everyone present needed to help stop it. Another rule was that Rachel (aka Nana) and Jill were responsible for discipline just like they would be at home and although the therapist might make a request it was not the therapist's job to discipline children. The rule that the therapist would decide what toys to use and when got added.

Joining with every member of the family and building the therapeutic alliance was infused into all steps and stages, especially the problem exploration stage where support of each family member was vital, as was a discussion of family strengths and limitations. Goals were co-created and recommendations, impressions, and insights around what was happening within the family and what changes people wanted to see were shared.

Amanda's goals were to do more things with the family and "make Nana and Jill be more like a mom and a dad" and if therapy was really working then she would be doing more things with her family and they would "feel more like a family." Henry's goal, interestingly enough, was to feel "dizzy" and it was determined that hugs helped. Henry said that he would help the family by taking care of them and asking Amanda if she wanted to play together more.

Jill's goals were to feel less "grumpy" and less worried about everything and everybody. And if therapy was working for her, Rachel would be less "testy, anxious, frustrated, and short" with her. Rachel's goal was to try to be more supportive to everyone in the family, especially Jill, and to try to be less angry at Jill.

Although there are a number of ways to organize the play genogram, from sending everyone away to do their own and then sharing with the rest of the family, to putting the genogram on a big sheet of paper and creating one genogram together, this family chose to do separate genograms and confine the genogram to the immediate members of the current household. Both children were adamant about leaving their mother, Elizabeth, out of the genogram construction at this time. Because this family was so diffusely organized and there were so many arms to the children's past including living with an abusive step father, a foster home, and occasional abandonment with virtual strangers when Elizabeth was using, we decided to expand the play genogram in later sessions to include Elizabeth and step and foster parents. Moreover, the issues that needed immediate attention and resolution of some description concerned these four family members. Play genograms can lead to transformation in the way a family thinks about a certain problem or has been attempting to solve that problem.

The instruction is to "pick a toy(s) that best shows thoughts and feelings about everyone in the family and yourself." Each member of the family was instructed as to how to make a family play genogram and they were asked to pick a miniature toy off the table. They were then told to place their choices on the genogram. Second, family members were asked to "pick a miniature that best describes your relationship between other people in your family (you and Nana; you and Jill; you and your brother/sister)." This can also be narrowed to one relationship that is somehow either special or difficult in some way. Interpretation is to be avoided and a far more effective therapeutic tool is to simply notice what is there and speculate on what objects might feel and think and say to one another.

The family play therapist can ask the family to sit together and make comments about the family play genograms or ask questions to others about it or just sit in silence and see what people have to say. Beginning from where one is drawn into the genogram and working from the assumption that everything is about something, by simply noticing the therapist helps to expand meaning. The therapist might notice the height of things, or one species versus another, or notice how things are angled and what direction they face in relation to one another, or where they are placed on the paper, or what is similar and what is different. The therapist might also ask something like, "If these objects were to face each other what is the first thing these things would say to each other?" Or, "If this object had a voice what would it say? Who would it say it to?" To massage and work the metaphor through the expanded language of play allows the therapist to tap the potential of the conversation to become deeper, more disarming, and more revealing. Emotions lend themselves to expression through metaphor.

There is a value in externalization and making the problems that the family brings to therapy simultaneously and paradoxically both abstract and concrete as well as miniaturized. When miniature toys are used on a family play genogram to assess and to identify underlying issues the apparently huge and overwhelming problems have been made small by putting them on a piece of paper in miniature. When one begins to manipulate and move things around, then one can start to think about managing things in a different way. When you begin to move the material in this therapeutic way and further decide that you are going to do something with it, then assessment becomes treatment and the iterative flow between assessment and intervention takes therapeutic shape and it is all accomplished within the metaphor of the toy and all it symbolizes. In the symbol is the bridge between the left and right hemispheres of the brain and the content from the conscious and unconscious mind begin to organize through the symbol.

In Amanda's genogram she represented herself as a miniature garden and Henry as a leopard. Amanda chose a huge, strong, rather terrifying and protective Hulk-like creature for Rachel, that embodied both the terrifying and protective aspects of the mother, and Jill became a pair of sunglasses "because she likes to wear sunglasses." The symbol for the relationship between Henry and Amanda was a beautiful and fantastic little creature with wings and a sword, a Nintendo Mario/Luigi-like figure sat between Amanda and Rachel, and between Jill and Amanda she placed a stethoscope, symbolic of both healing and illness.

Henry came to life on his genogram as a winged unicorn. Amanda appeared as a miniature pink carriage and Rachel was a lovely purple carriage. He symbolized Jill as a police car and the relationship between them as a miniature yo-yo. The relationship between Amanda and him was a heart-shaped eraser and the relationship between himself and Rachel was a relatively large miniature of a moose in a lotus pose.

In Jill's genogram she characterized herself as a globe, Rachel as a miniature dog, Amanda as a windmill, and Henry as a large funny faced rather sub-human looking creature with a big smile pasted on its face. Relationally, Jill's genogram was a study in movement and possibly escape where the relationship between her and Rachel was symbolized by a plane, between her and Amanda she placed a sports car, and between her and Henry she placed an army jeep.

In Rachel's genogram, she was a super hero, Amanda a butterfly, and Henry was a fishing pole. Jill was a monkey eating a banana. In the relational space between her and Amanda she placed a dolphin, between her and Jill she place a large brightly colored and rather scary looking bug, and between her and Henry she placed a sleek sports car with huge wheels.

Profoundly rich in metaphor, these family genograms and the toys chosen provide a means of exploring themes of loss, trauma, loyalty, protection of self and others, control, illness, escape, growth, hope, and healing. The loss of their mother and the early childhood abuse and trauma that both children had experienced left them struggling with exiles that were in a great deal of pain. Both had active manager parts that were repressing pain, grief, loss, shame, and self-blame and loathing, through dissociation in Amanda's case and anger and control in Henry's (HI). Moreover, Amanda's desire to "make Jill and Rachel more like "a mom and a dad" spoke to her need to address the difference in her family. She is being raised by her lesbian grandmother and her grandmother's partner, a union bathed in cultural shame and pathologizing discourse (HC). As the therapist noticed elements in the garden, it became clear that Amanda craved stability and "normalcy" and for the first time in this little girl's life she was dimly aware of the possibility of that occurring as a result of living with her grandmother and Jill. However, an exploration of cultural issue around gender and powerful themes of oppression, commitment, and love, as well as an individual and family exploration of the excruciating pain of the exiled parts and the swift and brutal actions of the family's firefighter and manager parts, were constraining movement toward that end.

Rachel, Amanda, and Henry were grieving Elizabeth's loss, whereas Jill's anger and refusal to allow the mourning would indicate a firefighter part who is desperately trying to control the pain of the exiles in all members of the family (HI). One result was the polarized positions within the couple which exacerbated the triangulation around the biological force field created by Rachel and her grandchildren. The stricter and less yielding Jill's firefighter parts became, in an attempt to control both her partner's and the children's pain, the more invested Rachel's protective managers became (HI). The metaphor of the super hero in Rachel's play genogram was explored in therapy again, through the art of "noticing."

Because the exiles in this family are in such pain, engaging Self-leadership in all family members is critical and is done through gently inviting the Self to take charge, exercising respectful collaboration along with unwavering faith in family members' ability to connect with their own inner resources and healing wisdom, and maintaining a nonblaming, nonpathologizing stance. An internal family systems approach facilitates the release of "legacy burdens" along with the retrieval and repair of parts that have been exiled through compassionate witnessing of individual and family pain. In Satir's terms, the therapist facilitates congruent and safe communication through family members leading with the Self. In this way, not only discussion of problematic issues becomes possible but so do agreed upon solutions. This is a deeply bereaved family in that many deaths have occurred and both the children and their grandmother constantly avoid talking about Elizabeth while simultaneously worrying that she will be found dead somewhere on the streets. Windmills, purple carriages, airplanes, and a moose in a lotus pose provide powerful meaning-laden metaphors that allow greater safety while exploring the family's current and preferred pictures.

While noticing the police car and the yo-yo in his genogram, Henry responded with, "They help. They hurt. They help you. They scare you. Up and down and I never know what's going to happen." If play is essentially about adaptive functioning in the areas of creative problem solving, coping, and perspective taking, and serves a purpose for children other than simply having fun (Russ & Niec, 2011), then Henry may be working through his relationship with Jill and commenting on the unpredictability and ambivalence he experiences. What is interesting from a solution focused and wishful perspective, however, is the potential for fun and play inherent in the symbol of the yo-yo and the protection inherent in the police car.

Through face-to-face communication as well as through the metaphor of the toy, sequences are created and observed and elements of sequences like recursiveness, where behaviors are influenced by other events in the sequence, thus increasing the probability that these same behaviors will occur and new ones won't, can be explored and understood as well as transformed. One highly recursive sequence of events occurs when Jill's and Rachel's fighting, which erupts in moments of tension, serves to block any attempts to problem solve. In response to the couple's fighting Henry consistently converted his anxiety to anger and Amanda would withdraw. Understanding the embeddedness of this sequence, the constraints it engenders, and the recursiveness of interactions was the precursor to the exercise that followed, the circle project.

Pictures were taken of the family play genograms and after some deliberation, discussion, fighting, and false starts, an agreed upon problem was taken from the genograms to work on. They chose the problem of family conflict. Through play, such a problem can be explored in ways as diverse as an examination of Bowen's transgenerational, S4 sequences, to Satir's exploration of survival stances (i.e., blaming, placating, super-reasonable, and irrelevant).

To symbolize this problem the family chose both the large, scary looking bug and the police car. These were moved to the innermost circle and the phrase "family fights" was written underneath.

A larger circle was drawn around that and the family chose from the table of miniatures objects that represented the first, second, and third steps in addressing this concern. Then they each chose objects that symbolized the available resources the family had to address the concerns as well as symbols for people who might be able to help them. The family chose, in total, twenty six objects which acted as different resources and people who might help. By the time they were finished, the outer circle was filled with toys symbolizing steps to address the problem, strategies to address the concerns, and people who could help achieve those goals. Finally, a single symbol was chosen to represent what it would look like if the problem of family fights were solved and it was placed on the outer edge of the outer circle. The family chose a large smiling sun to place on the outer edge of the circle. A picture was taken, printed immediately, and given to the family to take home and place in a prominent place in the household to remind them of their strengths and the strategies they had created to deal with the problem and what the problem would look like once it was solved.

The first, second, and third steps are about identifying what the family could do and the strategies are about identifying how the family would do it. Within the circle project the conflict gets smaller than the resources and the solutions and strategies far outnumber the problem at the center. The photograph of the circle project provided a striking visual for the family of the resources they had available to them and was a powerful reminder of the fact that they had many strategies to choose from to help them solve their "family fights."

A second family problem that was also dealt with in this way concerned the fact that both Jill and Rachel worked long hours outside the home. Hence, the family routine was chaotic, with the children going to different caretakers on a daily basis after school (HS). The solution that emerged was for Amanda and Henry to spend time at an after school day program and then spend an hour at home alone before Rachel and/or Jill arrived. Amanda was enrolled in a babysitting course and after a number of short, time-limited practice runs, was placed in charge of herself and her brother with support people to call should they need help. This served to increase Amanda's sense of responsibility and dampen oscillations through developing more age appropriate competence (HD). This new sequence accommodated age-appropriate changes in behavior for Amanda and the family as a whole and supported emergent competence.

Developmentally, the family was going through nodal as well as microtransitions and both in sessions and at home Jill was openly resentful and bitterly blaming toward Elizabeth for putting the couple in this position at this time in their lives (HD). Jill constantly reminded Rachel that in their mid-fifties they should not be raising children, let alone seriously traumatized children (HS). Because family problems can be located in either a child or a parent's acting out it became increasingly obvious that the couple "executive subsystem," in the language of structural family therapy, needed intense and reparative work separate and apart from what was occurring in the context of the family.

Because both children struggled with social and cognitive delays (HD) there were extra expenses, creating added anxiety between the couple as they watched their retirement funds dwindle and children's dental, medical, and educational expenses mount. As a result of the developmental delays and the nodal and microtransitional challenges that family members were facing, encouraging competence and weakening oscillations through new behavior would help to develop both children's sense of self. Moreover, because development at one level helps to facilitate development at another, as the children become more independent, age appropriate, and proficient the couple can begin to return to some semblance of being a couple. Dampening oscillations through age-appropriate development of competence in the children will help the entire family relieve the constraints and constrictions associated with the developmental metaframeworks. It is also possible that constraints throughout the family will shift at the relational level in that as the children become more competent, recursive relational processes such as liking and attraction, the coordination of meaning, and capacity for nurturing may also change significantly.

Play is a particularly significant intervention for this family due to the fact that it has little sense of itself as a family and is, in Whitaker's terms, "dedicated to chaos" (Keith & Whitaker, 1981) in the popular meaning of the word. Within this family, play provided a way to express feelings, limit verbal behavior between the parents, and encourage the working through of difficult emotions while simultaneously generating new more adaptive and positive behaviors. Play is at first a reaction to objects and then an exploration of objects and finally the symbolic use of objects. Play is intimately connected to development in children in that it reflects developmental levels, provides an opportunity to practice appropriate developmental skills, and creates developmental change (Russ & Niec, 2011). Family play therapists, much like child therapists, are in a "unique position" (p. 4) to encourage developmental change in the context of the individual and the family.

Further, because there is no normative map for how a family should be organized within the context of metaframeworks, this family was free to define through the act of play the organization and structure in whatever way worked best for its members (HO). The family leadership was in disarray, resulting in constraints that kept the family unbalanced and unable to function as a family and relate to one another through the elements of healthy sacrifice, caring, cooperation, and a sense of belonging. The most potent challenge to collaboratively exploring this family's constraints to improved leadership and harmony would appear to lie, in part, in the couple's inability to problem solve without the interaction deteriorating into the routine habitual and patterned conflict.

As stated, Elizabeth's return to a life of using and prostitution increased existing tensions within the couple and family as a whole while simultaneously relieving the tension of day-to-day living with a highly addicted dissociative individual. As well, the workload for both partners had increased substantially. Rachel's highly critical attitude toward Jill, her tremendous guilt around Elizabeth and her grandchildren (HS), and her tireless efforts to please and comfort her grandchildren, coupled with Jill's rising resentment toward the children and the resultant changes, created highly polarized positions on the part of both members of the couple, thereby constraining any capacity for leadership, harmony, and balance within an already seriously unbalanced system (HO): a system riddled with grief, loss, trauma, and culturally generated stigma.

Family play therapy is a perfect way to enter such powerfully pain filled areas in a family and explore, among other things, themes of leadership. Exploring leadership through nurturing skills such as teaching safety, self care, and self-soothing within and between individuals, as well as beginning to teach the children methods of caring for themselves and others, is treating both the estrangement and blame within family members as well as the trauma they all bring to the intersubjective space. Softening Jill and Rachel's symbiotic hostile dependent attitudes toward one another and Jill's toward the children, while loosening the defensiveness and guilt that keeps Rachel shackled, are all themes that can be examined through play. Moreover, the biologically driven triangulation around Rachel and the grandchildren could be explored through fantasy and make-believe and a metaframeworks perspective can function to focus the family play sessions.

Play engages both adults and children in cognitive and affective processes where fantasy and symbology facilitate one's ability to organize information and entertain divergent thinking. Obviously, it is far preferable to act aggression out through the toy rather than actual fighting. Working through powerful emotions such as aggression while using the toy as a vehicle for expression, enhances one's capacity to process and regulate emotions as well as integrate them with cognitions. Moreover, the act of playing and the toy are transformational catalysts due to the "inherently creative process which is intimately linked to pretend or make believe play" (Russ & Niec, 2011, p. 7) and, by definition, play is fun.

The family puppet interview (Irwin & Malloy, 1994) is both fun and invaluable for observing family patterns, studying symbolic communication between family members, and viewing decision making within the family (p. 21), all of which are intricately woven into the organization of the family and the family's capacity to establish effective balance, leadership, and harmony. Following the two cardinal rules of the family puppet interview (Gil, 1994), it has to be a made up story and can't be one you already know and you have to act it out as a family; this particular family's members chose from an array of diverse puppet figures that ranged from snakes to princesses and made up the story below:

In keeping with her role as a manager and a protector and director, Rachel chose a policeman puppet. Henry chose a clear symbol of a firefighter part with the fireman puppet, and Jill chose a monkey and a butterfly and endowed the monkey with magical powers. Other family members argued the point but Jill persevered and the monkey's magic remained. Amanda placed a queen puppet on her hand which she referred to as a fairy godmother. In watching the videotape of the family as they created the puppet show it was clear that Rachel was the director and the hostility between the couple almost derailed the entire process on two occasions. Had Jill not acquiesced the show would not have gone on.

The family decided on a list of animals that escaped from the zoo. The monkey (Jill) was an escapee, as was a big scary looking snake whose fangs were large and protruding and who Henry chose and spoke for. As the story unfolded, the puppets set out to hunt for the snake and when they found it the fireman (Henry) sprayed it with his hose. The fairy godmother (Amanda) took away the monkey's magical powers primarily because the monkey (Jill) used those magical powers to "jinx" everything the family tried to accomplish. Not only did the monkey "jinx" story events and characters' accomplishments but, ultimately killed the fireman (Henry) and the policeman (Rachel) which the fairy godmother (Amanda) then resurrected. All the other animals trapped the snake (Harry) and the fairy godmother (Amanda) removed the monkey's (Jill) magical powers and made him an "ordinary monkey" again. Once restored to life the policeman (Rachel) and the fireman (Henry) found the butterfly (Jill), who had gotten lost in the chaos. The story ended with the fairy godmother (Amanda) watching over everyone, especially the monkey (Jill), to make sure everyone was safe and the monkey never got his magical powers back.

This story opens the way for an exploration of power and powerlessness, transformation and change, escape and entrapment, and is rich in imagery and symbology. Processing trauma and loss as well as exploring family therapy constructs such as flexibility and cohesion are, among other things, a matter of allowing the narrative to unfold. Observe how the family tells the story and who plays what part. Notice the selection of the puppets. Notice what each family member picks up and pays close attention to, the story itself, and how family members relate to each other as they tell the story.

Thinking deeply and entering into the imagery of the family's metaphor by staying within the story and asking questions from within the story, as well as responding in a noninterpretive way both validates and expands the metaphor. Clinical issues such as creating safe space in which to process trauma, exploring themes of power and control, helplessness and transformation, and danger and safety along with clinical goals such as "feeling more like a family," being more supportive of one another, feeling "dizzy," or "less grumpy and worried about everything and everybody," or less "testy, anxious, frustrated, and short," guide the therapy. Working within the metaphor helps to both point toward and ground interventions.

By asking questions of the snake or the fireman rather than of Henry, the therapist keeps the metaphor alive and allows the family to safely explore possibilities and possible solutions. For example, asking the snake, "What would you like to say to the fireman who sprayed you with the hose?" or asking the fireman, "What was it like when you sprayed the snake with your hose?" function to keep family members working within the power of the metaphor enfolded in the story. Avoiding "why" questions, questions that can be answered with either "yes/no" and questions that ask for explanations help keeps the story grounded and moving.

The clinical issues are also deeply embedded in the relationships between family members. Jill's position as the outsider, Jill and Rachel's inability to collaborate, Henry's and Amanda's relationship to their traumatic past, the loss of their mother yet again and the impact of all of that on their current family, and Amanda's apparent powerlessness and profound dissociation, can all be examined within the metaphor of the puppets. Embodied in the metaphor of the snake and the monkey are deadly forms of danger but transformation and peace is possible. Jill is simultaneously the evil stepmother, as the monkey who not only disrupts everything but actually kills people, and the transformational symbol of the butterfly. She holds power in the family structure but her lack of attachment and sense of belonging impedes her ability to exercise it wisely. Rachel is, not surprisingly, the policeman, and Amanda, who seems the most avoidant and withdrawn is paradoxically the one who imbues herself with the power to keep the family safe and the monkey under control.

These systemic and relational themes can be examined and assessed and influenced by carefully tracking the beginning, middle, and end of the story, where in the beginning the family faces a threat. In this family puppet interview, dangerous beasts escape from their cages. In the middle of the story the therapist is looking for what the family does about the threat which, in this case, after a great deal of deadly jockeying for power and magic, has the family band together to capture the snake. Ultimately, by the end of the story the family aligns in a way that dampens the threat and they find transformation and safety. To some degree there is resolution but it entails living through death, rebirth, and transformation.

The family puppet interview also points to relational patterns that need strengthening, and family games like the secret handshake and the cotton ball blowing exercise can be used later in therapy to engage the family in playful connectedness. The cotton ball blowing exercise is a game specifically designed to enhance attachment between caregivers and children (Gil, personal communication) where attachment bonds are the weakest. Hence, making Amanda and Jill a team and Rachel and Henry a team, where the goal is to blow cotton balls into a net across the table, helps to realign family alliances and establish bonds. A similar kind of bonding can be encouraged within the metaphor of the family puppet interview by, for example, creating a tea party between characters such as the policeman and the monkey and the butterfly or creating subgroups that dialogue about the threat. Sessions are taped, played back at the next session, and interventions such as those mentioned above are implemented. Creating connections through the puppets can mitigate feelings such as loneliness and isolation, contain trauma, explore what will happen if the threat comes back, and create nurturing activities for the family.

Shortly into weekly therapy sessions, Henry's night terrors increased in intensity and frequency, adding yet more strain to the family system. A number of safety amplifying techniques for both children were implemented such as building a safe place in a sand tray and photographing it for future reference, creating a coping umbrella (Goodyear-Brown, 2010), and teaching breathing and relaxation exercises, along with more positive coping strategies. Exploratory and psychoeducational sessions on attachment and trauma with the couple helped them continue to implement strategies at home. And, because the night terrors were distressing to the entire family and Henry's yelling and screaming was waking up the household, a variation was created of the "Now and Later" technique (Goodyear-Brown, 2010) involving the whole family. Together, on a large piece of paper which we folding into thirds with "NOW" written on the first third and "LATER" written in the last third, and using the night terrors as the central problem, the family created a collage using a variety of material from tissue paper to paint to magazine images to express their experience of Henry's night terrors. They created a collage of "NOW" on the first third of the paper and a collage of "LATER" on the last third. They were then asked to create a collage in the middle third as to what might constitute one small step toward solving the problem. The family created many small steps in the middle section that proved to be a turning point in therapy in that the collage was richly decorated with images of family members supporting one another physically and emotionally in myriad ways. Further, the family decided to go on a week-long vacation to Ireland where Jill's family was originally from and where Jill and Rachel had wanted to go for their honeymoon.

Problems in communication are often the result of a disorganized family system that lacks leadership. Communication is a crucial aspect of healthy family functioning and if it is lacking between members of the executive subsystem (i.e., Rachel and Jill) then so is effective leadership and its many components, such as caring, nurturing, encouraging autonomy and connectedness, being fair and flexible, effective problem solving, regulating responsibility and conflict, and coordinating future goals. In planning a vacation for the entire family the couple made a substantial shift in providing leadership for the family and orienting it toward a meaningful future goal.

However, Jill's position in the family remained confusing in that it existed somewhere between being a lesbian step-parent who had agreed to be part of accepting and creating this family, and a step-parent who accepted the children as part of the relational "package," putting her squarely in the position of having to examine and ultimately drop her resentment and learn how to "blend blood and choice" (Weston, 1997).

Although research would indicate that there are far more similarities between lesbian mothers and heterosexual mothers than differences, and the children of lesbian mothers are no more likely to develop social, psychological, cognitive, and sexual difficulties than children raised by heterosexual mothers, feminist writers quite accurately point out that the gold standard remains the heterosexual parent against which the same sex parent is measured (Kranz & Daniluk, 2006). The culture continues to discriminate against same sex couples and Jill and Rachel have experienced discrimination and prejudicial treatment from the culture at large and from teachers and parents at the children's school. During a recent and particularly ugly incident another parent spit and yelled at Jill while she was picking the children up from school. Both Amanda and Henry witnessed the incident and refused to attend school for several days putting them further behind. The incident also had a profound effect on Jill in that it functioned to strengthen her commitment to the children who rushed to her aid.

The family, as stated, is connected to a global community and embedded in systems over which the family and its members have no control. The fact that the children have two "mothers" must be explored. Like any family, this one needs an identity, rituals and traditions, and a culture, but unlike many families this must be created within a cultural collective consciousness that is both misogynistic and homophobic. Within a metaframeworks model, both gender and cultural constraints can be examined in collaboration with the family, and through play these larger themes and experiential patterns can be communicated and expressed.

Facilitating change within these metadomains requires an understanding that the family is just one element in creating change and when securely attached and working as a team can come together, successfully face the threat, and establish safety within its sphere of influence. Because Satir believed that solving the current problems that the family was confronting was less important than learning how to problem solve in general, Swearer's (2006) problem solving play therapy was introduced. Five steps to problem solving were taught through the use of the acronym POWER, where P is for problem, O is for options, W is for which option is best, E is for execute the option, and R stands for rate it in terms of how well it worked. The scene in the school yard where Jill was spit on was reenacted through puppet play and explored in terms of POWER (problem, option, best solution, execute, and rate). Amplifying questions turned to safety and how the puppets could help to make things feel safer around the school yard, in their neighborhood, and within the family itself, which included a cell phone for each child. These ideas were recorded and built into a family sand tray image that embodied all the elements of safety that had been recorded. Moreover, because two options were to contact school officials about the incident and report it to police, social advocacy and legal channels of safety were explored and the children were able to experience the system as less adversarial and terrifying than in the past. Given cultural stereotypes and norms, however, engaging police is not always the best course of action. All of these issues and constructs can be examined, working within the acronym and exploring "W," or which solution(s) is the best. This course of inquiry can also lead to an opportunity to play out some of the children's previous experience with law enforcement officials.

As the family began to successfully build bridges over the rockier aspects of their communications and the couple became more congruent with each other and the children through understanding their polarized parts and positions, the disappearance of Elizabeth became a focal point in therapy. The children experienced another severe escalation in trauma symptoms, necessitating a return to games of bonding and safety such as the creation of safe space, relaxation, and breathing, along with supporting the family in safe therapeutic space and creating a holding environment strong enough to contain the traumatic memories that were emerging through support, clarity of boundaries, and skillful use of self and techniques.

Tracking therapeutic change using the broad theoretical strokes of systems theory and the critical eye of the postmodernist, the metaframeworks practice of organizing constraints according to internal family systems, sequences, development, organization, culture, and gender levels helps contain the intricate, complex, and many layered points of entry into this family system. Using play therapy within a metaframeworks model allows the therapist to employ a wide range of techniques inherent in the vast and fascinating field of play therapy, metaframeworks itself as a practice model, and the techniques derived from the rich history and current evolution of all models of family therapy. Working within the metaframeworks model these theories and practice techniques can be applied and evaluated in light of the biopsychosocial continuum of biology, person, relationship, family, community, and society.

If family therapy is going to become truly inclusive and if family therapy in the twenty-first century is going to be about all family members, then the body of theoretical and research literature must evolve and develop to be inclusive of children, and it must be taught to those in the field of family therapy. Family therapists need to become as adept and comfortable at including children of all ages, through newly developed theoretical foundations as well as best practice techniques, as they are at working through the intricacies of problem saturated couples' relationships. The metaframeworks model helps to keep the focus contained and the therapist can use the blueprint for therapy to maintain the flow of therapy overall, in the session itself, and in the moment. Within the metaphor of play, new meaning associated with actions and new actions associated with meaning can be explored. The work can be difficult and messy, which brings one back to the chaos inherent in growth, where chaos breaks down old structures in order to create new ones and the principle of self-organization asserts itself and the system gets bigger, more organized, and/or more complex or it dies. Both are possible but if self-organization is a matter of creating the conditions necessary for change and growth, then the family therapist is well situated to encourage and facilitate a more organized and complex way of operating in spite of the magnitude of the family's fear, trauma, loss, grief, and disappointment. When young children are a part of this, then family play therapy becomes a powerful medium through which transformation might be accomplished.

REFERENCES

Ariel, S. (2005). Family play therapy. In C. Schaefer, J. McCormick, and A. Ohnogi (Eds). *International Handbook of Play Therapy: Advances in Assessment, Theory, Research, and Practice*. New York, NY: Jason Aronson, 3-22.

Cederborg, A. (1997). Young children's participation in family talk therapy. *The American Journal of Family Therapy*, 25 (1), 28-38.

Chasin, R. (1989). Interviewing families with children. *Journal of Psychotherapy & the Family*, 5 (3),15-30.

Gil, E. (1994). *Play in family therapy*. New York, NY: The Guilford Press.

Golding, C. (2006). Redefining the nuclear family: An exploration of resiliency in lesbian parents. In Anne M. Prouty Lyness (Ed). *Lesbian Families' Challenges and Means of Resiliency: Implications for Feminist Family Therapy*. New York, NY: The Hawthorn Press, Inc.

Goodyear-Brown, P. (2010). *Play therapy with traumatized children: A prescriptive approach*. Hoboken, NJ: John Wiley & Sons, Inc.

Irwin, E., Malloy, E. (1994). *Family puppet interview*. In C. Schaefer and L. Carey (Eds). *Family Play Therapy*. Northvale, NJ. Jason Aronson. pp. 21-34.

Keith, D., & Whitaker, C. (1981). Play therapy: A paradigm for work with families. *Journal of Marriage and Family Therapy*, 7, 243-254.

Kranz, K. & Daniluk, J. (2006). Living outside the box: Lesbian couples with children conceived through the use of anonymous donor insemination. In A. Prouty Lyness (Ed.) *Lesbian Families' Challenges and Means of Resiliency*. New York, NY: Hayworth Press, Inc.

Piaget, J. (1962). *Play, Dreams, and Imitation in Childhood*. New York, NY: Routledge.

Russ, S., Fiorelli, J., & Cain Spannagel, S. (2011) Cognitive and affective processes in play. In S. Russ, & L. Niec. *Play in Clinical Practice: Evidence-Based Approaches*. New York, NY: The Guilford Press, 3-22.

Russ, S. & Niec, L., (2011). *Play in Clinical Practice: Evidence-Based Approaches*. New York, NY: The Guilford Press.

Scharff, J. (1989). Play with young children in family therapy. *Journal of Psychotherapy & the Family*, 5 (3),159-172.

Sklare, G. (2005). *Brief Counseling That Works: A Solution-focused Approach for School Counselors and Administrations* (2nd ed). Thousand Oaks, CA: Corwin Press.

Weston, K. (1997). *Families We Choose: Lesbians, Gays, Kinship*. Boston, MA: Beacon Press.

Chapter Five

Narrative Play Therapy with Families

Alan McLuckie and Melissa Rowbotham

In our experience as mental health therapists, families often frame their need for counseling or therapy in terms of problems. These problems can wield such influence within family systems that a family member (often a child) can even be identified as "the problem." Over time, these families can lose touch with who they are independent of their challenges and begin to doubt their skills, knowledge and strengths. Fortunately, in our experience, even the most problem saturated stories contain flickers of hope and evidence of "know-how." Tapping into a family's resources and harnessing these skills and "know-how" is not always easy, especially in situations where the problem has an extended history of influence on the family system. Marginalized families may also encounter difficulties resulting from oppressive forces (e.g., racism) embedded within society's structures and institutions (e.g., government, schools). In such situations, families may benefit from working with a counselor or mental health professional to help them reconnect with forgotten resources or help support the emergence of new possibilities. Unfortunately, counselors and mental health professionals too often amplify the influence of problems within families by using problem-based therapeutic approaches that locate problems within a child or family; by adopting a therapeutic stance that positions the mental health therapist as the expert or source of solutions; and/or by failing to address broader societal factors that negatively affect families.

OUR JOURNEY TOWARD NARRATIVE PLAY THERAPY WITH FAMILIES

Having trained as a social worker in the mid-1990s at undergraduate and graduate programs rooted in a mix of family systems and psychoanalytic traditions, my (AM) role in counseling agencies typically includes individual psychotherapy and family therapy. With a particular interest in children's mental health issues, my early practice drew upon psychoanalytic traditions that have influenced child psychotherapy and play therapy, including the works of Hermine Hug-Hellmuth (1921), Melanie Klein (1955), and Anna Freud (1969). Over time, my psychoanalytic tendencies gave way to an experiential paradigm (Poulter, 2005), operationalized in practice as Rogerian (1989) therapy with youth and adults and child-centered play therapy with younger children (Axline, 1969).

Working as a special education teacher, my (MR) journey as a mental health therapist began alongside children identified as "trouble" within the school system. Influenced by my employment setting and training in behavioral modification, my early therapeutic approach was consistent with a remedial-accommodative paradigm (Poulter, 2005). This practice paradigm assumes that there is a "normal" for children in the behavioral, social, emotional, and cognitive realms from which dysfunction, typically considered endogenous to the child, can be identified, remediated, and/or accommodated in order to rectify or reduce abnormality. Building on these experiences, my graduate training in counseling psychology reinforced the use of cognitive behavioral therapy (CBT) as a primary approach to mental health therapy.

Our separate journeys converged in the winter of 2000 when we both joined an interdisciplinary children's mental health program in a large urban center in Ontario. Here we provided psychosocial therapies to children, ages four to sixteen years, and their families. We quickly connected around our passion for working with vulnerable children and around our frustrations with problem-focused one-on-one therapies that too often pathologized children and seldom seemed to translate into meaningful change within the family system. Feeling like we were becoming a part of the problem saturated stories during therapy sessions and searching for more meaningful ways to include parents within the therapeutic process, we began to re-member and integrate narrative practices into our work with children and families. This narrative practice drew from, and built upon training that I (AM) was involved in with Michael White and Judith Myers-Avis (1997), which we modified to include key aspects of play-based therapy.

White's work along with his colleague David Epston ushered in a new paradigm of practice that harnessed the power of language and narrative as the means to positive therapeutic ends (White & Epston, 1990). Narrative therapy shifted how therapy was conceptualized and practiced by emphasizing the therapeutic value of social constructionist and postmodern thinking, an egalitarian collaborative relationship, and meaning-making with families. White's inclusion of structural-level forces (e.g., socio-political, gender, culture, socio-economic) as a therapeutic target was particularly appealing. This "new" non-problem saturated approach to therapy was energizing, created a sense of hope and opened up a world of new possibilities for engaging families and supporting change. We found that the stories shared by families with young children were more easily accessed, more thickly described, and more amendable to change using a narrative approach that incorporated play therapy principles and practices. Rather than rely on talk-based interactions as the main conduit for therapy, our developmentally informed approach to narrative therapy, views play as the child's "natural medium of communication" (Landreth, 1991, p. 10). We refer to this body of work as *narrative play therapy* (McLuckie, 2002).

In the early days of our work in this area, there was a paucity of literature examining the intersection of narrative therapy and play therapy. To inform our practice, we drew upon a range of works in the field of play therapy as well as works from the narrative genre including, *Playful Approaches to Serious Problems* (Freeman, Epston, & Lobovits, 1997), *What is Narrative Therapy?* (Morgan, 2000), and *Narrative Therapy with Children and their Families* (White & Morgan, 2006). These works are excellent resources but offer a perspective of therapy that is primarily grounded in the principles and practice of narrative therapy, with some play and art techniques incorporated in a largely atheoretical manner. A new perspective was offered by Ann Cattanach (2002, 2006, & 2008) whose writings synthesized many key principles and processes of narrative therapy into her model of practice play therapy practice rooted in drama therapy and Sue Jennings' (1999) developmental play therapy (Taylor, 2011). Her writings, *Narrative Play Therapy* (Cattanach, 2006) and *Narrative Approaches in Play with Children* resonate most with us and with the work presented in this chapter (Cattanach, 2008).

The goal for this chapter is to share ideas that contribute to the building of a community of practice for narrative play therapy. Specifically, we draw upon our experience working with young children and families and apply narrative play therapy as it applies to a family therapy context. A brief review of the relevant theories underpinning narrative therapy are examined and woven into practical play therapy approaches for working with children and families.

NARRATIVE PLAY THERAPY WITH FAMILIES: KEY THEORIES AND PRINCIPLES

Our approach to narrative play therapy integrates principles and practices of play therapy into a foundation of narrative therapy, essentially adapting White's model (White & Eptson, 1990) into a more developmentally accessible therapy for young children. Unlike prior writings in this area that encourage the eclectic use of "playful" elements (e.g., drawing) into otherwise "traditional" narrative therapy sessions, we encourage therapists to have a solid grounding in both play therapy and narrative therapy. This approach differs theoretically to some degree from Cattanach (2006), who drew upon principles and practices from narrative therapy to inform her core model of practice; a play-based model derived from drama therapy and Sue Jennings' (1999) developmental play therapy (Taylor, 2011). A further difference between our approach and those described by Cattanach (2006) is that we typically employ narrative play therapy within a family context (i.e., family-based therapy), rather than engage children in one-on-one therapy unless contraindicated.

Our intention in this chapter is not to get bogged down with an unnecessary review of theory. However, we advocate for clinicians to have a solid grounding in theories that inform narrative and play therapies, as in our opinion, the feckless application of techniques (i.e., externalization or puppet work) can contribute to therapy sessions that are inconsequential and non-influential (Jordan & Hickerson, 2003).

An in-depth exploration of the principles and theories underpinning narrative therapy, play therapy, and family therapy is beyond the scope of this chapter. However, where possible, additional resources will be suggested. In particular, we draw from the child-centered approaches (Axline, 1969), developmental play therapy (Jennings, 1999), and family-based play therapy/family play therapy (Gil, 1994). There are also a wide range of helpful play therapy resources that focus specifically on play-based techniques, including works by Heidi Kaduson and Charles Schaefer (1997) and Liana Lowenstein (1999, 2001, & 2010).

As extensive literature exists on these models of play therapy and in relation to family systems (Kaslow, Dausch, & Celano, 2003), we refer you elsewhere for a fuller discussion of their respective theoretical bases. The current chapter will be centered on illuminating the major theoretical concepts underpinning narrative therapy, as there is little writing that applies these concepts to therapy with young children and families.

The compressive and highly accessible work entitled *Narrative Therapy: The Social Construction of Preferred Realities* (Freeman & Combs, 1996) outlines four key principles that provide the philosophical and theoretical foundation to narrative therapy. These principles include: a) realities are socially constructed; b) realities are constituted through language; c) realities are organized and maintained through narrative; and that d) there are no essential truths (Freeman & Combs, 1996). The below brief review is focused towards the reader who may have had little exposure to narrative therapy and its theoretical underpinnings. For a more in depth exploration, we refer the reader to the excellent resource on narrative therapy created by Freedman and Combs (1996).

SOCIAL CONSTRUCTIONIST APPROACHES TO FAMILY THERAPY

Narrative therapy emerged as a mainstream model of psychotherapy in the 1990s offering a new paradigm of practice that espouses a social constructionist worldview (Gurman & Messer, 2003). Social constructionist thinking within therapy represents a departure from family systems thinking (i.e., that a person's reality, including life's problems arise from and are sustained by interpersonal interactions within the family environment). Simply stated, social constructionist thinkers believe that a person's reality (e.g., the personal narratives or stories we hold about ourselves and our world), including life's problems, arise from and are maintained through interpersonal interactions that occur within, and are influenced by, structural forces within the broader environment. The environment within social constructionist thinking includes the family unit but goes beyond its confines to include broader cultural, historical, and socio-political forces. Structural forces (e.g., gender, race/ethnicity, class) provide the context which shape people's personal narratives and influence the meaning given to daily events or interactions/exchanges with the world (Morgan, 2000). The developmental context (e.g., family context and broader environment) for some will foster a personal narrative replete of privilege while for others the context may help construct a personal narrative dominated by oppression.

An underlying assumption of social constructionist psychotherapies is that our stories about "who" we are as people are not constructed in isolation, independent of other people's influences and the influences of our social context. Our life stories, including who we are, do not simply arise as a product of genetic materials inherited from our parents or result from our family upbringing. Rather, these stories are co-constructed across time within a developmental context that is social in nature that has a pre-existing context of meaning, from which we draw meaning from in order to make sense of who we are (e.g., our personal narratives) (Brown & Augusta-Scott, 2007).

In our opinion, although it is not a social constructionist theory by design, Bronfenbrenner's (1979) ecological systems framework effectively depicts how an individual's story about him/herself unfolds or develops within a nested system, ranging from the broad sociocultural context (i.e., macrosystem) to the inner core of the family system or the parent-child relationship (i.e., microsystem) (see figure 4). Transactions occurring within each system, such as at the level of the family, are highly influential on an individual's life story (Bronfenbrenner, 1979). Transactions between systems also have marked influence on the realities of children and families. For example, children and families can be shaped by government policies related to such things as health care (i.e., macrosystem), and/or by experiences parents have with workplace policies (i.e., exosystem), and/or by the opportunities children have at school (i.e., mesosystem).

Unfortunately, Bronfenbrenner's (1979) model does not explicitly account for the fact that children and families do not all begin on equal footing within their particular social context, nor does it provide a blueprint to challenge oppressive structural forces. Socio-cultural forces are seldom experienced the same by all children and families. Not everyone has the same power, privilege, and opportunity within the various levels of society, includ-

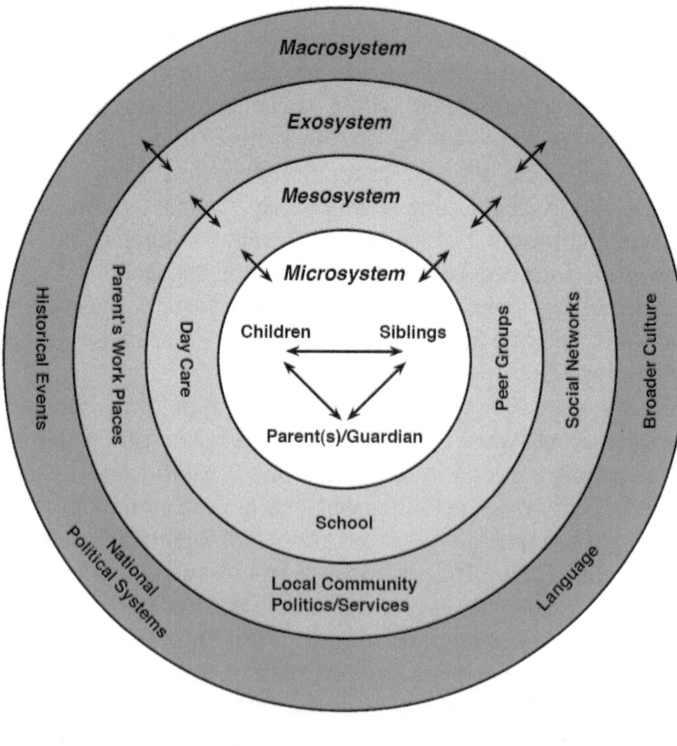

Figure 5.1. Constructing Problems and Solutions Adapted from Brofenbrenner, 1979

ing the broader macrosystem. Social structures are often socially constructed by the dominant group(s) in a fashion that maintains a privileged position within society for the dominant group(s), thereby resulting in oppression of other groups. For example, racism is alive and well in a North American context. Discrimination due to such factors as race/ethnicity, gender/sex, sexual orientation, age and physical ability, continue to erect barriers to young people and families within major institutions (e.g., school and the employment sector) and society. Real and potential sources of oppression with society must be acknowledged and challenged within the therapeutic context because these forces wield a negative influence on the development of children and families.

REALITIES: CONSTITUTED THROUGH LANGUAGE

Language is of the utmost importance to narrative therapists. In social constructionist and narrative doctrine, language constitutes realities (Freedman & Combs, 1996). Language is the vehicle through which people and societies construct reality. Language not only reflects our past and present social reality (i.e., cultural norms and societal values), but actively shapes our reality across time and within a cultural-linguistic context (Bruner, 2004). Lev Vygotsky (1962), developmental psychologist and social constructionist thinker, proffered that language functions as a tool through which cultural practices are transmitted to children and across generations, thereby shaping individuals, families, communities, and cultures across time.

Narrative therapists often point to pathologizing/stigmatizing labels as a prime example of the power language has to shape the realities of young people and families. In our experience, psychiatric diagnoses such as Attention-Deficit/Hyperactivity Disorder (ADHD) and Oppositional Defiant Disorder (ODD) can be useful to describe an aspect of the child's reality or personal narrative, albeit in a thin and often decontextualized manner. Diagnoses can help children and families access information and services by "legitimizing" the nature of the problem within the mental health/medical and educational systems. Unfortunately, such labels can shift from a position of describing an aspect of the child's reality (i.e., behavior) to a position of defining who the child is within the eyes of key relationships (e.g., parents and teachers) and intuitions (e.g., schools). When this reifying process goes unexamined within society, Freedman and Combs (1996) caution that human created tools designed to describe reality (i.e., a diagnosis from the Diagnostic and Statistical Manual [DSM-IV-TR]: APA, 2000) can begin to define reality (i.e., behavioral descriptors become synonymous with endogenous traits) and shape the story of who the child is in their world.

Due to stigma and the lack of education regarding mental health issues, it is common for members of the general public to equate pathologizing terminologies (e.g., ADHD and ODD) with “trouble maker” or “difficult child” or “dysfunctional parents.” These labels often carry such weight that the problem is seen more clearly than other aspects of the child’s story. We have worked with many families and educators who describe a child’s diagnosis of ODD, as if the child was experiencing an untreatable disease, rather than displaying a significant but amendable behavioral pattern. Such labels can also restrict children and parents from fully comprehending the nature of the problem, contributing to their losing sight of personal knowledge and skill that could be brought to bear against the problem. As mental health therapists and play therapists, we need to be cognizant of these reifying forces and be committed to critically examining the potentially oppressive aspects of labels and language used within our therapeutic practice.

Most narrative therapy literature, including writings focused on interventions with children, emphasize the importance of language to the model of practice and for positive therapeutic outcomes (Freedman et al., 1997). This literature privileges verbal interactions between the therapist and child and/or families as the primary conduit of therapy, with secondary emphasis on written interactions (i.e., typically letters or written recordings of important in-session occurrences). Only minor consideration is given to the value of play as a form of communication for young children, a key therapeutic conduit harnessed by play therapists. Virginia Axline (1969) underlines the importance of play to play therapists stating that, “play therapy is based upon the fact that play is the child’s natural medium of self-expression” (p. 9). Gary Landreth (1991), elaborating on Axline’s work, compares toys to the words that children use during communication and describes play as the “child's natural language of expression” (p. 11).

When play-based interventions are described within narrative therapy literature (e.g., dramatized role playing or playful interactions during externalization and/or art-based techniques, such as drawing/painting pictures of the “problem”), they are typically used as a means to engage the child or as an adjunct to talk-based communication/interactions. In many cases, these play-based interactions are highly appropriate and consistent with play therapy principles. However, in our opinion, play therapy interventions, especially when young children are involved, should be integral to the therapy and any de-emphasis of play’s importance as a form of childhood communication should be reconsidered. When working therapeutically with families who have young children, we consider play and play-based interventions to be the *great developmental equalizer*.

Piaget (1954) notes that play helps children to make sense of their reality and make sense of their lived real-world experiences. His work on cognitive capabilities relative to age also suggests that the concrete nature of play-based interventions may be well-suited to therapeutic work with children in the pre-operational (i.e., two to seven years of age) or concrete operational (i.e., seven to eleven years of age) stages of development (Piaget, 1954). Winnicott (1971) would likely agree with this perspective as he asserts that a "child does not usually possess the command of language that can convey the infinite subtleties that are found in play" (p. 39).

When conducting family therapy sessions, we believe that it is imperative to tailor therapeutic interventions to the *lowest common developmental level* within the family system in order to maximize the inclusivity of the session for all family members. Thus, with families composed of a range of ages/developmental abilities including pre-operational and concrete operational thinkers (i.e., children under seven years of age) and those capable of formal operations/abstract thought (i.e., parents/caregivers and siblings older than eleven or twelve years of age), we privilege play-based interventions over complex verbal interactions that require high levels of abstraction in order to maximize inclusivity. It takes effort on the part of parents and older siblings (and at times encouragement and support from the therapist) to engage in play-based activities, when they may prefer to engage in abstract discussions. However, parents and older siblings are cognitively/developmentally capable of "moving down" from abstract reasoning to a level of concrete reasoning (i.e., engaging in play activities such as drawing emotions), whereas it is not developmentally possible for younger children to "move up" to abstract reasoning. Therefore, we believe that family-based interventions should be targeted toward the lowest level of development, which includes play therapy when concrete operational thinkers are involved. For a fuller discussion of ways to incorporate play therapy within a family therapy context we recommend Schaefer and Carey (1994).

REALITIES: ORGANIZED AND MAINTAINED THROUGH NARRATIVES

Language forms the nucleus of narratives or stories which serve to organize and maintain the structures of society. The personal narratives we hold about ourselves or what we tell ourselves about who we are (Bruner, 2004), the stories we co-construct with others about who we are as people (Ernde, 2007), as well as the written and oral traditions within our societal institutions (e.g., family, schools, law) greatly influence, if not define, who we are as people. Bruner (2004) suggests that narratives imbedded within our social institutions organize and shape the very cultural fabric of our societies. Narratives organize and maintain the structures of society in the present, but also in the future through personal, familial, and social expectations and norms (Emde, 2007). For example, family traditions passed down through stories may shape how parents or children "should" act, as well as influence their future views of what is considered "normal" family functioning. Written traditions codified within law can also form powerful social narratives regarding what individuals, family systems, communities, and cultures consider normal and "abnormal." For example, by legalizing same-sex marriage, a traditional narrative of what is considered "normal" is challenged and expanded to include other possibilities for "married couples" and "families" that are no longer filtered exclusively through a heterosexual/hetero-normative lens.

Narrative therapists seek to understand the stories people hold about themselves; stories which give meaning to their experiences (White & Denborough, 1998). Specifically, narrative therapists seek to explore and deconstruct the dominant oppressive stories held by young people and families which are typically problem saturated. By engaging with an individual about their actions and inner thoughts (i.e., what someone tells him or herself about his or her lived reality), narrative therapists seek to understand the relative influence of the oppressive "plot" line of the story (i.e., dominant oppressive narrative). Therapists are also skilled to listen/watch for unique outcomes during interactions with children and families (e.g., what is said or done in the therapy session) that suggests the presence of an alternate or preferred narrative which will form the foundation of the family's new story (i.e., alternate or preferred narratives). In our experience, dominant oppressive narratives are often well developed within the stories of the young people and families who seek out therapy. Sadly, alternate stories that are non-problem saturated are vapor thin. During the course of therapy with a family system these narratives or competing "plot lines" (i.e., dominant versus preferred narrative) can co-exist as the family works to reduce the influence of the problem and firm up the action and thinking processes that allow the alternative story to take root.

Building on the work of anthropologist Clifford Geertz (1973), White (1997) emphasizes the therapeutic importance of seeking out thick descriptions of the narratives held by young people and their families, in order to understand their realities in a meaningful fashion. White (1997) views thick descriptions of action or thinking processes as making it possible for people (e.g., therapist and family members) to arrive at a shared meaning about these actions/thoughts. In our experience, play-based interventions are essential for therapists to access thick descriptions of children's narratives. Conversely, thin descriptions of a child's reality most likely result from therapy sessions that rely too heavily on spoken or written forms of communication or that de-emphasize the role that play-based and art-based interventions have for working therapeutically with children.

Freeman et al. (1997), White and Morgan (2006), and Morgan (2000) all include playful interventions and art techniques in their narrative therapy sessions with young children. However, they are often peripheral to the therapeutic interaction, which misses an opportunity to potentially thicken the description and enhance the shared meaning of the child's reality. Cattanach (2006 & 2008) and Taylor de Faoite (2011) position play and art-based interventions at the center of their interactions but do so in a manner that is somewhat distanced from key principles and practices that make narrative therapy helpful. Our perspective on narrative play therapy is that the key processes and practices of narrative therapy can be central to the play and art-based interventions within the family session to allow for a thicker understanding those who would not otherwise be able to fully participate in highly abstract verbal discussions.

POST MODERNITY AND MULTIPLE REALITIES: NO ESSENTIAL TRUTHS

Narrative therapy is informed by postmodern thought, which conceptualizes reality not as a single entity but as the co-existence of multiple realities negotiated between people or societies. Modern approaches to therapy are typically reductionist in nature, value objectivity, knowing with certainty, focus on the facts of a "case,"and have an outlook in therapy that something is "broken" and can be "fixed." In these approaches, there are essential truths about what is functional or dysfunctional (e.g., family functioning), normal and abnormal (e.g., family structure), and rational and irrational (e.g., thinking patterns of a young person or family member). Postmodern therapists are interested in subjectivity and meaning making, and believe that there are no essential truths about life. Rather, as noted by Freedman and Combs (1996), life is a "multiverse" (p. 34), where right or wrong is replaced by the best fit at the time for a particular individual or family and knowing with certainty is replaced by a position of partial knowing (Brown, 2007).

In our experience, postmodern approaches to therapy with children and families can be misconstrued as being synonymous with an anything-goes approach when this is not the case. For example, accepting that narrative play therapy is a postmodern model does not mean that all techniques are accepted practice within this model. It does mean, however, that there are multiple ways of doing narrative play therapy, as evidenced by our somewhat different approach than Cattanach (2006). This should be reassuring considering that a postmodern approach also sees young children and families as unique. Children's difficulties are not reduced to a single diagnosis, nor are family problems equated to a family relational difficulty such as "enmeshment." Postmodern therapists honor the belief that every child and every family will have different stories that need to be understood in a "thick" manner, free from assumptions. In our experience, it is likely that individuals and families will hold multiple stories of who they are, especially when they are engaged in a process of challenging dominant oppressive narratives and solidifying preferred narratives of they are and who they will be.

THERAPEUTIC STANCE: COLLABORATION, SCAFFOLDING, AND BEING DECENTERED

Forming and maintaining a collaborative relationship with children and families lies at the core of narrative therapy. Establishing such a relationship requires that the therapist recognize and respond to the power differences that exist within the therapeutic relationship. In order to effectively engage in a collaborative relationship, it is important for therapists to engage in a critical reflective process in order to be aware of and challenge forces (including personal factors of the therapist) that contribute to power differential between the therapist and families. These factors include power associated with the status inherent to the professional role (i.e., the power within the role of physician, social worker, psychologist), as well as other sources of power arising from factors such as age, gender, race, socio-economic status, and sexual orientation. Morgan (2006) states that the therapist is not separate from these power relations that shape lives and is never neutral. For an in-depth review of power within the therapeutic relationship, we refer you to Brown (2007).

Morgan (2006) underlines the importance of recognizing the power differential that exists in therapeutic relationships with children. In particular, there is a power imbalance associated with the differences in developmental/cognitive abilities between the therapist and child. As noted earlier, when working with families with children we believe that play is the great developmental equalizer and that therapists should use play-based interventions to engage at the lowest common developmental/cognitive level. Cattanach (2006, p. 92) would likely agree with this view as she states that, "the equality of the relationship facilitates the unfolding of the [child's] story" (p. 92) within narrative play therapy.

To navigate the power differential within the therapeutic relationship, Morgan (2006) advocates for therapists to reflect on how they position themselves in relation to the child and family. Specifically, she underlines the importance of therapists knowing where they stand (i.e., where their therapeutic stance falls) on a continuum (or axis) of professional expertise. At one end of the continuum, the therapist's stance is centered on, or privileges, his or her knowledge and expertise. At the other end of the continuum, in a decentered position, the therapist places the child and family's skills, know-how, and expertise at the center of the therapeutic work (Morgan, 2006). The family's know-how and skill developed through lived experience, including their knowledge of the problem, must be tapped and supported in order for a preferred narrative to emerge.

Vigilance and reflexivity are needed to remain decentered within the therapeutic relationship. Even the most experienced narrative therapist can slip from a decentered to a centered stance in therapy. Morgan states that she feels decentered when asking questions that leave room for children to make meaning of their experience, and slips toward being centered by asking questions "phrased in such a way to be likely to elicit a particular answer that I have in mind, or when I ask a question in a way that implies an answer" (Morgan, 2006, p. 64). The solution to the dilemma of possessing knowledge and authority, but wishing to remain decentered, has been for the therapist to adopt a position of curiosity or what Brown (2007) describes as partial-knowing, which better acknowledges the therapist's skill and knowledge more so than a false not-knowing position. Regardless of the specific language applied, the therapist's not-knowing stance does not mean the therapist abandons his or her prior knowledge, but rather is aware of the limitations of his or her ability to know about the family story, the nature of the problem, or the path to a new story (Cattanach, 2006).

Embracing a decentered therapeutic stance does not mean that narrative play therapists adopt a non-influential position. We are not advocating for a decentered, non-influential therapeutic stance, akin to a laissez faire approach to therapy. We agree with Morgan (2006) and Freedman and Combs (1996) that narrative therapists should strive to remain decentered, but also accept that they possess skills and knowledge helpful to influence change in the family story. Morgan suggests that a key facet of being influential is not in directing the outcome of the therapy (or the person's story) but in skillfully and influential manner scaffolding therapeutic questions (and play-based techniques) and providing responses within therapy that enable the skills and knowledge of the child and family to be more richly known and brought to bear against the dominant oppressive narrative.

White agrees with Morgan that narrative therapists are influential within the therapeutic process due in a large part through their efforts to help scaffold the family from their dominant narrative to their preferred narrative (White & Morgan, 2006). A distance typically exists between what is known and familiar (i.e., familiar ways of thinking and acting) and what is possible for family members to know and accomplish (White, 2006). White proffers that this gap "must be traversed" (White, 2006, p. 40) in order for people to form a new and lasting story and/or a new relationship with the problem. White goes on to say that it is "rarely possible for people to traverse this gap without the appropriate scaffolding . . . the sort of scaffolding that is the outcome of social collaboration" (White, 2006, p. 40). To make sense of this scaffolding process, White draws upon the work of Vygotsky. Although Vygotsky's (1986) work is focused on early childhood learning and development White postulates that Vygotsky's theory related to the zone of proximal development (ZPD) is relevant to narrative therapy (Vygotsky, 1986). In particular, White applies Vygotsky's theory of ZPD to help conceptualize how therapists scaffold new learning (i.e., new possible ways of thinking and doing) within therapy sessions through their conversations, questions and interactions. Vygotsky (1978) defines the ZPD as:

> The difference between what children can already do comfortably on their own and their potential development as determined through problem solving under adult guidance or in collaboration with more capable peers (p. 86).

In Vygotsky's (1962) view individuals do not develop, learn, grow, or change independent of others. Rather, development occurs as an outcome of social interaction. In relation to the therapeutic context, White (2006) suggests that scaffolding a narrative conversation in an influential and decentered manner is what provides family members with the opportunity and needed support to proceed across the ZPD in manageable ways.

However, White fails to acknowledge the importance that Vygotsky placed on play as a principal factor acting within the ZPD. As noted above, we view play as the great developmental equalizer that provides the necessary scaffolding to allow children to participate in co-creating preferred narratives within family therapy. Vygotsky (1962) goes further to suggest that play is key to young people making strides forward in relation to any developmental milestone by sharing the following reflection on play and the ZPD:

> Play also creates the zone of proximal development of the child. In play the child is always above his average age, above his daily behaviour; in play it is as though he were a head taller than himself . . . in play it is as though the child were trying to jump above the level of his normal behavior. The play-development relationship can be compared to the instruction-development relationship, but play provides a background for changes in needs and in consciousness of a much wider nature. Play is the source of development and creates the zone of proximal development . . .The child moves forward essentially through play activity. (p. 16)

By integrating play-based interventions with narrative therapy questions and interventions, children are provided with developmentally appropriate and necessary scaffolding to break things down into manageable pieces (i.e., abstract things such as emotions or problems) in order to imagine new possibilities for their preferred narratives. Furthermore, engaging therapeutically with the whole family (as opposed to one-on-one therapy with the child) allows the therapist to scaffold interactions between the child and adult guidance (i.e., parents and the therapist) and more mature peers (i.e., siblings); key to growth within the ZPD. Through play, questions, and the therapeutic relationship, the therapist helps scaffold the thickening of the child and family's know-how, skills, and preferred narrative (Freedman et al., 1997).

THE PROCESS OF NARRATIVE PLAY THERAPY WITH FAMILIES

As narrative play therapists, our goal is to work collaboratively with children and families to deconstruct their personal and family stories in a manner that offers access to a thick meaningful understanding of their lived reality. We work with the expertise of the child and family to recognize the influence of the dominant oppressive stories. Equally, we work to identify the actions and knowledge possessed by the family that, when linked together and harnessed in meaningful ways, will form new or rediscovered narratives (i.e., alternate or preferred narratives) that will challenge the problem saturated narrative.

We turn now to describe how we engage in the process of narrative play therapy with families. Although presented in a linear fashion, this approach should not be considered a linear process to be followed in prescriptive manner. Therapists should expect that this process will unfold in an organic way moving between phases across multiple sessions (our average is six to eight sessions). To develop this process of applying narrative therapy we have drawn on the works of other narrative therapists (see Freedman & Combs, 1996; White & Epston, 1990; White & Morgan, 2006; Young, 2008).

Typically, the therapist and family begin by moving from "setting the agenda" and "getting to know the family away from the problem" into an exploration of the influence of the problem including the important stage of externalization and "naming the problem." From there, the therapist will begin to gain a thick understanding of the influence of the problem by exploring the 'impact of the problem' and the "requirements of the problem," including understanding how the family was recruited into the dominant oppressive story. From there, the therapist will work to understand the family's "statement of position" to garner what has happened such that the family now stand against the problem. Sparkling moments that shine a light on "unique outcomes" and "unique accounts" are thickened through the therapist's use of curiosity-based questions and play-based techniques that tap into the family's preferred narratives (Morgan, 2000). The process typically concludes with the family and therapists examining how the family has and will engage in "unique circulation," spreading the word that the child and family's story is no longer dominated by the problem. Throughout this process, as described below, we provide examples of how we have synthesized play therapy into our work with children and families. We do not consider this process to be the only way of practicing narrative play therapy. Rather, the process outlined below is offered as a guide to beginning narrative play therapists in their journeys to help scaffold their ability with this approach rooted in social constructionist and postmodern principles.

ENGAGEMENT AND BEGINNING PHASE

Setting the Agenda

At the outset of therapy our role as a narrative play therapist is to meet with families, begin forging a collaborative relationship and work to understand their therapeutic agenda. To establish an agenda for therapy, we use questions and play-based interventions (see below) to explore the family's hopes for the focus of our time together. Unlike modern approaches (as opposed to postmodern approaches) to family therapy, we are not setting specific or rigid goals with the family. Rather, we are beginning a process of exploring new possibilities within the family story that are no longer dominated by problems. In our experience, this is often a time when parents/caregivers will focus on the difficulties experienced in their family or with a specific child. This is an important opportunity for the therapist to be influential within the family's story by declining to speak in-depth about the problem, choosing instead to ask the family about their hopes. We respectfully decline to explore the problem in a highly transparent manner, asking the family if it is possible to first get to know the family distinct from the problem and understand their hopes, and return to fully explore the influence of the problem at a later stage of therapy.

Example Play-Based Activity

After introductions and housekeeping (e.g., informed consent, paper work), we invite the family to engage in a play-based activity involving paper-bag puppets. The focus of this activity is for the family to introduce themselves as well as their hopes in a playful and engaging manner. We invite each family member to create paper-bag puppets using brown paper lunch bags and a variety of art supplies, including markers and crayons. See Lowenstein (2002) and Hall, Kaduson, and Schaefer (2002) for additional insight regarding puppets as a play therapy intervention. Specifically, we invite each family member to create a puppet representation of his or herself or their "character" in their "family story." In our experience, this "character" is often a caricature with amplified qualities or attributes. We have had our greatest success with this intervention when we begin by asking each family member to put their hand inside the paper bag and "to find the puppet's mouth" (e.g., the natural fold of the paper bag will open and close like a mouth) while we demonstrate using our own paper bag. This helps to guide the family to draw the puppet character in a manner that is conducive for the puppet to "speak."

We also encourage family members not to worry about this being an art or drama class, but instead to create a puppet that best represents him or herself within their family story.

When the puppets are complete, we ask the family if we can talk with their puppets and, with permission from the family, proceed to have a direct conversation with the puppets (controlled by the family members). We ask the puppets to introduce themselves and their family, their reasons for attending therapy, as well as their hopes for their family and for what will come of our time together in therapy. Our discussion is non-scripted, but often includes questions such as, "What do you wish would come of our time together?" "How might we begin to work towards this?" "What hopes do you have for yourself and your family?" and "In which ways can our time here together help with these hopes?"

Alternate Activity

We have also had a great success when working with younger children to ask about their hopes in a playful manner including questions such as "If you were a family of superheroes what would your mission be? Would there be any villains? Will there be heroes?" or "If you were a detective, what would the mystery be? Do we know any clues about how the mystery might be solved?"

Getting to Know the Family Away From the Problem

During the beginning phase of therapy it is key to forge a collaborative relationship and for the therapist to get to know the child and family away from the problem. This phase of therapy is entered seamlessly from setting the agenda with the family members. Most likely, conversations and play-based interactions with family members will move back and forth between exploring who the family members are, as well as their hopes. In getting to know the family distinct from the problem(s), we are interested in arriving at a thick understanding of the family's story or who they are (past, present, and future) using storytelling, drama, and play-based activities. At this phase, we continue to resist invitations to explore the problem-based story by remaining curious and asking questions about aspects of the family story unrelated to the problem. In our opinion, this helps create the necessary space during therapy and within the family system for new stories to begin and/or for old know-how and skills to resurface in the form of the alternate narrative.

Example Play-Based Activity

To get to know the family, we typically continue to interview the paper-bag puppets asking questions such "Can you tell me the 'story' of your family, making sure that there is a beginning, middle, and end?" In our experience, it can be very helpful to interview each family member (directing questions at their puppets) asking them each questions such as, "What things do you like to do as a family?" or "If everyone has a job in the family, what job do you have?" or "What are you the best at . . . what is your family good at doing?" We also find it helpful to be playful in this approach by asking the family to pretend that they are being interviewed for television or that they are making a movie about their family that tells all the important parts. In our experience, it is important to also ask simple circular question to family members such as, "Who gets along best in the family?" or "Are there parts of your family story that your Mom or Dad or brother or sister do not know about?" See Brown (1997) for a fuller description of the basic use of circular questions within family-based therapy.

Alternate Activity

We are often successful at getting to know the family by inviting them to draw on a large piece of paper (i.e., chart board paper) an ecomap, showing the people and activities of importance to their family story. As life and family stories have both ups and downs, we invite the family to include all the things in their life, both positive and negative, that are important to help us understand who they are. We make available a range of art materials including markers, crayons, stickers, and magazines from which to cut pictures (with symbolic meaning for the child or family member). We have had our best results with this activity when we provide a quick demonstration of how to draw an ecomap.

For further information on ecomaps as a therapeutic tool for working with families see Hartman (1995). For variations on this tool that are play-based see Lowenstein's (1999) activity, *People in My World*. After completing the ecomap we invite family members to share their "part of the story." We typically ask questions to facilitate this process including asking "Who are the people in your family, your class, who you work with?" or "What parts of your story make you feel successful or proud?"

Alternate Activity

Invite the family to draw a family portrait, kinetic family drawing, or have each family member to draw their family as "animals." Please refer to Arad (2004), Kerr (2010), or Oaklander (1998) for fuller descriptions of these activities. After the pictures are complete, engage the family in a narrative conversation about their family pictures in order to develop a thicker understanding of the family story, separate and distinct from the problem.

DECONSTRUCTION-EXTERNALIZATION PHASE

Naming of Problem

The main task during this phase of therapy is for the therapist and family to work together to name the problem. Selecting a name is key to successfully externalizing the problem, which until this point has likely been attributed to an internal/endogenous trait or characteristic of a family member (typically a child). Externalizing is a central technique to narrative therapy and a central philosophical position to this approach that involves viewing children and families as separate and distinct from the problems they experience. Simply stated, the person is the person and the problem is the problem.

It is our experience that family members and mental health professionals may use different names to describe problems. For example, mental health professionals may use formal diagnostic terminology such as ADHD or ODD, whereas families may use terms such as "busy" or "trouble." We encourage therapists to be patient during this phase and to allow families to identify and select the name that best matches their experience with the problem. We have been most successful when we invite families to use the name they commonly apply to the problem in the home environment or when they discuss the problem outside of the therapeutic environment. Finding a name that is meaningful and accessible to all family members is key to externalization because it allows the family to bring to the therapy their personal knowledge/expertise regarding the problem. This knowledge will be helpful when working in the next phase of therapy to understand the influence of the problem on the family system.

In our view, a child or family commonly experience more than one problem or they experience several interrelated problems. For example, we often see children and families impacted by learning and behavioral problems where it is difficult for families to distinguish where one problem stops and the other starts. In these situations, it is often helpful to externalize the problems as separate, rather than assume that that they are one big problem. For example, when we asked children and families, "Does Bored have any friends?" (in reference to a problem previously described in a thin way as ADHD), it is not uncommon to hear responses such as, "Yes, Trouble hangs out with Bored all the time!" Through further externalization conversations, it is clear that Bored's presence in a classroom setting is a strong invitation for Trouble to join in and add to the child's problem. In our experience, it is helpful to separate these problems because different steps may be needed to address the influence of these problems over the child's story. See Morgan (2000) for a fuller discussion of the externalization process.

Externalization is often criticized due to a misconception that this process invites children and/or family members to be irresponsible. For example, there may be fears that this technique will contribute to a claim that "I didn't do it! ADHD did it!" However, our experience is quite the opposite. When using this technique with children, we observe that the problem becomes more accessible to children and families, in part because it has become more concrete and congruent with developmental levels, but also because externalizing removes the shame and stigma of the child being "the problem." To us, young people and families who engage in therapy, externalize their difficulties, and challenge dominant narratives, show a profound ability to accept responsibility and actively work to influence their problems. Unfortunately, in our society we have confused the idea of accepting responsibility for a problem with a person admitting that "they are the problem."

When working with children, it is important to use play-based and art-based interventions to achieve a thick description of the problem. This should not be surprising as play is the natural manner in which children share or externalize their personal narratives (i.e., internal worlds) in order to make sense of their experiences (Freedman et al., 1997). Narrative play therapists harness play as a means of engaging children and families more fully in the externalization process that helps invite change in the family story.

Example Play-Based Activity

If the family is receptive to the technique, we typically continue using paper-bag puppets and dramatic play-based interactions in this phase of therapy. We have had great success using puppets as a means of externalizing the problem, likely because this technique literally "externalizes" the problem into the form of a puppet. We have had less success with drawing pictures of the problem because pictures are more static in nature compared to puppets. Puppets are a dynamic medium that can be brought to life (i.e., directly manipulated/controlled) by a child or family member throughout the course of dramatic playful activities, interactions, and conversations, all the while acting as a symbolic representation of "the problem."

Building on the paper bag puppet activity, we invite the family, or a member of the family, to create a paper bag puppet of the problem using art supplies, such as markers and crayons. It may be helpful to ask the family to create the puppet collaboratively. Depending on the situation and/or family dynamic it may be more helpful to select a particular family member to create the puppet. If completing the puppet collaboratively, ask one family member to begin drawing and then at an agreed upon interval of time (e.g., two minutes) have the puppet passed to another family member, until the family agrees the puppet is complete. In our experience, the activity is most powerful and most consistent with the theoretical premise of externalizing when the "problem puppet" is created by the family member (typically the child) who identifies as having the "closest relationship" to the problem, is the identified "patient," and/or the person scape-goated by the family as being the "problem".

Once the "problem puppet" is complete, it is helpful for therapists to engage with the families in externalizing conversation (Freedman, et al., 1997). In this process the therapist asks questions of family members and of the "problem puppet" in a manner that amplifies the separation between person and problem, while still understanding the influence and impact of the problem. In our experience, it is very empowering/symbolic to have the scape-goated child or the "problem family member" take on the puppet-master role, controlling and voicing the words for the problem puppet. Although we have done so less often, there may be times where it is advantageous to have other family members control the "problem puppet." This technique may suit situations where the "problem" is viewed as having a "close" relationship with several family members (e.g., parent-child conflict). In this event, the puppet represents the same problem, but the therapist and family are able to gain a thicker understanding of the puppet's influence by having two different perspectives of the "problem." It is also possible to combine this intervention with prior family puppet activities by having family members control their "family puppets" so that they can interact with the therapist and the "problem puppet."

The externalizing conversation facilitated by the therapist is not scripted but typically begins by asking the "problem puppet" for its name. This reaffirms/solidifies the naming of the problem. Other questions we have asked include, "Do you have a nickname?" "What do you (directed at the problem puppet) get the family (or child) to do that they wouldn't normally do?" or "If you (directed at the problem puppet) do the talking for the family (or child), what kind of things do say?" or "What powers do you have?" or ask "What are some of the tricks that you play on this child and/or family?" It is very important that when engaging in externalizing conversation, the therapist use externalizing grammar, which does not attribute the problem to the child (Freedman et al., 1997). The therapist should also be conscious of facilitating an externalizing dialogue between family members so that they are describing the problem akin to it being another family member, rather than talking about any one specific family member as if they were the problem. For a fuller discussion of narrative based questions that can be asked to understand the influence of the problem please refer to Morgan (2000) or White and Morgan (2006).

Alternate Activity

We have also invited family members to draw a picture of the problem using a range of art supplies. Once complete, we invite each family member to share a story about their picture (or contribution to the collaborative picture).

The therapist engages in an externalizing conversation using externalizing language to invite the family to see themselves and the "problem family member" (likely a child) as separate from the problem depicted in the picture (Freedman et al., 1997).

Impact of the Problem

At this stage, the therapist begins to explore with the family the relative influence of the problem. In particular, we are curious about how the problem is influencing the actions and thinking of family members, as well as how it is impacting key relationships. For example, how might the problem influence how family members act toward each other and how might the problem contribute to thoughts (often negative) family members may have about themselves or other family members? Building on the externalization phase, we are interested in finding examples of times that the problem dominates the family story. It is equally important for the therapist to listen for and highlight times when the problem is less influential in the family story (i.e., actions or ways of thinking that are consistent with the alternate or preferred narrative). By *deconstructing* the influence of the problem we simultaneously identify know-how and skills possessed by family members that lay the foundation for the development of an alternate storyline.

Example Play-Based Activity

Returning to the concept of the family ecomap, we invite the family to draw three separate circles on three separate pieces of large paper (e.g., chart board paper). These circles represent the "frames" (just like picture frames) of their family story in the past, present, and future. We explain that this activity is about understanding how big a part of the family story the problem is at (a) the current time (first picture to draw); (b) in the past (second picture to draw); and (c) in the future (third picture to draw). We have the family put titles on each of the "frames" (i.e., past, present, future). We invite family members to use symbols (or circles) to fill in the story frames with all the important parts (people, activities, roles) in their family story in a similar way to how they completed the ecomap in a previous session (see the Getting to Know the Family phase outlined above).

We ask the family to distinguish the importance of each aspect of their story by varying the size of the symbol relative to its importance in the family story (i.e., big circles for people or activities that are a big part of their story). The therapist makes sure that the family understands to depict the "problem" on the same scale of "big" and "small." In our experience, families typically draw their ecomaps with the problem being different size timeframes of their story. It seems to coincide that when the problem is a bigger part of their life, other aspects of their story also change in influence/size (e.g., a parent, friends, or school may become a bigger/smaller part of their life relative to the influence of the problem). In our experience, it is helpful if the therapist gives an example from their life showing how big (or small) parts of their life are (e.g., job, family, sports).

For the past "family story," we typically ask the family to select six months or a period of time that is meaningful to the family (i.e., coinciding with a key life event likely linked to the problem, such as a divorce or death). It is often helpful when working with younger children to use concrete timeframes (e.g., start of school, a birthday), rather than abstract time references such as six months. It is helpful to ask the family questions about the changing influence of the problem and to link this to the unique outcomes (actions they take against the problem) and unique accounts (what meaning the family makes of these actions and/or what this says to the family members about the unique possibilities that arise from taking these actions). It is especially important to explore the anticipated influence the problem may have on the future family narrative/story. This activity can be done as a family (collaboratively on several larger pieces of paper) or as individual family members using three pieces of paper each.

The therapist then facilitates a therapeutic conversation related to the changing family story. This discourse is not scripted, but typically begins by asking questions such as, "Did you notice that the problem seems to get bigger/smaller?" and "How do you, your friends, your family and your teacher like it when the problem hangs around?" or "How do they like it when the problem is around less, or not at all?" For a description of a similar use of drawings to depict the relative influence of the problem see Perry's (1998).

Alternate Activity

Invite family members to use a sandtray to tell the story of how "the problem" influences their family/family story. It is also possible to invite the family to co-create this story by creating a sandtray together. We make sandtrays available to the family and assortment of symbolic toys and materials to be used as "props" in their stories. In our experience, children need little prompting to play out a story using a sandtray, as they are quite familiar with playing in the sand. However, we have found it helpful to explain the rationale for play-based activities, such as sandtray, to older siblings and parents, who may be less comfortable with engaging spontaneously in this medium. Specifically, we explain that sandtray is a helpful medium to allow young children to share narratives/stories about the problem's influence on the family; a concept which would otherwise be abstract in nature and outside of their developmental "comfort zone." For additional reading on sandtray or sandplay therapy, we refer you to a number of excellent resources

(Boisk & Goodwin, 2000; Homeyer & Sweeney, 2011; McNally, 2001). Freeman and colleagues (1997) also do an excellent job of demonstrating how to integrate sandtray work with children and families into narrative therapy.

Requirements and Recruitment of the Problem

This phase of narrative play therapy explores what conditions are needed for the problem to exist and explores how the problem gained influence within the family story. In our experience, it is helpful to explore with the family what event(s), relationship dynamics, and/or contextual factors may have contributed to the problem's influence within the family story. Remember that in our experience it is not uncommon for the problem to receive its power/influence over the family story from broader socio-cultural factors (e.g., racism being linked to bullying or unrealistic media messages regarding beauty and weight being linked to disordered eating patterns/eating disorders). It is important for narrative play therapists to explore the sources of the problem's power/influence within the family system and the broader context (e.g., school environment, community context, and socio-political environment).

Example Play-Based Activity

We typically explore requirements and recruitment during the previous activity, when families share their narrative about the changing influence of the problem in the past, present, and future. In particular, we listen to the family's story and ask, "How did the problem decide to visit the family?" or "What invitations were sent to the problem?" or "What makes the problem comfortable or uncomfortable, happy, or unhappy" or "What make the problem feel more or less powerful" or "Does the family or people at school or in the community do anything that helps the problem or gives it power?" or "Does anyone in the family or at school do anything that makes the problem less powerful?"

Taking a Position

This stage of therapy examines the metaphorical crossroads within the family story to highlight and amplify the point where the family decided to take a stand against the problem and pursues alternate or preferred narratives. This sets the stage for the thinning of the problem saturated storyline/plot (i.e., dominant oppressive narrative) and thickening of the counterplot (i.e., the alternate/preferred narrative) (Freedman et al., 1997). At this point in our exploration of the family narrative, we work to solidify who is a member of the "support team" and is working in support of the preferred narrative and against the dominance of the problem. In many cases, where the child was the "identified problem," we work with the family to determine who is "with the child" and who is "with the problem." In our experience, when we or the family are unclear about why the support team is committed to taking a stand against the problem, it is difficult to develop the alternate or preferred story in the upcoming phases of narrative play therapy. See Morgan (2000) for further insights regarding the important role of support teams.

Example Play-Based Activity

We have experienced success organizing formal support teams that include real life "heroes" and/or individuals important to the family who also have know-how and skills to help support the family solidify their preferred narrative. Typically, we work with the family to identify and invite as many "heroes" onto the support team as possible. Support team members typically include family members, teachers, peers, pets/animals, other helping professionals (i.e., pediatrician, psychiatrist, religious professionals), and occasionally young people and/or families who have experienced similar problems. Together with the family, we send invitations in the form of letters, emails, phone calls, or personal invitations outlining the nature of the mission. Collaboratively organizing the support team with members of the family to support the family against the problem is an important step that will be used through the reconstruction process including the "unique circulation" phase.

We have also experienced success organizing support teams comprised of members who are meaningful to the young person or family but may not be available to directly participate in the team events/activities. This part of the team includes, for example, members of the family who may have passed away, persons not known to family but respected for their character or skill (e.g., historic figures of importance to the family's culture), or imaginary characters (e.g., characters from books, films, television, or the imagination of the child or family member) who have demonstrated qualities that resonate amongst the family in their mission again the problem. In our experience, the skills and know-how and support that are gained through these "make-believe support teams" can rival the actual support provided from the "real support teams." Incidentally, we use the term "make-believe" rather than pretend or fantasy as this term has a more positive connotation, is familiar to young children, and is consistent with the play-based therapeutic environment. Furthermore, young people and families have often reported that in drawing from the strengths of these "make-believe" teams has helped to make them believe in the abilities and skills within themselves and their families long buried by the influence of the problem.

We invite the "support team" to adopt a meaningful team metaphor, such as detectives or crime fighting teams that are working to uncover clues about the problem and find evidence of sparkling moments (Morgan, 2000). We encourage families who engage in this process to meet regularly with their "teams" outside of therapy sessions in order to keep on the case. For additional ways of engaging families in this manner we refer you to a resource outlining one family's quest to take back their lives from worry/fear, documented in an article by McLuckie (2005). During "support team meetings" held during therapy sessions we explore the statement of position of team members by asking questions such as, "What happened that you got tired of the problem (use the problem's name when possible) always being the boss/making all the rules?" or "Who is on your side against the problem?" and "How come they are on your side?"

RE-CONSTRUCTION PHASE

Unique Outcomes

This phase of therapy represents the thickening of the alternate or preferred family narrative. The central goal of this phase (and through the therapeutic process with families) is to identify sparkling moments or times that the child, parent, siblings, family, or teacher engaged in actions less influenced by the problem (or actions not influenced by the problem). In particular, we explore the actions and behaviors that challenge the problem saturated narrative. Freedman and Combs (1996) and others describe such actions as falling on the landscape of action, which is one of two landscapes believed to underpin narratives; the other being the landscape of consciousness (inner knowledge typically explored in the next phase of therapy: unique account) (Bruner, 2004).

In our experience, it is not enough to validate the ability of the child or family to engage in actions against the problem. We believe that for the child and/or family to weave this skill into a lasting narrative (i.e., alternate or preferred narrative) we must work to link this ability across time into a story about who the child/family is. The therapist must support the stability of these moments in the child/family story by eliciting what knowledge and skills were engaged by the entire team that allowed this moment to surface. By challenging the child and family in this manner, the process of creating these unique outcomes becomes integral to the child/family wielding lasting influence on the dominant oppressive narrative. For a helpful discussion of ways to discover and explore unique outcomes and sparkling moments we refer you to Morgan (2000).

Example Play-Based Activity

We have had success engaging with young children and families in playful conversations about "superheroes" and "villains" in order to uncover knowledge about the "sources of power" that are drawn upon by family members, as well as by the problem. We begin by identifying the heroes (real and make-believe) in the lives of young people (which will be useful in the next phase examining the statement of position), along with the super-powers (i.e., strengths) these people have. We also explore times in which a family member has been heroic (which will be helpful again during a subsequent phase where we identify unique outcomes). Freedman and colleagues (1997) indicate that heroic elements are often present in children's narratives when the alternate story emerges. For additional information on the use of the superhero metaphor in counseling, please refer to Rubin (2007).

Our focus at this stage is to identify the power that the "villain" (i.e., the problem) has, where this power originates, and how it is sustained. In our experience, children engage quickly with this concept as many of their superhero stories include superheroes or villains who gain or lose powers. To explore this concept, we invite young children and family members to role play either their heroes or the villains within the family story. We utilize masks created by the family (i.e., masks of the "hero" or "villain" persona) from paper plates. We then facilitate a therapeutic conversation with the family asking questions such as, "How has the problem been tricking its way into your family?" or "What powers do you have (speaking directly to the problem being role played by a family member)" or "What powers does the problem have?" or "As detectives, what clues did you find about the mystery of the problem?" or "Can you tell me about times you were the boss over the problem?" or "Can you tell me about times that you out-smarted/tricked the problem?" or "Can you tell me about times that you/your family were able to take away the problem's powers?"

Alternate Activity

Building on the popularity of card games such as *Yugio,* we have also had success working with children and families using similar cards created by the family. Specifically, we invite family members to create cards for the heroes and villains within their family story to identify the strength/powers and sources of strength. We use these cards with the family to "play out" strategies to overcome the power of the "villainous" problem.

Unique Account and Unique Possibilities

This stage of therapy explores how the child and family account for the actions or behaviors (typically explored in the unique outcomes stage of therapy) that run contrary to the problem-dominated story and consistent with the preferred narrative. Simply stated, this stage explores what it is about the child and family that made the actions, explored in the previous stage, possible. In this stage, we seek to understand how the child was able to engage in the actions/behaviors, including what knowledge they were able to access in order for these actions to occur. Freedman and Combs (1997) refer to this knowledge or know-how as being located on the landscape of consciousness.

In our experience, therapists will explore unique outcome, unique account, and unique possibilities in an integrated manner. We have separated them here as distinct therapeutic phases to amplify the importance of exploring this landscape. In our experience, focusing only on the actions/behaviors and failing to explore and thicken the "know-how" of the family vis-à-vis the problem can make it difficult for the preferred narrative to gaining traction within the family narrative. Without tapping into the family's know-how, action by itself does not seem to result in a significant or lasting change to the family narrative or their relationship with the problem. By threading together the actions and knowledge that enable the child and family to challenge the influence of the problem, they seem most likely to weave a new lasting preferred narrative.

In order to thicken up the unique account, we also examine the unique redescription and unique possibilities associated with the child and family's actions. Unique redescription refers to what the child and/or family believe or think about themselves that allowed for the action/behavior to occur (i.e., unique outcomes). Unique possibilities refers to what future possibilities are available to the child and/or family through these new ways of thinking and acting against the problem. Inviting a future outlook for the family helps to promote a sense of hope and enables the child and/or family to live the belief that they have the power to establish a new story.

Example Play-Based Activity

We explore the unique accounts which the child and family provide for their "heroic" actions while examining the unique outcomes. We explore these unique accounts by asking questions such as, "How were you able to do X, Y, Z (i.e., whatever action the child/family did to stand up to the problem)?" or "How did you figure out that you could trick/outsmart the problem (use the name of the problem) in this way?" or "What were the most important clues to figuring out the mystery of the problem (use the name of the problem)?" In our experience, with young children it is also important to ask questions about their character and their internal know-how that made it possible to take specific actions. For example, we often ask children, "What does your ability to do X, Y, Z (i.e., whatever action the child did to stand against the problem) say about you?" As this question is quite abstract and complex, we often offer options for the child including, "Do you think it means that you are brave (use a descriptor that best fits the situation)?" Often children will pick from a list of descriptors the characteristic that best suits them relative to their action. It is also important to explore how the child and family's know-how and skill will change their future story if they continue on this path. For example, we ask questions such as, "If you had a crystal ball and could see into the future what would your future be like if you keep doing X, Y, Z? (i.e., whatever action the child/family did to stand against the problem)" or "If you keep tricking the problem by doing X,Y, Z how will this help you in your family, class, with friends?" or "When you grow up what will the problem (use the name of the problem) be doing?" Focusing on the future in this manner helps to thicken up the child or family's alternate or preferred story.

Alternate Activity

We have also had good outcomes using role plays to tap into the child's and family's unique know-how by inviting them to engage in role plays with the problem. In our experience, inviting the child and family to engage in non-competitive and non-confrontational role plays with the problem (paper-bag puppets) can be helpful to understand and thicken the know-how of the child and family regarding the problem and their resources to overcome the problem. For example, we have invited children and families to be teachers and teach the problem things that it needs to stop being a problem. Although this may sound counterintuitive by sharing ideas with the problem, this is only an issue if the stage has been set for the child/family to "battle" against the problem or to "compete" with the problem. Through engaging in an "education" session with the problem, the young person and family are able to access a wealth of knowledge and engage in a dynamic process provide a means for the problem to subside. See White (2006) for a fuller discussion of the various metaphors that can inform the exploration of the child and family narrative.

Throughout such role plays we will ask questions such as, "What does the problem (use the name of the problem) need to learn about you/your family to cause less difficulties?" or "What does the problem not know yet about you/your family that it keeps causing difficulties?" or "What will happen in the future if the problem learns these things?"

Unique Circulation

This phase of therapy represents the culmination of the preceding steps and of the reconstruction of the family's narrative. Although narrative play therapy is not a linear process and its separation into distinct phases (done so in this chapter to demonstrate the aspects of the model) is somewhat artificial, the ending phase of therapy typically ends with circulating the family's new (or rediscovered) story. This phase of therapy is not merely a passive termination process whereby the therapist and family reviews the work accomplished. In our experience, this phase is essential to solidify the new story for individual family members and for the family.

Circulating the news of this new non-problem dominated story (i.e., preferred narrative) moves the change beyond the confines of the therapeutic relationship, and even the family system, spreading the news of the changed story throughout the support team and throughout the many facets of the family members' lives. Spreading the news in this manner exemplifies the social constructionist orientation to this work, as narrative play therapists believe that the family's preferred narrative becomes more real with each telling and re-telling. Spreading the news of this new story can be done through the use of ceremonies and letters that recognize the skill and know-how of the child and family, but also bring together an audience to witness the change, which helps make the change real.

Example Play-Based Activities

Building on the prior activity that identified the child and family's support team (see the Taking a Position phase above), we have experienced success activating the support team members to function as witnesses to celebrate and solidify the child and family's new story. As the preferred narrative becomes prominent within the stories and accounts shared during therapy sessions, we invite the child and family to reflect on what ceremonies or rituals would best honor their process and help "spread the news of their new story." In our experience, children and families are open to holding ceremonies during the final therapy session as well as at home. We identify a guest list to see who the family would like to invite to this final ceremony, which typically consists of members of the support team (e.g., extended family members, peers, and teachers). We facilitate this invitation in collaboration with the young person and family, sending out invitations detailing the reason for the ceremony. For those individuals who are unable to attend the ceremony, we request that they forward a letter of commendation to be read at the ceremony. Specifically, we ask members of the support team to share what skills and knowledge they have witnessed from the child and/or family consistent with a new non-problem oriented story. We also invite these individuals to reflect on what these demonstrated skills and knowledge may mean to the family's new story in the future. In our experience, the participation of support team members and/or their letters are very meaningful to the child and family, especially as a source of validation that others have faith in them and have noticed the emergence of this new story.

During the actually ceremony, which is typically the final therapy session, we invite the family members to bestow awards on other families, recognizing their skill, know-how and support to stand-up to the problem. We provide a series of awards and cards from which young people and family members can select in preparation for this session. We also ask family members to make speeches or share what was most important to them in their journey. At this time, the child and family members are invited to share meaningful play-based activities with the audience, including showing art work or creations (e.g., puppets). We encourage families to engage in play-based activities, such as a puppet show if helpful, to demonstrate their skills and know-how. Having an audience, including the therapist and support team members, can be very beneficial to thicken up this preferred narrative. We invite the child and family to take home the art or materials created during the therapy sessions and encourage them to continue utilizing these techniques at home (e.g., home-based support team meetings can continue to include puppets).

As therapists, we also facilitate the ceremony in an unscripted manner asking questions designed to thicken and circulate the preferred narrative including, "Who would have known that you could stop the problem?" or "Who will be the first to notice that you could stop the problem (use the name of the problem)?" or "Who would have known that you could do X, Y, Z (whatever action the child/family member did to stand against the problem)?" or "Who would have NOT been surprised that you could stop the problem (use the name of the problem)?" or "What does (name of support team member) know about you or your family that makes them believe you can do it?"

We also provide each family member with a certificate and a personalized card or letter detailing the journey of the family to bring forth a preferred story highlighting the skills and know-how witnessed. This correspondence makes specific reference to play-based activities engaged during the therapy session (e.g., the use of puppets to discover the problem's tricks) and offers reflections about how the family will continue to solidify this preferred narrative into the future. We also invite the child and family to leave a message for other young people and families in the "message book of hope." This book allows young people and families to share anonymous messages of hope and encouragement to families dealing with similar challenges and further broadens the concept of support teams. Please refer to Morgan (2006; 2000) for additional ideas related to creating audiences for the family's preferred story and to Morgan and Freeman and colleagues (1997) for ideas related to certificates, letters, and ceremonies. Novy (2002) also provides further insight into the use of audience as a therapeutic tool in describing her

Biography Laboratory Project. Other play therapists including Lowenstein (1999) also value the use of certificates and letters and offer examples of their therapeutic use.

In conclusion, this chapter explored our conceptualization of narrative play therapy, including the underlying theories, key principles, and therapeutic processes of the model. Consistent with our belief in a postmodern reality, we do not suggest that this is the only effective way to do narrative play therapy. Rather, our work builds on the clinical experience and literature of writers and practitioners in the fields of narrative therapy, play therapy, and family therapy. Furthermore, our work builds upon what we have learned through our collaborations with children and families who have consulted with us in therapy. We are particularly appreciative of others who have contributed to the dialogue pertaining to narrative therapy practice with children and families and those practicing narrative play therapy. Our intention in writing this chapter is to share our experiences with narrative play therapy and hopefully scaffold the learning of other therapists seeking new ways of working with children and families. In summary, we invite you, the reader, to be a part of this conversation and join a growing community of helping professionals interested in hope-based, non-problem orientated ways of collaborating with young children and their families to make meaning, challenge oppressive forces in society, and create space for new possibilities.

REFERENCES

American Psychiatric Association [APA]. (2000). *Diagnostic and statistical manual of mental disorders (4th ed. revised)*. Washington, DC: American Psychiatric Association.

Arad, D. (2004). If your mother were an animal, what animal would she be? Creating play-stories in family therapy: The animal attribution story-telling technique (AASTT). *Family Process, 43*(2), 249-263.

Axline, V.M. (1969). *Play therapy*. New York, NY: Ballantine Books.

Boisk, B.L., & Goodwin, A. (2000). *Sandplay therapy: A step-by-step manual for psychotherapists of diverse orientations*. New York (NY): W.W. Norton.

Bronfenbrenner, U. (1979). *The ecology of human development*. Cambridge, MA: Harvard University Press.

Brown, C. (2007). Situating knowledge and power in the therapeutic alliance. In C. Brown & T. Augusta-Scott (Eds.), *Narrative therapy: Making meaning, making lives* (pp. 3-22). Thousand Oaks, CA: Sage Publications.

Brown, C., & Augusta-Scott, T. (Eds.). (2007). Introduction: Postmoderism, reflexivity, and narrative therapy. In C. Brown & T. Augusta-Scott (Eds.), *Narrative therapy: Making meaning, making lives* (pp. 9-47). Thousand Oaks, CA: Sage Publications.

Brown, J. (2007). Circular questioning: An introductory guide. *Australian and New Zealand Family Therapy, 18*(2), 109-114.

Bruner, J. (2004). Life as narrative. *Social Research, 71*(3), 691-710.

Cattanach, A. (Ed.). (2002). *The story so far: Play therapy narratives*. London, UK: Jessica Kingsley Publishers.

Cattanach, A. (2006). Narrative play therapy: A collaborative approach. In C. Schaefer & H. G. Kaduson (Eds.), *Contemporary play therapy: Theory, research and practice* (pp. 82-99). New York, NY: The Guildford Press.

Cattanach, A. (2008). *Narrative approaches in play with children.* London, UK: Jessica Kingsley Publishers.

de Saussure, F. (1974). *Course in general linguistics* (W. Baskin Trans.). London, UK: Fontana/Collins.

Emde, R.N. (2007). Engaging imagination and the future: Frontiers for clinical work. *Attachment & Human Development, 9*(3), 295-302.

Freeman, J., Epston, D., & Lobovits, D. (1997). *Playful approaches to serious problems: Narrative therapy with children and their families.* New York, NY: W.W. Norton & Company.

Freedman, J., & Combs, G. (1996). *Narrative therapy: The social construction of preferred realities.* New York, NY: W.W. Norton & Company.

Freud, A. (1969). *The psychoanalytical treatment of children: Lectures and essays.* New York, NY: Schocken Books.

Geertz, C. (1973). Thick description: Toward an interpretive theory of culture. *The interpretation of cultures* (pp. 3-30). New York, NY: Basic Books.

Gil, E. (1994). *Play in family therapy.* New York, NY: The Guilford Press.

Guerney, L. (1983). Introduction to filial therapy. In P. Keller & L. Ritt (Eds.), *Innovations in clinical practice: A sourcebook, vol. 2* (pp. 26-39). Sarasota, FL: Professional Resource Exchange.

Gurman, A.S., & Messer, S.B. (Eds.). (2003). *Essential psychotherapies.* New York, NY: The Guilford Press.

Hall, T. M., Kaduson, H.G., & Schaefer, C.E. (2002). Fifteen effective play therapy techniques. *Professional Psychology: Research and Practice, 33*(6), 515-522.

Hartman, A. (1995). Diagrammatic assessment of family relationships. *Families in Society, 76,* 111-122.

Homeyer, L.E., & Sweeney, D.S. (2011). *Sandtray therapy: A practical manual (2nd ed.).* New York, NY: Routledge, Taylor & Francis Group.

Hug-Hellmuth, H. (1921). On the technique of child analysis. *International Journal of Psychoanalysis, 2,* 287-305.

Jennings, S. (1999). *Introduction to developmental playtherapy.* London, UK: Jessica Kingsley Publishers.

Jordan, C., & Hickerson, J. (2003). Children and adolescents. In C. Jordan & C. Franklin (Eds.), *Clinical assessment for social workers (2nd ed.)* (pp. 179-213). Chicago, Il: Lyceum Books Inc.

Kaduson, H., & Schaefer, C. (Eds.). (1997). *101 favorite play therapy techniques.* Northvale, NJ: Jason Aronson.

Kaslow, N.J., Dausch, B.M., & Celano, M. (2003). Family therapies. In A.S. Gurman & S.B. Messer (Eds.), *Essential psychotherapies: Theory and practice (2nd ed.)* (pp. 400-462). New York, NY: The Guilford Press.

Kerr, N. (2010). My family as animals. In L. Lowenstein (Ed.), *Creative family therapy techniques* (pp.50-51). Toronto, ON: Champion Press.

Klein, M. (1953). The psychoanalytic play technique. *American Journal of Orthopsychiatry, 25,* 223-237.

Landreth, G.L. (1991). *Play therapy: The art of the relationship.* Bristol, PA: Accelerated Development.

Landreth, G.L. (2001). *Innovations in play therapy: Issues, process, and special populations.* Philadelphia, PA: Brunner-Routledge.

Lowenstein, L. (1999). *Creative interventions for troubled children & youth.* Toronto, ON: Champion Press.

Lowenstein, L. (2002). *More creative interventions for troubled children & youth.* Toronto, ON: Champion Press.

Lowenstein, L. (Ed.) (2010). *Creative family therapy techniques.* Toronto, ON: Champion Press.

McLuckie, A. (August, 2002). Narrative play therapy: Rediscovering our hidden heroes. Oral presentation for the *Summer Play Therapy Institute—The International Society for Child and Play Therapy*, Kingston, ON.

McLuckie, A. (2005). Narrative family therapy for pediatric obsessive-compulsive disorder. *Journal of Family Psychotherapy, 16*(4), 83-106.

Morgan, A. (2000). *What is narrative therapy?* Adelaide, South Australia: Dulwich Centre Publications.

Morgan, A. (2006). Creating audiences for children's preferred stories. In M. White & A. Morgan (Eds.), *Narrative therapy with children and their families* (pp. 99-119). Adelaide, South Australia: Dulwich Centre Publications.

Novy, C. (2002). The biography laboratory: Co-creating in community. In A. Cattanach (Ed.), *The story so far: Play therapy narratives* (pp. 209-229). London: Jessica Kingsley Publishers.

Oaklander, V. (1988). *Windows to our children.* Highland, NY: The Gestalt Journal Press.

Perkins McNally, S. (2001). *Sandplay: A sourcebook for play therapists*. Lincoln, NE: Writers Club Press.

Perry, L. (1998). Sarah-Jane's story. In C. White & D. Denborough *(Eds.), Introducing narrative therapy* (pp. 77-88). Adelaide, South Australia: Dulwich Centre Publications.

Piaget, J. (1954). *The construction of reality in the child.* New York, NY: Ballantine Books.

Piaget, J. (1969). *The mechanisms of perception*. New York, NY: Basic Books.

Poulter, J. (2005). Integrating theory and practice: A new heuristic paradigm for social work practice. *Australian Social Work, 58*(2), 199-212.

Rogers, C.R. (1989). *On becoming a person: A therapist's view of psychotherapy.* New York, NY: Houghton Mifflin Company.

Rubin, L.C. (2007). *Using superheroes in counselling and play therapy.* New York, NY: Singer Publishing Company.

Schaefer, C.E., & Carey, L. (1994). *Family play therapy*. New York, NY: Aronson.

Taylor de Faoite, A. (Ed.). (2011). The theory of narrative play therapy. In *Narrative play therapy: Theory and practice*, (pp. 26-49). London, UK: Jessica Kingsley Publishers.

Turner, B.A. (2005). *The handbook of sandplay therapy.* Cloverdale, CA: Temenos Press.

Vygotsky, L.S. (1962). *Thought and language*. Cambridge, MA: MIT Press.

Vygotsky, L.S. (1967). Play and its role in the mental development of the child. *Soviet Psychology, 5*(3), 6-18.

Vygotsky, L.S. (1978). *Mind in society: The development of higher psychological processes*. Cambridge, MA: Harvard University Press.

Vygotsky, L.S. (1986) [translation newly revised and edited by Alex Kozulin]. *Thought and language.* London, UK: The MIT Press.

White, C. (2006). Narrative practice with families with children: Externalising conversations revisited. In M. White & A. Morgan *(Eds.), Narrative therapy with children and their families* (pp. 1-56). Adelaide, South Australia: Dulwich Centre Publications.

White, C., & Denborough, D. (1998). *Introducing narrative therapy: A collection of practice-based writings.* Adelaide, South Australia: Dulwich Centre Publications.

White, M. (1997). *Narratives of therapists' lives.* Adelaide, South Australia: Dulwich Centre Publications.

White, M., & Epston, E. (1990). *Narrative means to therapeutic ends.* New York, NY: Norton.

White, M., & Morgan, A. (2006). *Narrative therapy with children and their families.* Adelaide, Australia: Dulwich Centre Publications.

Winnicott, D.W. (1971). *Playing and reality.* New York, NY: Basic Books.

Young, K. (2008). Narrative practice at a walk-in therapy clinic: Developing children's worry wisdom. *Journal of Systemic Therapies, 27*(4), 54-74.

Chapter Six

Filial Therapy and Theraplay

Evangeline Munns

INTRODUCTION

Filial and Theraplay are two models of play therapy whose prime purpose is to enhance the healthy attachments between parents and their children. These models are opposite in technique (Filial is nondirective and Theraplay is directive), but both have some similar core beliefs: that the child has the potential to grow and heal itself and should feel valued, accepted, respected, and cared for.

FILIAL THERAPY

Filial play therapy originated in the late 1950s and early 1960s by the founders Drs. Bernard and Louise Guerney, who were both clinical psychologists (Guerney, 1977) that were strongly influenced by the client centered approach of Carl Rogers. They adapted Virginia Axline's (1969) nondirective play therapy methods to training parents in this approach and called it Filial. Today it is practiced around the world with increasing empirical findings to support it (Bratton, Ray, Rhine, & Jones, 2005; VanFleet, Ryan, & Smith, 2005). This research has shown some of the following results: improvement in child behavior and social-emotional growth, in parenting skills, in parental empathy, in lowering parental stress and in enhancing parent/child relationships (Dillman, Taylor, Purswell, Lindo, Jayne, & Fernando, 2011).

Filial therapy is essentially a form of family therapy that uses play as its main means of establishing parent/child connections. It is a psych-educative model where parents learn to play with their children in an attuned, empathic, accepting, nonjudgmental way that helps their children to express their conflicts, fears, wishes, and creative solutions to some of their most troubling issues. Play is the language of the child. Children learn about their world and some of its limitations through play in their own unique way. (Landreth, 2002; Sweeny & Landreth, 2011).

In Filial, parents are the primary agents of change. Reasons for involving parents include the following: parents usually know their children intimately; they are the most important people in their children's lives; they already have a relationship with their child that Filial builds on, so the child does not have to form a new relationship with the therapist; parents gain a new understanding of their child that they can apply after treatment ends and they can extend these new skills to other children (siblings) in the family; Filial strengthens parent/child relationships and finally, Filial provides an avenue where parents and child can have fun with each other. Laughter can heal.

Two of the most recognized Filial adaptations are: Child-Parent Relationship Therapy (CPRT) developed by Drs. Landreth and Bratton (Landreth & Bratton, 2006) and Filial therapy developed by Dr. VanFleet (VanFleet, 2003, 2011). These clinicians were originally taught by the Guerneys so their methods are similar. Bratton and Landreth's program is shorter while VanFleet sometimes includes Filial sessions with all of the children in the family besides the targeted child (VanFleet, 2011). In the present chapter, Vanfleet's model has been emphasized.

Filial is considered a short-term treatment method usually requiring ten to twenty sessions. However, when there are more severe parent/child difficulties, additional sessions are often required and/or other treatment methods are sometimes used. For example, this may happen when Filial is extended to a more seriously dysfunctional population such as those suffering from trauma and/or reactive attachment disorder (Vanfleet, 2011).

Filial has been used for a wide range of social, emotional, and behavioral problems (both internalizing and externalizing disorders), as well as children on the autism spectrum, those with attachment difficulties, self-regulation disorders, and those coming from homes where there is domestic violence and substance abuse (VanFleet, 2011). Filial has also been modified in its application to a wider age range including adolescents (Ginsberg, 1977).

Phases

After first assessing the family and gaining an in-depth family, developmental, and social history of the child, there are five phases: (1) play therapy demonstration by the therapist, (2) training of the parents, (3) supervised parent/child play sessions, (4) home play sessions, (5) ending.

1. *Play Therapy Demonstration*

   While the parents observe, the therapist conducts a play session with their child, following Axline's nondirective method (Axline, 1969) including letting the child lead, reflecting its feelings, supporting and accepting the child without judgment, and setting limits if necessary.

2. *Training Phase*

   The parent is guided in the selection of toys and learns the following four main play therapy skills:

   - *Structuring:* What to say to the child when starting and ending each play session. For example at the beginning of the session the therapist might say: "This is our special play room and in here you can play with any of the toys in most of the ways you would want to." Toward the end of the half hour play session the therapist might say: "In five minutes our play time will be ended." At the end, a second warning is given. The therapist might say: "Johnny our session will end in one minute." At the very end the therapist might say in a pleasant, but firm voice: "Johnny our play session is ended for today."
   - *Empathic Listening*: The adult pays full attention to what the child is expressing in the play while letting the child lead the play. Use of tracking and reflection of feelings helps the child to feel understood.
   - *Child-Centered Imaginary Play*: How to respond and/or join in when the child invites you into a make-believe role.
   - *Limit Setting*: How to set limits and enforce consequences using a three-step approach.

3. *Supervised Parent/Child (Filial) Play Sessions*

   The parent practices the above four skills with the therapist playing the role of the child, while the parent practices being the therapist. The therapist frequently praises the parent for his/her efforts during these practice sessions and focuses on what the parent did right rather than wrong. When the therapist feels the parent has learned the four skills, the parent then practices playing with his/her child for fifteen to twenty minutes while the therapist observes without participating or interrupting. After each play session, the therapist gives feedback to the parent concentrating first on the play therapy skills and later, on the interpretation of the child's play including exploring possible themes that might be revealed in the child's play.

   Later on, the feedback also includes a check on the child's progress at home and school. The therapist usually supervises five to six sessions before the next phase.

4. *Home Play Sessions*

   At the beginning of this phase, one session is held to plan the play sessions at home such as time, best location, selection and use of toys, handling of interruptions, etc.

   The parent holds the special play sessions at home once a week for thirty minutes and records problems, successes, questions, and primary themes to be discussed later with the therapist. After one to two home play sessions, the parent meets with the therapist in her/his office to hold these discussions. After four to twelve home sessions, treatment usually comes to the end phase.
5. *Ending Phase*

   When the child's behavior has improved at home and school, the parent is encouraged to expand the use of play therapy skills (structuring, empathic listening, imaginary role playing and limit setting) to everyday situations. Parents are also encouraged to have special times with their children after treatment ends.

Group Format and its Modification

Filial can be used in a group format where six to eight parents typically meet for two hours each week over sixteen to twenty sessions. This can include single parents or couples (Guerney, 1980). The phases of treatment are similar to working with a single family with a few modifications. More time might be spent at the beginning with participants getting to know each other. For this purpose the present author has used group Theraplay games (Munns, 2009) such as "hello-thank you" activity where a person throws a bean bag to someone calling out their name first; "handstack"—placing hands in turn on top of another's hand as the stack of hands grows going up and then down; tossing balloons in the air without allowing them to touch the floor, etc. This helps the parents to become more comfortable and free-er with each other.

After the fun games described above, the leader explains the fundamentals of Filial, demos a mock play session with his/her co-leader and has the parents practice a mock play session with each other using the client-centered approach. The four skills of structuring, empathic listening, imaginary role play, and limit setting are each demoed and then practiced by the parents. Feedback is given by the leaders after each skill is taught and practiced. This training phase takes place over four to six sessions, followed by the home training phase. Here the parents are asked to hold a play therapy session with their child in their home and to video this and to bring the tape of this session to the Filial meeting. If a parent does not have a video camera, then the parent and child can come to the clinic or agency, where the therapist can observe them in a play session.

When parents meet again in a group, their videos of their home play sessions are viewed by the group and feedback is given, as well as discussion regarding possible themes emerging in the play. This takes place over several sessions so each parent can take a turn showing their video. This continues until the leaders feel the parents have gained sufficient mastery of the skills to continue home sessions. Parents are encouraged to extend their play skills and understanding of their child to everyday life. When their child's behavior has improved at home and school, the Filial sessions stop, but parents may continue special times such as baking together, taking bike rides or walks together, etc. where they can continue to enjoy each other and grow in their relationship.

Conclusion

Filial therapy is a model of play therapy where parents learn to interact with their children following a client-centered play approach. They become the main therapeutic agents of change in their children. In this process, parents and their children strengthen their relationship and attachment with each other (VanFleet, 2011). As well, not only does the behavior and emotional well-being of their child usually improve, but parents gain a new understanding of their child. They gain skills in responding with empathy and unconditional positive regard (Ginsburg, 2011) that they can apply in the future to all of their children for lasting family change.

THERAPLAY

History of Theraplay

The founder of Theraplay, Dr. Ann Jernberg, was a psychologist who was given a federal grant to improve the attachment between mothers and their children in the Head Start program in Chicago in the late 1960s (Jernberg, 1979). She established the Theraplay Institute in Chicago in 1971 which still serves as the international headquarters for Theraplay training today. Theraplay now is practiced around the world (Booth & Jernberg, 2010).

Philosophy

Theraplay is based mainly on attachment theory (Bowlby, 1988; Cassidy & Shaver, 2008). It is believed that the first relationship a child experiences forms the template for further relationships. If that relationship or attachment is not a secure one, then other relationships later in life are likely to be problematic (Karen, 1994; Zeanah, 1994; Fearon, Bakermans-Kranenburg, Ijzendoorm, Lapsley, & Roisman, 2010). Theraplay goes back to that first relationship and strives to make it a stronger, healthier one. Activities that are often used with younger children are incorporated in order to touch base with those first connections between a young child and its caretakers. Treatment is geared to the emotional age of the child, but as treatment progresses, more age appropriate activities are included. The emphasis in Theraplay is on replicating normal parent/child interactions (Munns, 2000, 2009, 2011a, 2011b).

Theraplay is not a verbal or interpretive type of therapy, but rather one where playful interactions and nurturing touch is emphasized. The focus is on the healthy, positive aspects of the child, which leads to heightened self-esteem and self-confidence. Bizarre behavior is ignored. No toys are used. Theraplay is short-term. The family is usually seen from twelve to eighteen sessions (or longer) once a week for one-half of an hour followed sometimes by one-half of an hour of parent counseling (Munns, 2000, 2009).

Theraplay is applicable to a wide age range—from very young children to the elderly (Munns, 2008; Munns, 2011a). It has made significant positive changes to many kinds of troubled children and their families: from the withdrawn, fearful child to the externalizing, aggressive child (Munns, 2009). It has been particularly effective with adoptive parents and their children (Lindamen & Lender, 2009). Research with randomly assigned control groups, has verified its effectiveness in reducing aggression (Munns, 2009, 2011b), enhancing attachment and in raising the self-esteem of clients (Siu, 2009; Meyer & Wardrop, 2009; Coleman, 2010).

Parents actively participate, first observing a few sessions, as the therapist models interactions with the child, and then with direct contact with their child under the therapist's guidance. Theraplay is characterized by being playful, physical, and fun.

Underlying Dimensions

After observing hundreds of interactions between normal children and their parents, Dr. Jernberg categorized them under four main dimensions (Jernberg & Booth, 1979; Booth & Jernberg, 2010):

Structure

Even with the very young child there is structure in the child's life. Routines such as feeding, nap, bathing, and play times are scheduled so there is a regularity and rhythm in the child's world giving it a sense of predictability and security. Parents are in charge, making decisions that a young child should not be expected to make. Rules are in place—the child can crawl around, but not touch the hot heater; the child can throw his soft toy, but not his glass of juice, etc. This helps the child to learn to control his impulses and to learn what is acceptable and what is not.

In Theraplay the therapist structures the session by leading the activities and by preplanning each activity according to the child's needs. Toward the end of treatment, more of the leading is given to the parents. There is a clear beginning and ending to each session. Rules such as "no hurts" help to establish a sense of safety in the session.

Children who are impulsive, acting out, disobedient, defiant, controlling, hyperactive, or distractible, are in need of structure in their lives, so in Theraplay this dimension is emphasized for them.

Challenge

At home the young child is usually challenged in a way that ensures his/her success. A toy is held within reach of the infant. Cushions help the baby to learn to sit up and hands are held of the toddler who is learning to walk and finally let go. Increasing challenges are given to the child as he/she grows older and with each success the child's self-confidence and self-esteem grows. The child learns that taking appropriate risks can be rewarding, empowering, and stimulating.

In treatment, challenges are given that the child can master. Through challenging tasks the child can gain a sense of competence and strength. Challenging activities are especially suitable for children who are fearful, timid, overanxious, withdrawn, dependent, or overprotected. These activities are also recommended for children with a lot of underlying tension or aggression as a way of releasing some of their feelings in acceptable ways.

Engagement

There are many enticing ways that a parent normally uses to engage his/her child bringing delight to both. For example, parents will use games such as "peek-a-boo," "patty-cake," "this little piggy went to market," etc., to playfully interact with their young child. Engagement often involves intruding into their child's world, but as long as this is done with sensitivity to their child's cues, the result is often pure enjoyment for everyone. The child becomes aware of himself in relation to another, learns about body boundaries, learns that surprises can be fun and learns that he can be a source of joy to others.

In Theraplay, the therapist engages the child in a variety of activities that are usually new and stimulating to him/her. The therapist strives to gain the child's interest and responsiveness. This is especially important for children who are withdrawn, rigid, avoidant, or who have high, protective barriers such as children with autism.

Nurture

This is the most important dimension of all, leading to the child's sense of self as someone who is loved, valued, important and worthy of care. Ideally parents cradle, rock, caress, hug, feed, bathe, and powder, etc., their child in a warm, affectionate manner and in a timely way so the child knows that his needs will be met. As well, they respond empathically to the child and try to calm and soothe the child when needed. Nurturing a child consistently helps the child to develop a sense of inner security and positive attachment to his/her caretakers.

In Theraplay, therapists first model nurturing care and then guide the parents in such activities. (Sometimes parents need to be nurtured as well.) Nurturing activities might include the following: powdering or lotioning hurts on the child's hands or feet, feeding of a favorite snack, rocking the child in a blanket while singing a special song about the child and feeding him/her a lollipop, freezie, or baby bottle, etc. Activities are suited to the emotional age of the child, which typically, is younger than his/her chronological age. Toward the end of treatment, activities are geared more to the chronological age of the child.

No hurts are allowed. If the child or parent accidently gets hurt then immediate attention is given to that hurt.

All children require nurturing touch (Field, 2000), but this is especially important for children who come from deprived or abusive backgrounds. Theraplay is used with children who have been traumatized through physical or sexual abuse, but it is modified so that the therapist is slower and more gentle in her approach to the child. If the child refuses to do an activity, this is respected, for these children must be empowered (James, 1994). An emphasis in treatment is placed on nurturing and self-esteem enhancing activities, but at a pace that is responsive to the child's cues. Desensitizing the child to touch, is important for such children (Ford, 1993; Hindman, 1991) but must be done carefully, so the child is not retraumatized.

Goals

The goals of Theraplay are to enhance positive attachments, and/or relationships, to increase trust and to heighten self-esteem and self-confidence of both child and parents, to help the child to regulate, and to increase parents' attunement to their child's cues and needs.

Theraplay is well suited for children where there are relationships or attachment issues such as those found with adoptive, foster or step-children, autistic disorders, etc.

Phases of Treatment

Overall, there are three phases of treatment in Theraplay.

Phase 1 Beginning

Exploration In the initial stage of Theraplay the therapist introduces him/herself to the child in a cheerful, but sensitive manner letting the child know that there will be a regular time and place where they will meet each week. The therapist playfully engages the child where they get to know each other. They may explore the size of their hands, the height of the child, how many freckles does the child have, the sparkle in his eyes, and his nice, rosy cheeks, etc. The therapist helps the child to become more aware of his physical self in a positive light.

Honeymoon The child tentatively accepts the therapist and initially goes along with the activities. At times the child can appear watchful and cautious, but also can show enjoyment and laughter. It appears as if the child is starting to trust the therapist and is becoming more comfortable with the activities. Both parents and therapist are happy things are going so well.

Phase 2 Middle

Negative Period The child starts to resist. The child wants to regain the control he is used to having in his life. This is especially true of children who have become tyrants in their own home. They are used to being "the boss." This may also be true of children who have a great need to control everything, because this is the way they have tried to make the world safe for themselves. The latter may be seen in children, who in their past, have been traumatized. The resistance may be passive where the child becomes limp, lies down, doesn't want to do anything, pouts, etc., or the child may be actively resistant by yelling, screaming, swearing, running around, crying, or becomes aggressive.

(At this point the parents might start getting alarmed fearing that their child is getting worse instead of better.) The therapist remains calm and tries to carry on with the activities. A child may, for example, try to change the rules of a game, so he can always win. When the adults remain firm about the rules, the child has a temper tantrum. The therapist gives the child a choice; he can join the game obeying the rules or he can sit out (in the same room) for a few minutes to calm down. When the adults are consistent about this, the tantrums tend to disappear fairly rapidly.

The length of the period of resistance varies, as does its intensity, with each child. Not every child goes through a negative stage. However, when it does happen, it is essential for the therapist to remain with the child giving him the feeling that no matter how his behavior escalates, he is still there for the child and accepting of him. Sometimes it seems the child is testing the therapist: "Will you still like me, even when I show you my worst part of me?" The therapist must always give the underlying message (often unspoken) that he still cares for the child.

Growing and Trusting Period The child becomes increasingly cooperative, maintains eye contact, seeks proximity to the therapist, smiles and laughs more often, obviously enjoying the activities. The parents, who have been observing up to this point, are now brought in for direct participation with their child. Sometimes when the parents come in, the child's old negative patterns emerge briefly, but soon usually disappear.

Progress continues with the child and his/her relationship with his parents. Both parents and child enjoy more intimacy and enjoyment of each other for longer periods of time. The child obeys his parents and is less defiant or the timid child has become more self-confident and outgoing. Parents and child appear to be much closer in a healthy way. Parents often report that their child's behavior has improved at school as well.

Phase 3 End

Termination When referral problems have disappeared or been substantially reduced, the therapist discusses termination of treatment. The child is told that there will be only several sessions left as he/she is doing so well. In the second to last session, the family is asked what favorite activities they would like to include in the last party session. Parents are asked to bring the child's favorite food and drink for the party. In this last session, after the Theraplay activities, participants may exchange party hats, food is eaten, a small present is given to the child, and the family's progress is celebrated. The first of four checkups is scheduled with the first checkup occurring a month or so later. The family is encouraged to continue the Theraplay activities at home (as they have been doing throughout treatment).

Case Studies

The following cases typify what can happen with two different kinds of children.

Case 1

Referring problem: Sally, a six-year-old girl, is withdrawn, passive, fearful, clings to her mother, has no friends, and is resistant to any change. She presents as a very insecure, anxious child. Although she shows some symptoms that are sometimes associated with children who have been abused, there is no known abuse in her history.

Phase 1 Beginning In the first phase of treatment, the therapist appealingly moves in, tries to draw her out, and gently entices her to play and to have some fun. She gradually complies and starts to enjoy herself. This is the honeymoon phase.

Phase 2 Middle The therapist continues to challenge Sally. They have thumb wrestling matches, paper punch activities, paper sword fights, cotton ball throws at each other, etc., all in an effort to have Sally become more assertive and to let go of some of her defenses so she can be more emotionally expressive. This almost works too well and Sally starts "talking back," becomes a little resistant, and "naughty." Parents express their apprehension that she seems to be getting worse instead of better. At the same time she is much more independent and self-assured. The therapist helps the parents become aware of her growing self-confidence.

Sally continues to "spread her wings," but she also wants the approval of the adults around her, so she has become more cooperative. She has formed a positive relationship with her therapist, who has remained supportive and accepting throughout her treatment. Sally looks forward to all of her sessions. Parents, who have been previously observing, now are brought in and gradually the responsibility of leading the activities is shifted to them. They are also encouraged to do Theraplay activities at home. Sally continues to become more outgoing and happier: she is less clinging at home and is able to take more risks. Parents are less overprotective.

Phase 3 End The termination of treatment is agreed upon with the parents as there appears to be a consolidation of Sally's gains: she is much more self-assured, more independent, more emotionally expressive, but appropriately so and is happier. About three sessions in advance, the child is told that Theraplay will end soon, because she is doing so well. A party is held in the last session that includes her favorite activities and snacks. A small gift is given to the child. Games are played where the positive attributes of the child can be talked about—i.e., everyone prints out something they like about Sally on small rectangular pieces of colored construction paper and with some masking tape, a chain necklace is quickly made, which Sally takes home as a memento of the Theraplay sessions. An appointment is made for the first of four checkups. A goodbye song is sung and the therapist walks the family to the door after hugs and handshakes with the promise of seeing them again in about one or two months' time for their first checkup. Knowing that he/she will see the therapist again helps the child with separation anxiety from the therapist.

In Sally's case, although she was much more confident and outgoing at home and school, she needed further help with making friends, so a socialization peer group was recommended.

Case 2

Referring problem: Johnny is an eight-year-old boy, who is continually in trouble at home, at school, and with his peers. He is aggressive, impulsive, disobedient, defiant, stubborn, controlling, and often feels alienated. He has no friends. His parents have lost patience with him and are often angry, resentful, and rejecting toward him. There is a physical and emotional distance between them.

Beginning Phase Johnny, in spite of his reputation, complies fairly well at the beginning of treatment. He is surprised that his "problems" are not talked about and instead the therapist, who is warm and welcoming, points out his positive physical features, lotions his "hurts," and gently cares for him. This is a change for him—an adult that seems to accept him and admire him. She is not critical or disapproving, even when he does not fully cooperate at times.

Middle Phase Johnny is used to being in control and has learned to get attention through negative behavior. He is accustomed to people viewing him as the "bad" child and he has identified with that image, which he is not about to relinquish. He starts to openly resist by turning away, sulking, becoming aggressive, or screams or cries. The parents become concerned that their child is not being helped. However, they are learning an important lesson as they watch the therapist stay with their child through his tantrums and help the child to comply. The therapist remains calm, cheerful, but persistent in what she wants the child to do. Johnny must learn to comply with the rules of the game or they don't play. He learns that no hurts are allowed and if there is a hurt then it is immediately cared for. If he has caused a hurt, then he is guided to help care for the hurt ie., gently rubbing around the hurt or putting lotion on it or a Band-Aid. This "restitution" of hurts leaves him with the feeling that he has helped to alleviate the harm he has caused to someone, so he is part of the solution and not only the problem.

A strong part of the therapy is to nurture Johnny. A child like Johnny often gets criticism and rejection rather than warm affection. He is taken back to a stage when he was a baby, where he wasn't getting into any trouble and he was accepted just as he was. This is recreated by activities such as rocking him in a blanket while singing a favorite lullaby, or cradling him in his parent's arms while feeding him a lollipop or bottle and singing a special song about him. This is an attempt to have parents and child connect again in a very basic, but positive way. For a short while he shows some regressive behavior such as sucking his thumb and reverting to baby talk. This regressive period is short lived lasting only a few weeks at most, but it is a turning point for Johnny and his parents. They start to see Johnny as the needy child he is and they are more accepting and less blaming. Through nurturing activities Johnny learns he is valued and cared for. He is given positive attention without any demands on his part.

Johnny gradually becomes more cooperative and less controlling as parents learn to be firm and consistent in their directives to him. There is more spontaneous affection between them. They start to enjoy each other and there is more eye contact and more smiles and laughter in their play together.

Johnny learns that he can be a source of delight with his parents instead of the constant "headaches" he was previously causing.

End Phase Johnny not only becomes more obedient at home, he is more cooperative at school as well. As he receives more praise than reprimands, his basic image of himself continues to become more positive. He is more aware of his strengths and is more motivated to please the adults in his life as he begins to more strongly identify with their values and standards. His inner controls improve. The parent/child relationship continues to become stronger and healthier. Termination is planned for with a party celebrating this positive growth. The first of four checkups is scheduled and the parents are encouraged to continue Theraplay activities at home.

CONCLUSION

Filial and Theraplay are increasingly recognized as two effective, evidence-based ways of enhancing parent/child attachments. Which method is most appropriate? Some families could benefit from both. The present author has found that in her experience, parents who are relatively healthy and free of their own personal issues, can be effectively treated through Filial. For more complex parents whose personal issues are more deep-seated and/or long standing, and whose children might be more acting out or aggressive, then Theraplay may be the treatment of choice

REFERENCES

Axline, V. M. (1969*) Play Therapy*. (Rev. Ed.). New York, NY: Ballentine Books.

Booth, P. & Jernberg, A. (2010). *Theraplay: Helping Parents and Children Build Better Relationships Through Attachment Based Play* (3rd Ed.) San Francisco, CA: Jossey Bass.

Bowlby, J. (1988). *A Secure Base, Parent-Child Attachment and Healthy Human Development*. New York, NY: Basic Books.

Bratton, S. C., Ray, D., Rhine, T., & Jones, L. (2005). The Efficacy of Play Therapy With Children: A Meta-analytic Review of Treatment Outcomes. *Professional Psychology: Research and Practice*, 36 (4), 376-390.

Cassidy J. & Shaver, P. (2008). *Handbook of Attachment*. New York, NY: The Guilford Press.

Coleman, R. (2010). Research Findings That Support the Effectiveness of Theraplay. In P. Booth & A. Jernberg. (Eds.) *Theraplay: Helping Parents and Children Build Better Relationships Through Attachment-Based Play* (3rd ed.), (pp. 85-97) San Francisco, CA: Jossey-Bass.

Dillman, D., Taylor, D., Purswell, K., Lindo, N., Jayne, K., & Fernando, D. (2011). The Impact of Child Parent Relationship Therapy on Child Behavior and Parent-Child Relationships: An Examination of Parental Divorce. *International Journal of Play Therapy*, 20(3), 124–137.

Fearon, R., Bakermans-Kranenburg, M., Ijzendoorn, M., Lapsley, A., & Roisman, G. (2010). The Significance of Insecure Attachment and Disorganization in the Development of Children's Externalizing Behavior: A Meta-Analytic Study. *Child Development, 81* (2), 435-456.

Field, T. (2000). *Touch Therapy*. New York: Churchill Livingstone.

Ford, C.W. (1993). *Compassionate Touch: The Role of Human Touch in Healing and Recovery*. New York: Simon and Schuste.
Ginsberg, B. (1977). Parent Adolescent Relationship Development Program. In B.G. Guerney (Ed.) *Relationship Enhancement*. San Francisco, CA: Jossey-Bass, Inc.
Ginsberg, B. (2011). Congruence in Nondirective Play and Filial therapy: Response to Ryan and Courtney. *International Journal of Play therapy*. 20(3), 109-123.
Guerney, L. (1977). Filial Therapy. In K.J. O'Conner & L.M. Braverman (Eds.), *Play therapy and Practice: A Comparative Presentation* (pp. 131-159). Somerset, NJ: Wiley.
Guerney, L. (1980). Filial Therapy. In R. Herink (Ed.) *The Psychotherapy Handbook*. (pp. 227-229). New York: the American Library, Inc.
Hindman, J. (1991). *The Mourning Breaks*. Oregon: Alexandria Associates.
James, B. (1994). *Handbook for the Treatment of Attachment-Trauma Related Problems in Children*. New York, NY: Lexington Books.
Jernberg, A. (1979). *Theraplay: A New Treatment Using Structured Play for Problem Children and Their Families*. San Francisco, CA: Jossey-Bass Publishers.
Jernberg, A. & Booth, P. (2010). *Theraplay: Helping Parents and Children Build Better Relationships Through Attachment Based Play* (3rd Ed.) San Francisco, CA: Jossey-Bass Publishers.
Karen, R. (1994). *Becoming Attached*. New York: Warner Books.
Landreth, G. (2002). *Play Therapy: the Art of the Relationship* (2nd Ed.). Philadelphia, PA: Brunner-Routledge.
Landreth, G. & Bratton, S. (2006). *Child-Parent Relationship Therapy: A 10 Session Filial Therapy Model*. New York, NY: Taylor and Francis.
Lindamen, S. & Lender, D. (2009) Theraplay with Adopted children. In E. Munns (Ed) Applications of Family and Group Theraplay. New York, NY: Jason Aronson.
Meyer, L. & Wardrop, J. (2009). Research on Theraplay Effectiveness. In E. Munns (Ed.), *Applications of Family and Group Theraplay* (pp. 17-24). Northvale, NJ: Jason Aronson.
Munns, E. (2000). *Theraplay: Innovations in Attachment-Enhancing Play Therapy*. Northvale, NJ: Jason Aronson Inc.
Munns, E. (2008) Theraplay With Zero to 3 Year Olds. In C. Schaefer, S. Kelly-Zion, J. McCormick & A. Ohnogi (Eds.) *Play Therapy for Very Young Children* (pp. 157-170), New York, NY: Jason Aronson.
Munns, E. (2009). *Applications of Family and Group Theraplay*. New York, NY: Jason Aronson.
Munns, E. (2011a). Integration of Child-Centered Play Therapy and Theraplay. In A. Drewes, S. Bratton, C. Schaefer. (Eds.) *Integrative Play Therapy* (pp. 325-340), Hoboken, NJ: John Wiley & Sons.
Munns, E. (2011b). Theraplay: Attachment Enhancing Play Therapy. In C. Schaefer (Ed.) *Foundations of Play Therapy* (2nd Ed). (pp. 275-296), Hoboken, NJ: John Wiley & Sons.
Munns, E. (2009). *Applications of Family and Group Theraplay*. Northvale, NJ: Aronson.
Sui, A. (2009). Theraplay in the Chinese World: An Intervention Program for Hong Kong Children with Internalizing Problems. International Journal of Play Therapy. Jan. 18(1), 1-12.
Sweeney, D. & Landreth, G. (2011). Child-Centered Play Therapy. In C.E. Schaefer (Ed.) *Foundations of Play Therapy*. (2nd Ed.) (pp. 129-152). Hoboken, NJ: Wiley.
VanFleet, R. (2011). Filial Therapy: Strengthening Family Relationships with the Power of Play. In C.E. Schaefer (Ed.) *Foundations of Play Therapy*. (2nd Ed.) (pp. 153-169) Hoboken, NJ: Wiley.
VanFleet, R. & Guerney, L. (Eds.). (2003). *Casebook of Filial Therapy*. Boiling Springs, PA: Play Therapy Press.
VanFleet, R. Ryan, S. & Smith, S. (2005). Filial Therapy: a Critical Review. In L. Reddy, T. Files-Hall, & C. Schaefer (Eds.) *Empirically based Play Interviews for children*. (pp. 241-264). Washington, DC: American Psychological Association.
Zeanah, C. (1994). Intergenerational transmission of relationship pathology: a mother-infant case study. Paper presented at the International Conference on Attachment and Psychopathology, Toronto, Ontario, September.

Chapter Seven

Working with Adoptive Families Using Sand, Water, Miniatures, and a Sandtray

Theresa Fraser

Theorists such as Bowen, Bronfenbrenner, Haley, Satir, Minuchin, and Whitaker taught clinicians who work with families that family therapy involves an understanding of the family system as a whole as well as an understanding of the parts that make the whole. Gaining insight into how the parts are connected and the processes that occur to develop or enhance this connectedness is the goal at both intake and treatment stage of intervention.

> The family emotional unit consists of living person related through marriage, birth, adoption and strong continuous attachment. In this view of family, there are no generational boundaries. The family emotional unit functions and adapts as a single interlocking set of relationships, guided by relationship forces which have automatic responses to threats and stresses.(Smith, 2001, p. 101)

When adoptive families are referred to my practice, my experience is that they are anything but a single interlocking set of relationships. Adoptions in Canada occur when a single person (or couple) adopt a baby, child, or youth internationally, privately, via a kin adoption, step-child adoption, or from a Canadian Child Welfare agency. The struggle to create a strong continuous attachment is the most common referring issue. Each family member comes to the process with systemic patterns of behavior; however, these patterns are often based on a history not shared because children may have had multiple parent figures and not necessary attachment figures including biological, kin, foster, and perhaps previous unsuccessful adoptive parents. These experiences may be compounded by stories with many missing words because the children were young when the stories were being constructed and there is no one around to fill in the blanks.

Traumatic experiences of abuse and neglect may have occurred even preverbally. What follows are that seemingly ordinary experiences trigger intense emotional reactions that adoptive parents may assume are current family system issues but in reality may be old stories or a mixture of old and new. This is a dynamic that can break down adoptive placements (Edwards, 2000).

Frances[1] grew up having to make meals for himself as well as meals for his siblings. His new adoptive parents sought his input in meal preparation. One morning one of his adoptive dads asked him what he wanted and then made toasted waffles. When the child was given the food, he exclaimed that is was "disgusting" because it wasn't toasted to his liking. His adoptive dad was hurt though later could recognize that this reaction was a defensive one from a child who is unable to receive acts of kindness with appreciation. Frances also would smell all food and closely check out plates which was a routine established after living in houses with lots of cockroaches and mice feces. Adoptive parents needed to be reminded of these early beginnings when they suspected that he was being mistrustful of their attempts to nurture him.

Each family member or subset of members (in the case of sibling adoption) may demonstrate different automatic responses to threats or stresses. For example, Jovan would become hypervigilent when a police siren could be heard. On a few occasions he would run into the house and hide in his room in case the "cops were coming." He experienced many episodes of being chased by police cars while driving with a drunken birth father. He also was prepared to hide under his bed in case police came in order to act on a warrant. Many sessions of play therapy occurred before Jovan ultimately began using police figures as protective factors for little children. His adoptive parents also arranged to have him attend a specially arranged police station tour and ultimate community open house.

The child's life script may be that they are undeserving, the cause of conflict, or unlovable and this script is in direct conflict to the new family's mantra which may be, "we are your family now." Chantal was caught taking her adoptive mom's laptop in her bedroom after everyone had gone to bed. She was caught and the laptop removed so she then began to pack her belongings as she felt that she would be "sent back" to the child welfare agency as this was her previous experience in foster care when she had "stolen" electronics. Her adoptive mom had to explain that even when caught making errors that she was not being returned to foster care.

The research of Dr. Bruce Perry and others confirms that the brain creates template patterns based upon the first set (or early experiences) and then new experiences are compared to these original templates. If new experiences vary greatly then new memories can be created with much repetition (Perry, 2001). This is why in this therapist's practice, family homework is often given so that the parents and children are creating new memories and templates based on repetitive experiences.

The play therapist who works with adoptive families needs to ensure that the play tools reflect the adoptive family client population. Miniatures need to reflect various cultural and generational family groupings as well as families who have same-sex parents. These tools are necessary so that these reflect old, present, and future familial experiences of the builder.

Clinicians need to be mindful that the underlying purpose of the therapeutic process is therefore to help the family to create a "secure/safe haven in which and from which each member is able to begin to form a coherent autobiographical narrative . . . by engaging in intersubjective experiences that are generated within the family" (Hughes, 2007, p. 2).

Therapists who specialize in adoption therefore often take on the role of parent coach so the child sees the parent as the expert who will provide safety in and out of the sessions. Raj was the adoptive father of a three-year-old girl. The family had two older biological sons. He verbalized not knowing what to do with a little girl and it was clear that even though he too took a parenting

Figure 7.1. Same-Sex Moms

leave that the child would consistently focus all of her attention on her new mother. During a therapy session (involving father and daughter) the little girl fell and she immediately ran toward the female therapist. Therapist picked her up and passed her to Raj verbalizing that daddy will want to check your arms and legs to kiss your boo boos. He was able to respond appropriately to his daughter with this cue.

Thus, each family system is unique and each child in the family has a unique past with a compilation of experiences and templates created from (sometimes) many family systems. The play therapist who works within adoptive family systems has much to be cognizant of. Also, families who adopt older children may require specialized therapeutic intervention and consideration (Elbow, 1986). Thus, intake needs to take into consideration the following areas of functioning:

- the current and emerging parent /child relationship (with each parent in the family)
- the couple relationship
- adopted family identity in relation to child's biological family and/or most recent family (perhaps foster family)
- adopted family identity in relation to their extended families
- the new family's overall emerging identity
- the new or changed parent identity
- the bio and/or adopted sibling group relationships
- the child's or children's individual treatment issues

> Making therapy fit the family is particularly important in adoption or fostering because the constellation and intensity of difficulties experienced can make achieving the very basics in daily life extremely challenging for parents, carers and children. (Hart & Luckock, 2006, p. 34)
> The inability of some practitioners to recognize the potentially colossal impact of children's legacies of abuse and neglect on family life is well documented. (Howe 2003 in Hart & Luckock, 2006)

Therefore, once information is gathered at intake it is paramount for therapist to collaborate with parents to ascertain what the most immediate goals of treatment are to be. Given supporting the parent/child attachment is a consistent underlying focus of intervention, it is always the therapist's role to support the parent's decision making so to support the emerging parent's identity. Dependent on the focus of intervention, the therapist may use one or various modalities in order to work both systemically but also in an integrated manner (Drewes & Bratton, 2011) or prescriptive manner (Schaeffer, 2001). This also means that the therapist may work with the whole family, subsets of family members, the parents themselves, or children individually dependent on the area of focus and at different phases of the therapeutic relationship. For example, a MIM (Marschak Interactional Method) observational assessment can be quite helpful in understanding the four dimensions of the parent/child relationship (Boothe & Jernberg, 2009). Registered play therapist Carla Sharpe's Build a House technique is also useful in ascertaining individual and overall family views of safety, roles, and rules (Sharpe, 2005). The therapist who specializes in adoption work can use a variety of assessment tools in order to develop the initial treatment plan including various play therapy approaches.

> Play therapy, within the framework of the Bowen theory, encourages participation from all family members, points to the interactions of the family members with each other, and links these systemic patterns to the reason why the family was referred to therapy (Nims & Duba, 2011, p. 83)

De Domenico developed Sandtray-Worldplay (STWP) theory, techniques and methods and this approach is utilized by play therapists who work with children, teens, adults, groups, and families. This play therapy approach is related to the pioneering work of Margaret Lowenfeld—Worldplay, and Dora Kalff—Sandplay (De Domenico, personal communication, April 25, 2005). It involves sand, a sand tray, water, and images (miniatures) that reflect, process or communicate experiences of the builder(s). This therapist studied with Dr. De Domenico over six years from 2004-2010 in Lansing, Michigan. This therapist utilizes the STWP method in her work with individuals, couples, groups, and families both in teaching and in the play therapy process.

In various areas of work with adoptive families, this therapist has utilized sandtray play directively and non-directively with individual family members as well as the entire family unit. Much has been written about this method and the protocol and stages of this intervention, thus these will not be repeated here. Description of sessions with various adoptive families will illustrate the use of sandtray play as a psychodynamic process that can be utilized to address some common themes that are often identified as concerns by the newly formed adoptive family. Using sand in family work is a powerful tool:

> The internal deformation of a grain of sand speaks metaphorically of the intrapsychic pain that many of our clients bring to us. Sand is a product of its history and so are we. (Carey, 1999. p. xii)

THE CURRENT AND EMERGING PARENT/CHILD RELATIONSHIP: RULES, ROLES, COMMUNICATION, AND PROBLEM SOLVING

In an initial session each family member (being two parents and four adoptive children-two biological sibling groups) were invited to pick a sandtray miniature (image) that represented their presence in this newly formed family (Gil, 1994). They each were then asked to place their image in the world and then silently family members were invited to move these images until they felt that this world was a safe place for their family to exist in. Additional images could be added and images could be taken away. The family continued to play silently until they all felt that the world was the way it should be.

This process assisted the therapist and family members to gain an understanding of family rules and norms both spoken and unspoken. In the family processing or experiencing part of the session, family members were able to identify how they felt when another member moved closer to a parent or when their image was moved or taken out of the world. Very quickly the family was able to draw connections between behavior played out in the world and behavior demonstrated in the home milieu. This connection between inner and outer world is not a requirement of the Sandtray-Worldplay method as psyche plays what psyche needs to play (De Domenico, personal communication, April 25, 2005).

However, pursuant to this play activity, this family was able to identify safety rules that needed to be present in their family so that all members felt respected. The older children were also able to verbalize how displaced they felt at times with the arrival of these younger and attention seeking family members.

The Couple Relationship

Jim and Patrice had adopted an eleven-year-old male who appeared to have no issues with Jim but was always in conflict with Patrice. This caused stress in their couple relationship because Jim felt that Patrice was being too strict and Patrice verbalized that she felt unsupported. Both parents were invited to create their own worlds in silence. They then were invited to "tour" each other around their built worlds. It was during this experience that Patrice was able to identify that she was grieving the hope she had held for adopting a younger child that might need her more. They had initially felt a little girl would be a better match for their family but saw their son at an adoption event and felt that he shared common interests given he had expressed an interest in traveling and liked working with his hands. Jim and Patrice had a home renovation business and during quiet seasons traveled around the world.

It also became clear during this session that Jim was working through his past experiences with his mom whom he viewed as controlling and unsupportive. He was able to identify that he was allowing their son to "split them" as a couple based on a faulty belief that Patrice had mismatched expectations of their new son. In reality, their new son was connecting more easily with Jim because Patrice had taken the parenting leave and had become the primary disciplinarian. Once both parents were able to be "on the same page" and were comfortable saying, "let me check with dad or mom" their son's attempts to manipulate decreased.

Additionally, the couple identified that their sex life had decreased and their date nights had become non-existent because they were strongly working on building a good attachment with their son. Ensuring that they spent time with each other became a priority and this decreased the lack of support they felt from each other. Patrice ended up attending therapy for a few individual sessions to work through her feelings of loss regarding the adoption of a younger female child. Jim too attended a few individual sessions to come to terms with the outstanding relationship issues he shared with his mother who was not meeting his expectations as a new grandmother.

During a subsequent couple session, both Jim and Patrice's identity as new parents in relation to their extended families was identified as still emerging. They struggled with managing the many pieces of unrequested advice that were shared particularly at family events with an audience. Outside of sandtray work we role played responses to unsolicited questions regarding their son's history. We also used this session to identify how these new parents could supportively respond to their son when he compared them individually and his new family to previous parent figures that he had lived with.

UNRESOLVED SEPARATION AND LOSS: THE CHILD'S INDIVIDUAL TREATMENT ISSUES

Mr. and Mrs. Martin were referred for intervention and asked if an initial session could occur with the youngest of their new children first. This child was tantrumming daily, not sleeping well, and always hypervigilent about who might be visiting or calling the home. The only instructions Maria was given in her session was to build a world either in the presence of the therapist or both her mother and therapist who would act as witnesses to the world. She initially chose the former (with therapy door open) until the world was created and then she invited her mother to come play with her. In her initial world there were children, parents, and then monsters that wanted to hurt the children. She then created another world in a sandtray adjacent to her world where she banished all the monsters. She identified that these were really from the past but still had an impact on the children's present.

When mom joined the play Maria directed mom to play with a particular image but warned her that though it was her job to protect the children from the monsters, the likelihood of having success was limited because these monsters had a lot of practice hurting the children and the children held little hope for change. The children also felt a little responsible for the monsters so it was hard for them to ignore the monsters even when they felt angry and scared by them. The children knew the story of the monsters and the protective mother didn't.

Adoptive mom was intuitive and quickly gave voice to the superhero female image that had become the protector of children. She protected the children from all aspects of the world even at times with her back turned to the monsters because as the safe mother she always "knew what the children might need." She then went on to state that the monsters may not intend to hurt the children but maybe didn't have mothers to teach them how to be good with children. She volunteered to help the monsters as long as they could follow the safety rules established in the world, namely that children's needs come first. Once she had this conversation with the monsters, Maria was able to rest in the world. The play quickly came to a close. The images chosen for the children began to play in the world (instead of being ready to run and hide) and the children even sought out affection from the protector mom. Maria also identified that the biggest female monster could also rest now because she had found peace.

When the session had ended, Maria's mom was told that for the process to be healing she did not need to draw connections to real life experiences. Maria's new mom left the session with tears in her eyes as she had finally experienced the feeling of trust with her newest child. Both parents reported that Maria began to talk more about her future in the Martin family and less about feeling responsible to find her biological mother and ensure that she was okay. It is also important to note that beginning a session with Maria and mother set a trusting tone for future work with the family. Maria and her brother had been in therapy before and once her brother saw how helpful her first sandtray play session was (based on her eagerness to come again and diminished tantrums) he too was open to participating in the family therapy process.

PARENTING DEVELOPMENTALLY

Often the most important concept integrated by new adoptive parents after participating in family play therapy process is the recognition that their children need to be responded to developmentally instead of chronologically.

Given the often traumatic children's history, this means that adoptive parents respond as they would with younger children. Additionally, behaviors such as lying as stealing need to be viewed as self-protective behaviors instead of as evidence of parental or family rejection. The work of the Child Trauma Academy and National Institute for Trauma and Loss reinforces this value in attachment based parenting. Being able to see how the children view what goes on in their sandtray worlds can be very powerful. Past themes, current worries, and future fears may show up in the play and often provide parents with both insight and understanding about the developmental stage of their child.

Stevie was a ten-year-old boy who was placed on adoption placement at nine and a half. He had experienced previous adoptive placement disruptions and his longest foster placement was an elderly woman with no car that rarely exposed Stevie to community activities or resources. Stevie struggled in his peer relationships and would be described by teachers as defiant, rude, and annoying to peers especially in new situations, prior to transitions or routine changes. His new dad, though very patient, often felt inept in his ability to parent Stevie as his intense tantrums appeared to "come out of nowhere" and his first response to most invitations was the word "no." When Stevie was invited to build a world he titled the world, *Children all alone,* after of course noting that he thought building would be boring. There were no toys, no friends, only a television set. Subsequent worlds had little human interaction, protective factors, or elements of safety in them. His parents were able to recognize that Stevie's lack of early environmental stimulation impacted his social skill development and greatly explained his ability to play on his own for long periods of time without talking or interacting with others. With this awareness, Stevie's parents attempted to *grow Stevie up* by beginning to parent him as he would a toddler who needed consistent routines, cues prior to routine changes, and reassurance that his mom and dad would be there when he needed them.

Emerging Family Identity

The Adams parents indicated that their new children argued about every rule or expectation in the home and were constantly trying to take control. In the family play therapy session, the family was broken into dyads. The therapist carefully matched parent with the child whom they were most in conflict with. Each dyad was instructed to create a world with no rules. Upon completion of these worlds, each dyad gave the other parent/child a tour of the new world. The whole family then had a discussion about what a land with no rules felt like. The children then determined that common rules made sense and the family proceeded to compile rules that fit for their family (Fraser, 2010).

Re-Connecting with Birth Parents

This therapist is also a foster/adoptive parent. Our eleven-year-old son has been with us since he was eighteen months old. His status as a chosen child has always been openly discussed with a promise to assist him in finding birth parents if he chose to when eighteen. Around Father's Day we began to see a little boy who was irritable and teary. He was able to share that though he had memories of his birth mother whom he visited until he was two and a half, he had no memories of his birth father. He wanted to know what birth dad looked like and why he was no longer a part of his life as an infant.

As a couple we decided that we would begin to search for our son's birth dad and within a few days were successful locating him on Facebook©. We contacted him and explained that we were only looking for written contact at this point if he was able and willing to reconnect with his birth son. Without breaching this man or our son's confidentiality, the reasons for their separation will not be shared publicly; however, their reunion could be no more positive than it has been. A private family Facebook group has been set up given family lives in different parts of Canada and all members of the paternal side of the family have enjoyed seeing photos and sharing short emails with each other.

This is a common issue or concern that impacts older child adoption. How can parents honor the birth family particularly when they have often been privy to the abusive or neglectful details of events that precipitated the child from being removed from their biological parent's care?

The Forest family had five children who ultimately were adopted by two different families and the oldest child was transferred to a kin placement. Each child had different memories of birth parents and grandparents. One daughter's adoptive parents invited grandparents to visit and stay with them, while the parents of two younger children needed to explain that it was upsetting for their children to have contact with grandparents and at this time contact needed to be suspended. This was made clear to them after touring their child's world where the child later verbalized that seeing grandparents made them worry that they were going to have to return to their biological parent's care as their previous experience was that grandparents drove them back home when they were leaving foster care on multiple previous occasions.

Play Therapy

Sandtray therapy and other forms of play therapy can provide the opportunity for adoptive families to work within a metaphor and create their new narrative. Play therapy approaches can address initial issues but also support the emerging family identity. They can also assist family members in obtaining a sense of belonging and acceptance for all members.

Family therapy with adoptive families requires focus and consideration in the many areas and dimensions of the family's functioning. Sandtray Wordplay is an intervention that can be utilized with individual family members or the entire family system in any or all of these areas.

> Then inclusion of all family members, particularly children in family therapy provides the sandtray therapist the opportunity to observe patterns of communication, roles, coalitions and triangles, rather than making assumptions based on the self-report of one partner or a few individual family members. (Homeyer & Sweeney, 2011. p. 70)

Play therapists who work successfully with adoptive families can utilize play therapy approaches including Sandtray-Worldplay to focus on strengths instead of challenges or deficits, and well as to help the family to choose and build on external resources so that they can create collaborative support systems in cases where ongoing resources may be required (Espe-Sherwindt, 2008). Consequently, many adoptive families benefit from online support groups or facilitated groups where they can be supported in their trauma focused parenting. Parents are often able to verbalize that connecting with other parents who share the unique experience of adoption revitalizes them and prepares them for upcoming challenges such as children wondering or seeking out birth family contacts.

Check-up Sessions

Check up or *check in* sessions have proven to be extremely important in supporting the adoptive family given pieces of work may need to be revisited as the adoptive child enters into new developmental phases. Often, however, only one or two sessions are required for the family to begin to feel that they are getting back on track. On these occasions it can be helpful to review photos of sandtrays created at different phases of therapy as these can serve as a reminder of the narrative created by the builders (child as well as overall family system) or create a new sandtray! The therapist may also need to be cognizant of who the check-up session is for: child, parent, or entire family system. Scheduling these as a matter of process rather than a reaction to a crisis can also normalize that therapeutic intervention is part of their family supporting each other.

NOTE

1. All names have been changed to protect identity.

REFERENCES

Booth, P., & Jernberg, A.M. (2009). *Theraplay: Helping Parents and Children Build Better Relationships Through Attachment-Based Play*. Hoboken, NJ: John Wiley & Sons.

Carey. L. (1999). *Sandplay therapy with children and families.* New York, NY: Jason Aronson, Inc.

De Domenico, G. (2011, August 30). Retrieved from http://www.vision-quest.us/vqisr/The%20Sandtray-Worldplay%20Method%20of%20Sandplay.pdf.

Drewes, A., & Bratton, S. (2011). Integrative play therapy. Hoboken, NJ: John Wiley & Sons.

Edwards, J. (2000). On being dropped and picked up: Adopted children and their internal objects. *Journal of Child Psychotherapy, 26*(3), 349-367

Elbow, W. (1986). From caregiving to parenting: Family formation with adopted older children. *Social Work, 31*(5), 366-370.

Espe-Sherwindt, M. (2008). Family-centred practice: collaboration, competency and evidence. *Support for Learning, 23*(3), 136-143.

Fraser, T. (2011). *Adopting a child with trauma and attachment disruption experiences.* Ann Arbor, MI: Loving Healing Press.

Fraser, T. (2010). A land with no rules. *Creative Family Therapy Techniques: Play, Art and Expressive Activities to Engage Children in Family Sessions*. (Edited by L. Lowenstein). Toronto, Ontario: Champion Press.

Gil, E. (1994). *Play in family therapy*. New York, NY: Guilford Press

Hart, A., & Luckock, B. (2006). Core principles and therapeutic objectives for therapy with adoptive and permanent foster families: *Adoption and Fostering, 30*(2).

Howe D. (2003). Attachment disorders: disinhibited attachment behaviours and secure-base distortions with special reference to adopted children, *Attachment & Human Development,* 5(3), 265-70.

Homeyer, L., & Sweeney, D. (2011). *Sandtray therapy a practical manual.* New York, NY:, Routledge,Taylor and Francis Group.

Hughes, D. (2007). *Attachment focused family therapy.* New York, NY: W.W. Norton and Co. Inc.

Nims, D., & Duba, J. (2011). Using play therapy techniques in a Bowenian theoretical context. *The Family Journal: Counseling and Therapy for Couples and Families, 19*(1), 83-89.

Perry, B. (2001) Adapted in part from: *"Maltreated Children: Experience, Brain Development and the Next Generation"* (W.W. Norton & Company, New York, in preparation)

Schaefer, C.E.(2001). Prescriptive play therapy. *International Journal of Play Therapy*, Vol 10(2), 2001, 57-73.

Sharp, C. (2005). *The Build-a-House Technique*, Kailua, HI: Self-published Retrieved from: http://carlasharp.com

Smith, W.H.Jr. (2001). Child Abuse in family emotional process. *Family Systems, 5*(2): 101-126.

Index

About the Contributors

Nancy Riedel Bowers, RSW, Rpt-S, PhD, holds positions within the Seminary and Faculty of Social Work at Wilfrid Laurier University, Waterloo, Ontario, Canada. She currently teaches the one of only graduate courses in play therapy at a graduate school of social work at an accredited university in Canada and serves on masters and doctoral committees internationally. A researcher and international workshop presenter, Dr. Riedel Bowers studies the psychotherapeutic process particularly in the area of child and play therapy. Her numerous chapters and research publications recognize the treatment phases involved in careful intervention planning and selective choice of models for intervention. She is currently completing an international study on the "Redefinition of Play." Nancy holds the positions as an APT-continuing education provider and is a registered supervisor with APT and CACPT.

Anna Bowers is a master's student in school psychology at the University of British Columbia. She grew up in Kitchener, Ontario and completed a BA in psychology at the University of Waterloo. As an undergraduate student, she was a research assistant in both a cognitive development and social psychology lab, and examined the intellectual functioning of children with ADHD, Asperger's Syndrome, and learning disabilities. Anna has experience working with children and their families in educational and therapeutic settings and hopes to continue learning about preschool assessment to optimize the functioning of young children with developmental disabilities. Her current research is examining parents' experience of the diagnostic process for Autism Spectrum Disorder (ASD) for their young children. Anna also has an interest in the use of play-based treatment approaches for children and their families. Anna enjoys running, tennis, and traveling with her family.

Kristin Trotter, PhD, is a family therapist who has been in private practice for many years. She holds a doctorate in clinical social work and is registered with the Ontario and American Associations for Marriage and Family Therapy. Kristin works with children, adults, families, couples, and individuals. She also has expertise in the area of trauma and works with survivors of childhood sexual and physical abuse as well as survivors of torture and many other forms of trauma. She also teaches at a local university and her research interests include the trauma of war and its impact on the family, the effects of trauma and war on refugee children's learning, and understanding the impact of drug facilitated sexual assault.

Alan McLuckie earned his PhD in social work from the University of Toronto and MSW from the University of Calgary. He is a registered social worker and an experienced mental health therapist, specializing in working with children and families. Dr. McLuckie is a supervisor of play therapy with the Canadian Association for Child and Play Therapy and Play Therapy International, as well as a clinical fellow with the American Association for Marriage and Family Therapy. He teaches and conducts research at Dalhousie University where he is an assistant professor with the School of Social Work, lecturer with the Department of Psychiatry, and researcher with the Sun Life Chair in Adolescent Mental Health. Dr. McLuckie is also supervisor of the Family Therapy Consultation and Training Program, a joint training program of the IWK Health Centre and Dalhousie University, Department of Psychiatry.

Melissa Rowbotham, BEd, MEd, is the manager of Community Education and Engagement at Integra Foundation, a children's mental health center specializing in treating youth with learning disabilities and co-occurring mental health disorders located in Toronto, Ontario. She provides training for and promotes collaboration between schools, students, parents, and community agencies around children's mental health and LDs. She has worked as a special education teacher for children with behavioral difficulties, learning disabilities, and social and emotional issues in Alberta and Ontario. Melissa also holds a master's degree in psychology from OISE/University of Toronto and has worked as a mental health therapist with children and their families using individual, group, family, and play therapy in a hospital setting.

Evangeline Munns, PhD, is a certified psychologist who was formerly the clinical director of play therapy services at Blue Hills Child and Family Services in Aurora, Ontario, which had the largest training school in Theraplay in Canada at that time. She is a popular presenter of Theraplay and other workshops throughout Canada and internationally. Dr. Munns has edited two books on Theraplay and has written chapters in over a dozen books. She has received the Monica Herbert Award from the Canadian Association for Child and Play Therapy for "making an outstanding contribution to play therapy in Canada" and was listed by CACPT as one of the top five play therapists in Canada.

Theresa Fraser, CYW, MA, CPT-S, trauma and loss clinical specialist is a professor at Sheridan College and a child and family therapist that utilizes play therapy in her work with children, teens, groups, and families. She has authored a few books on foster care and adoption. She and her husband have been treatment foster parents for over twenty years and in addition to a few biological children of their own, they are also adoptive parents. She is an international lecturer for both play therapists and foster/adoptive parents. Theresa studied with Dr. Gisela De Domenico and is passionate about sharing STWP tools with clients. Theresa had the priviledge of bring supervised by Dr. Nancy Riedel Bowers in her journey to become a Certified Child Psychotherapist Play Therapist. She is the current president of the Canadian Association for Child and Play Therapy.

www.ingramcontent.com/pod-product-compliance
Lightning Source LLC
LaVergne TN
LVHW101448200926
848483LV00001B/85